The Character of the Manager

Humanism in Business Series

The Humanistic Management Network is an international, interdisciplinary, and independent network that promotes the development of an economic system with respect for human dignity and well-being.

The Humanistic Management Network defends human dignity in face of its vulnerability. Since human persons realize themselves through social cooperation, economic relations and business activities can either foster or obstruct human life and well-being. Against the widespread objectification of human subjects into human resources, against the common instrumentalization of human beings into human capital and a mere means for profit, we uphold humanity as the ultimate end and principle of all economic activity.

In business as well as in society, respect for human dignity demands respect for human intelligence and freedom. Collective decision-making, in corporations just as in governments, should hence be based on free and equal deliberation, participation or representation of all affected parties. Concerns of legitimacy must, in economics like in politics, precede questions of expediency.

We believe that market economies hold substantial potential for human development in general. To promote life-conducive market activities, we want to complement the quantitative metrics which hitherto define managerial and economic success with qualitative evaluation criteria that focus on the human dignity of every woman and every man.

As researchers, we work towards a humanistic paradigm for business and economics, trying to identify and facilitate corporate and governmental efforts for the common good.

As a think-tank, we set out to spread intellectual tools for culturally and ecologically sustainable business practices that have the human being as their focal point.

As teachers, we strive to educate, emancipate, and enable students to contribute actively to a life-conducive economy in which human dignity is universally respected.

As practitioners, we act towards the implementation of a humanistic economy on an individual, corporate, and governmental level.

As citizens, we engage our communities in discourse about the benefits of a human-centred economy.

Titles include:

BUSINESS SCHOOLS UNDER FIRE

BANKING WITH INTEGRITY

HUMANISTIC MANAGEMENT IN PRACTICE

HUMANISTIC ETHICS IN THE AGE OF GLOBALITY

HUMAN DEVELOPMENT IN BUSINESS

INTEGRITY IN ORGANIZATIONS

THE CHARACTER OF THE MANAGER

The Character of the Manager

From Office Executive to Wise Steward

Gregory R. Beabout
Saint Louis University, USA

palgrave
macmillan

First published 2013 by
PALGRAVE MACMILLAN

Palgrave Macmillan in the UK is an imprint of Macmillan Publishers Limited, registered in England, company number 785998, of Houndmills, Basingstoke, Hampshire RG21 6XS.

Palgrave Macmillan in the US is a division of St Martin's Press LLC, 175 Fifth Avenue, New York, NY 10010.

Palgrave Macmillan is the global academic imprint of the above companies and has companies and representatives throughout the world.

Palgrave® and Macmillan® are registered trademarks in the United States, the United Kingdom, Europe and other countries

ISBN: 978–1–137–30405–6

This book is printed on paper suitable for recycling and made from fully managed and sustained forest sources. Logging, pulping and manufacturing processes are expected to conform to the environmental regulations of the country of origin.

A catalogue record for this book is available from the British Library.

A catalog record for this book is available from the Library of Congress.

To Cindy

Contents

Acknowledgments

Many people and institutions have helped and supported me while I was researching and writing this book.

Thanks to Claus Dierksmeier and the Humanistic Management Network for including this book in the Humanism in Business Series and to the editors at Palgrave Macmillan.

My department chair at Saint Louis University, Ted Vitali, has supported me in many ways during my research and writing of the book. I am very grateful for the opportunity to teach courses and seminars that complement my research. Fr. Vitali supported my application for a research leave both at the beginning and near the end of the writing phase. I very much appreciate his support, especially over the last five years. My research, writing, and editing has been made much easier because of various forms of support, including a summer research grant, a sabbatical leave, a Provost research award, and a Vice President's research award. I have benefited from the opportunity to present many sections of the book at various professional meetings. Travel to those meetings was supported by a Mellon grant, departmental travel funds, and support from Saint Louis University's College of Arts and Sciences. Jamie Hendrix in the department of philosophy has been a great help, especially with travel forms. Thanks to my research assistants, Jeremy Skrzypek and Samuel Murray. I very much appreciate all of the support from Saint Louis University and the department of philosophy.

I have taught many wonderful students at Saint Louis University. My experiences in the classroom, at all levels, have afforded me the opportunity to work through the ideas in this book. Our department and university have a deep commitment to the academic study of philosophy, to the history of philosophy, the tradition of the virtues, and to interdisciplinary dialogue. I feel blessed to work in a setting where the themes of my research pervade almost every class I teach: the introductory courses in "Historical Introduction to Philosophy" and "Ethics," sections of business ethics, and upper-level seminars that have provided the opportunity to focus intently on virtue ethics, narrative ethics, rhetoric, Plato, Aristotle, Kierkegaard, and MacIntyre. I am particularly grateful for the opportunity to engage with fine students in a context where the size of my classes and seminars has been conducive to intensive engaged dialogue, and to the many students whose participation in classes involved discussing ideas in this book.

The Department of Philosophy at Saint Louis University has an active calendar of colloquium presentations, and I have benefited from the opportunity to work in an environment where we regularly bring philosophers to our campus for talks and conferences. In addition, I have learned much from my colleagues, including conversations about various aspects of my work, especially with George Terzis, William Charron, John Greco, Jack Marler, Ted Vitali, and the late John Kavanaugh, S. J.

I benefit from working at an institution that prizes interdisciplinary conversation. This includes my work with Hal Bush and Dan Finucane planning the events of the Arts and Sciences Interdisciplinary Forum along with the participants in these and many other interdisciplinary conversations on our campus, including opportunities to interact with SLU's Center for Health Care Ethics, the John Cook School of Business, and Parks College of Aviation, Engineering, and Technology. I have benefited from conversations about medical humanities and business humanities with many people at SLU, especially Vince Casaregola, Sara Van den Berg, Jim Fisher, Ellen Harshman, and Mike Barber. I miss the frequent conversations I had with Tom Walsh. I appreciate that Jerry Katz of the Cook Business School allowed me to participate in his course on management theory and practice; I have found stimulating the opportunities to participate in courses and programs in our business school as well as interactions with advanced students who are management practitioners. My work with the executive leadership seminars offered through the Center for Aviation Safety Research has provided opportunities to discuss questions of character and leadership with managers in high consequence positions. I am especially grateful to Ed Sabin, Director of SLU's Industrial–Organizational Psychology graduate program, for many conversations about ethics, leadership, and organizations.

A few sections of the book are substantially revised versions of my previously published work. I gratefully acknowledge permission granted to use material from "Management as a Domain-Relative Practice That Requires and Develops Practical Wisdom," *Business Ethics Quarterly* 22 (2012) 405–432, and "The Profile of the Manager in *Caritas in Veritate*," in *Human Development in Business*, edited by Domènec Melé and Claus Dierksmeier (New York: Palgrave Macmillan), 2012.

The argument of the book began to come into focus for me in 2007, and many sections of the book are revised versions of papers that I presented at universities, conferences, and professional meetings over the last five years. In many such instances, a formal commentator provided a detailed response; I benefited from those, and from questions and criticisms raised in discussions at those meetings. I am grateful to those who have engaged my work in its various stages by offering responses, raising questions, and helping me think through concerns and possible objections along the way. Aspects of the book's argument were presented at the conference on friendship, character, and community at Baylor University, October, 2007; the symposium on environmental law at the University of St Thomas, Minneapolis, MN, September, 2007; the Midsouth Philosophy Conference at the University of Memphis, February, 2007; the conference on business education at the University of Notre Dame, June, 2008; the conference sponsored by the Abbeville Institute at Lindenwood University, July, 2008; the conference sponsored by the International Society for MacIntyrian Philosophy at St Meinrad, IN, July, 2008; the fall meeting of Legatus of Western Massachussets in Springfield, MA, September, 2008; the Third Annual Conference of the International Society for MacIntyrean Inquiry at the University College Dublin, Ireland, March, 2009; the conference on the thought of Alasdair MacIntyre at Lincoln University, Jefferson City, MO, October, 2009; the Saint Louis University Arts and Sciences Interdisciplinary Panel, March, 2010; the International Kierkegaard Conference at St Olaf College, July, 2010; the curriculum project on business education at the University of Portland, July, 2010; the meeting of the International St Thomas Aquinas Society held during the Eastern Division meeting of the American Philosophical Association, Boston, MA, December, 2010; the International Society for MacIntyrean Inquiry, Providence College, July, 2011; the annual meeting of the Society for Ethics Across the Curriculum, November, 2011; the symposium on human development, the economy, and the common good at Fontbonne University, April, 2012; the conference on free markets and localism at Lindenwood University, April, 2012; the business education conference on renewing mission and identity at the University of Dayton, June, 2012; and the panel on virtue ethics and business at the meetings of the Society of Business Ethics, Boston, MA, August, 2012. I am particularly grateful to Michael Naughton for the opportunity to work with interdisciplinary scholars from humanities and business schools, especially Andrew Yuengert, and for Patricia Johnson, for the opportunity to write several papers with her on teaching moral philosophy to business students.

A special sort of acknowledgment goes to Alasdair MacIntyre, whose work I engage in this book. Over the last decade and more, I have benefited from an intensive study of MacIntyre's virtue ethics. When I first read MacIntyre's *After Virtue* while I was a graduate student in the 1980s, I was rather critical of the book, partly because the account of Kierkegaard seemed misguided, and partly because MacIntyre's treatment of Thomas Aquinas seemed thin compared to the complexity and depth of the Thomistic debates I was learning from scholars that seemed much more immersed in the Aristotelian–Thomistic tradition. I did not consider MacIntyre's work seriously again until I encountered *Dependent Rational Animals*. A conference session in 2000 on that book and subsequent conversations with panelists Scott Moore, John O'Callaghan, and Thomas Hibbs impressed upon me that I should revisit MacInytre's work. Reading *Dependent Rational Animals* inspired me to reexamine the trilogy of books in MacIntyre's "After Virtue Project." Around the same time, Anthony Rudd's book, *Kierkegaard and the Limits of the Ethical*, helped me focus on ways in which the concerns of MacIntyre and Kierkegaard share a great deal in common.

I began using MacIntyre's work in my teaching, and that got me thinking in an intensive way about the similarities and differences between the managerial character criticized by MacIntyre and the way that the character of the aesthete is encountered in Kierkegaard's writing. Looking back, I now see that in my initial response to MacIntyre, I was too quick to dismiss his project. To be honest, in some of my earlier work, I used rather harsh language to criticize MacIntyre. Perhaps I should have been more kind in the words that I chose, but I still maintain that the interpretation of Kierkegaard presented in *After Virtue* is seriously incorrect. I appreciate the way that MacIntyre responded to his critics and revised his interpretation. I have had limited face-to-face interaction with Alasdair MacIntyre, but I have spent countless hours reflecting on his written work. I have participated in many fruitful conversations that grew out of discussions and criticisms of MacIntyre's work.

The outlines of the argument of this book began to germinate over a period of years when David Solomon was first organizing the conferences of the Center for Ethics and Culture at the University of Notre Dame. Those meetings, which I attended annually, allowed me to hear Alasdair MacIntyre lecture multiple times while allowing me to deepen my study of MacIntyre's virtue ethics while interacting with a community of scholars concerned with issues of virtue, character, social practices, and institutions.

I am certain that I have been shaped by extended conversations about character and virtue ethics with Randy Colton, Brad Frazier, Alex Gamble, Aaron Meyer, Linsey Dieckmeyer, Bre'Anna Liddell, Katie Burke,

Brian Carl, Randy Rosenberg, Fiona Barker, Bryan Cross, Beth Rath, Nick Setliff, Alex Plato, Ron Belgau, and many others. I have also benefited from the conferences of the International Society for MacIntyrean Inquiry. I am grateful for the work of the organizers of those meetings. I learned much during ISME meetings and from the presentations of the scholar–participants, including especially Geoff Moore, Ron Beadle, Chris Lutz, Bruce Ballard, and many others.

I am genuinely grateful to have that most important sort of support, the blessings of good friends and a wonderful family. Mike and Claire McGlynn have listened to countless conversations about my work, as have Joe and Mary Catherine Hodes. Gene Vanek has been a friend and, during an exciting chapter in my life, a wonderful business partner. I am grateful for conversations with members of my family and their willingness to share their direct experience in the world of managers, especially my brother Doug, and my father. I am profoundly grateful for the support of my entire family, especially my mother and father, and also my children and their spouses: Kevin and Kathy; Rachelle and Russell; Mark, John, and Therese. In the most special way, I am thankful to Cindy, to whom this book is dedicated.

Introduction

This book's argument proceeds in four parts: i) we need a better way to conceive of the manager and a better way to understand the role of moral philosophy in contributing to our notion of the character of the manager (Chapters 1–2); ii) Alasdair MacIntyre's work problematizes the manager as a character while providing a deeper diagnosis of contemporary inadequacies (Chapters 3–8); iii) a humanistic approach is needed, one that retrieves philosophy's task of offering character transforming arguments (Chapters 9–13); iv) the manager as wise steward is proposed as the term of such a process, including the character itself, the virtues and powers central to this character, the social context in local and global perspective, and suggestions for institutionalizing this ideal (Chapters 14–16).

This book is a sustained argument advancing a transformed conception of the character of the manager as a wise steward. One way of entering the book's line of reasoning is to see it as a long answer to a series of questions posed implicitly and inchoately by the 2011 Occupy Wall Street movement. Protesters, first in New York and later in many other cities across the globe, demonstrated to bring attention to CEO greed, corruption, undue influence by corporations on civic life, increasing disparities in wealth, and the lack of accountability for those who played key roles in bringing about the global economic crisis of 2008. I do not mean to claim that the Occupy Wall Street protesters are model citizens in the way they engaged in civic public discourse and shared deliberation. They have been criticized, perhaps with merit, for being an unfocused, leaderless movement driven by a narrow ideology with a willingness to resort to lawbreaking, sometimes even violence, rather than authentically working with others in a civil manner to pursue the truth and the common good.[1] Despite such shortcomings, the protesters point to questions that deserve a serious response. What is the societal role of the modern executive? What is the place of the manager in the contemporary social order? Should those responsible for organizing, planning, directing, and executing the activities of organizations be evaluated not only in terms of efficiency and effectiveness, but also in substantive moral terms such as justice and wisdom with regard to advancing the common good?

On the face of it, it is easy to grasp intuitively the sort of managerial character criticized by the Occupy Wall Street protesters: the anonymous, highly compensated office executive, CEO, top-level administrator, or senior manager of a large company whose task involves organizing a firm to accomplish quantifiable short-term results. Such a person typically values efficiency and effectiveness, takes advantage of economies of scale, tends to rely on outsourcing while frequently treating employees as replaceable units, and tends to treat instrumentally various stakeholders: the workers, consumers, those who inhabit a specific geographical area, the natural environment, and the broader society. The manager as office executive appears to be not merely neutral with regard to ethics, but personally fragmented and morally hollow. Focusing on this character gives rise to several questions. Is it possible to manage in a responsible manner, with an eye to efficiently and effectively organizing a group to accomplish a given, quantifiable purpose while comporting oneself in a manner that is honest and just with a concern for the common good? Has the time come to reevaluate the role of the manager? Is there a way to reconceive the manager as a virtuous character, that is, as one whose role is to act as a wise steward? Is it possible for a manager to practice the virtues?

Such questions are philosophical in character. What role can philosophers play in encouraging others to ask these sorts of questions, and in working toward reasoned responses to such an inquiry? The argument of this book is a reply to such questions.

The manager, considered as a type or a social role, is a modern character. During the final decades of the 19th century and into the early 20th century, this new sort of social authority emerged as an important figure in modern life. More than a century ago, writers from various industrialized nations began describing and analyzing this character. The Frenchman Henri Fayol famously developed a general theory of business administration that outlined the functions of the modern manager: planning, organizing, leading, commanding, and controlling. Fayol's theory continues to shape the self-understanding of countless contemporary managers. Frederick Taylor, with his time-and-motion studies of workers at Bethlehem Steel in the 1890s, exemplified the concerns of the modern manager. In early-20th-century Germany, Max Weber offered a sociological account of the modern manager as office executive.

For many decades, the modern manager exemplified by Taylor and praised by Fayol and Weber, has been the subject of sustained criticism. The complaints of the Occupy Wall Street protestors reprise well-worn objections. CEOs, administrators, executives, and all sorts of management personnel have been frequently accused of corruption, of acting without accountability, of placing profits over people, self-interest over justice, and acting in a manner that destroys the common good. Within these protests and objections, there is a yearning for virtue.

A few words of background might help to further frame the argument I advance in this book.

While I have been the owner, co-owner, and operator of several successful small businesses, I write as a moral philosopher. I acknowledge that my own experience as a manager is rather limited. In a successful entrepreneurial venture as the co-owner of a limited liability corporation, I was the business manager and publisher of a regional magazine. In that role, I was responsible for helping to develop a business plan and a budget. I was accountable for meeting a payroll, hiring and firing personnel, organizing and communicating plans to the members of the organization, structuring schedules, motivating others to accomplish their tasks, overseeing their progress, encouraging their development, negotiating agreements, and establishing networks of communication within the organization as well as with suppliers and customers. I learned what all business managers discover: managing is a constant balancing act. As a business manager, I learned first hand about finances and accounting, marketing and sales, entrepreneurship and economics, and the concrete responsibilities that go with managing a small business.

With that said, this book is written primarily in the voice of a moral philosopher. Since the 1980s, I have been a philosopher at a university. My teaching and research has engaged both the history of philosophy and contemporary questions of applied and professional ethics, especially business ethics. The argument of this book arises, in part, out of several dissatisfactions with my own previous efforts as a philosopher concerned with business ethics. Increasingly, I have come to think that substantive questions about management require a response that is framed in terms of the development of character and the cultivation of the virtues in human persons. Is it possible to be a manager while practicing the virtues? How does the account of the virtues and the description of the character of the manager developed by Alasdair MacIntyre complicate this question?

MacIntyre, perhaps more than any thinker in our day, has helped shift the focus in ethics away from a debate about competing moral principles such as utility or duty toward concern for virtues, habits of character, and the traits that make for a good life. In MacIntyre's virtue ethics, the manager emerges as a central *character* in the social drama of the present age. As I detail in the body of the book, MacIntyre envisions the manager as an amoral character entirely unconcerned with and unable to embody the virtues. "Once the executive is at work," writes MacIntyre, "the aims of the corporation must be taken as given."[2] Considered this way, the executive is a technician in pursuit of efficiency. MacIntyre aims to warn his readers that this character is dangerous. As we heed MacIntyre's warnings, we become awakened to the moral emptiness of the manager as office executive, and to deep contradictions within this sort of character.

Despite MacIntyre's criticisms of the contemporary manager, his argument has not gone far enough. On a few occasions, MacIntyre has hinted that we need a new sort of manager, but with regard to the work of filling out and building up a transformed conception of the manager, MacIntyre has done woefully little. To take up that task, this book proposes a way to reconceive both the activity of managing and the excellences needed to manage well. Retrieving two ancient characters, the "steward" and the "person of practical wisdom," this book is an argument for how moral philosophy might help bring about a transformed conception of the character of the manager.

While MacIntyre has been a prolific writer, he has not published any books on business ethics. As Ron Beadle put it, "MacIntyre is not a management thinker, and has written little about management or business."[3] MacIntyre has not focused on business ethics; in fact, he has been critical of contemporary applied ethics.[4] When asked why he declined an invitation to address a conference on business ethics, MacIntyre reportedly explained that he refused for the same reason that he "wouldn't attend a conference on astrology."[5] Despite this sort of dismissive attitude, there has developed in recent years a steady conversation within the business ethics literature engaging MacIntyre's work, and this has given rise to a variety of questions.[6] Some have debated the precise object of MacIntyre's criticism: Is it the manager that MacIntyre opposes or is his criticism aimed at modernity, enlightenment liberalism, and contemporary emotivism, with the manager serving as a mere symptom of a deeper problem?[7] Others have questioned whether

MacIntyre's account of the manager is based "on broad generalizations"[8] with too little empirical data.[9] So, I am extending a conversation that has been ongoing within the scholarly literature of business ethics and organizational studies.

Many of the writers who draw from MacIntyre's virtue ethics to discuss moral questions with regard to management are scholars who hold academic positions in business schools. Geoff Moore of Durham Business School in Britain has been a leading voice among those who think that, despite MacIntyre's criticisms of the manager and the market economy, "a MacIntyrean virtue ethics approach provides both a better diagnosis and also a better prescription."[10] In a series of articles, Moore has brought into focus the grammar and framework of MacIntyre's virtue ethics as these might be applied to business organizations, focusing on "practices and institutions, internal and external goods, and the place of the virtues within them."[11]

Concern with organizational virtue in corporations might seem out of place to those familiar with Joel Bakan's popular book, *The Corporation*, or the documentary film with the same title.[12] The tone of Bakan's work is signaled in his subtitle: "The Pathological Pursuit of Profit and Power." Bakan focuses on the corporation as a legal person, that is, as a person designed by law to be concerned only with increasing shareholder value. Such corporations compel executives "to prioritize the interests of their companies and shareholders above all others and forbids them from being socially responsible."[13] Bakan is comparatively less focused on managers and executives as individual human persons. Such individuals tend to compartmentalize their lives. They live as decent people who function quite normally outside the corporation, with warm and loving relationships with family and friends, by drawing a very sharp distinction between work and home, between "the contradictory moral demands of their corporate and noncorporate lives."[14]

Bakan's criticisms are directed almost entirely at the corporation rather than individual human persons who make up and work as management executives. Bakan uses the language of "traits" to describe the "corporation's institutional character."[15] Corporations, according to Bakan, are pathological and psychopathic in their persistent pursuit of profits; because the corporation has no conscience, it is a legal person that relates to other persons in a manner that is superficial, manipulative, grandiose, asocial, lacking in empathy and accountability, and unable to feel remorse.[16] The collapse of Enron, according to Bakan, "can be traced to characteristics common to all corporations: obsession with profits and share prices, greed, lack of concern for others, and a penchant for breaking legal rules. These traits are, in turn, rooted in institutional culture, the corporation's, that valorizes self-interest and invalidates moral concern."[17] In the final analysis, Bakan advances a moral indictment against the corporation as a legal person; his book and documentary film are directed against "the corporation's flawed institutional character."[18]

Part of what is dissatisfying about Bakan's analysis and evaluation is that his proposed solution, increased government regulations, seems tired and unlikely to provide an adequate response.[19] A more helpful way forward involves encouraging both individual and organizational reform that shapes our lives, our institutions, and our cultures in a manner that builds up those qualities of character that make for a good human life.

Thomas Wright and Jerry Goodstein, in their survey of the recent literature, boldly state their conclusion in the title of their essay, "Character is not 'Dead' in Management Research."[20] Wright and Goodstein provide a broad overview of "character across time and culture," from antiquity to the early 20th century; after the 1950s, "decades passed without serious consideration of the topic of organizational character or virtue in the social sciences literature, and it was left to business ethics scholars to draw attention to the importance and relevance of the topic of character and virtue for business organizations."[21] Their review of the revival of virtue ethics distinguishes between two perspectives: individual and organizational.

One strand of the renewed focus on character draws from the stimulus of the positive psychology movement under the umbrella of "Positive Organizational Scholarship."[22] To date, this approach has not produced a single, unified theory. Instead it has involved a range of studies, some empirical and others more conceptual, aiming to understand organizations in terms of happiness, excellence, thriving, flourishing, abundance, resilience, virtuousness, and similar themes.

Another rather significant strand includes Geoff Moore, Ron Beadle, and the other MacIntyreans who have drawn from MacIntyre's virtue ethics, extending his project into management, institutions, and questions of organizational virtue. My approach is related to but slightly different from an organizational virtue ethics perspective that focuses on institutionalizing organizational features such as a just purpose, an organizational structure that balances power among constituencies, the development of processes that promote critical dialogue and questions, and a culture that promotes virtue. I see the argument that I advance as complementing that of the organizational virtue ethicists even as it differs from it in subtle ways. In my own view, while social practices and institutions are crucial both for cultivating good dispositions and for the formation of character, virtues, properly speaking, are qualities of living persons, not institutions, organizations, or legal persons. My goal is a transformation in character, especially in the character of individual human persons. In contrast, I would characterize the goal of Moore and Beadle as the transformation of institutions. With that said, my sense is that all of us would agree that both individual and organizational transformation are needed and interconnected.

The argument of the book proceeds in four parts. First, we need a better way to conceive of the manager and a better way to understand the role of moral philosophy in contributing to our notion of the character of the manager (Chapters 1–2). Next, I examine in detail how Alasdair MacIntyre's work problematizes the manager as a character while providing a deeper diagnosis of contemporary inadequacies (Chapters 3–8). Then, I show that a business humanities approach is needed; I explain and employ such an approach, retrieving an older, deeper conception of the role of philosophy in the process of character transformation. MacIntyre's work provides a beginning; additional insights are drawn from virtue ethics, including the writings of Kierkegaard and the ancient Greeks (Chapters 9–13). Finally, the manager as wise steward is proposed as the term of such a process, including the character itself, the virtues and powers central to this character, the social context in local and global perspective, and suggestions for institutionalizing this ideal (Chapters 14–16).

A significant part of the argument of the book might be characterized as an effort to engage in a creative retrieval. I borrow this notion not only from Martin Heidegger, but more especially from Marshall McLuhan, who encouraged his readers to investigate the ways in which advances in human technology involve a subtle interplay between retrieval and reversal as figure and ground. McLuhan proposed a series of probes as "a means of focusing awareness of hidden or unobserved qualities in our culture and it is technologies, they act phenomenologically...to get at hidden properties, or concealed effects, of language and technology alike."[23] Whether it is a poem, a new form of communication technology, or a new way of organizing work, McLuhan proposed that understanding could be deepened by asking what a new development extends, pushes aside, retrieves, and reverses. For example, automobiles extend transportation, push aside horses, retrieve a sense of adventure, and when pushed to an extreme in urban sprawl, congestion and pollution, automobile culture reverses into a creative retrieval involving renewed interest in walking, jogging, bicycling, urban nature preserves, and a fascination with localism. McLuhan famously coined the phrase, the "global village" because he thought that electronic communication had the effect of moving beyond urbanized mass culture to retrieve a transformed sense of the village.

The argument of the book involves two such retrievals. Part of the book's purpose is to draw attention to the way that MacIntyre has called for a transformation in the character of the philosopher by drawing out our need for a creative retrieval of the sense that philosophy is a pursuit of understanding that serves the common good. The now standard approach to business ethics as a debate between utilitarianism and duty ethics has reached, it seems to me, a stalemated saturation point. The argument of this book is a proposal for a way forward that involves reconceiving the project of philosophers engaging questions of management and business administration, that is, a call to move forward by way of a creative retrieval.

In addition to arguing for a transformation in our understanding of the practice of philosophy, the book is primarily an argument for a transformation in the character of the manager, from office executive to wise steward. The philosopher Laurence Rohrer has raised an important objection to my argument. Rohrer notes that MacIntyre is able to reconceive what it means to a philosopher "only because he can reach back into the previous tradition, which was in a comparatively better working order. In this tradition, the role of the philosopher, his virtues, were connected to a genuine practice, aimed at the human good."[24] However, with regard to the manager, Professor Rohrer wonders whether there is anything to reclaim. Isn't the character of the manager thoroughly informed by and embedded in the larger development of advanced capitalism, and this to such a degree that there is nothing genuinely virtuous to reclaim? Aren't we just stuck in a world with amoral office executives?

In response, I propose a transformation in the character of the manager that relies on retrieving two ancient characters: the person of practical wisdom and the steward. The *phronimos*, the person of practical wisdom, is a person with experience and maturity who knows how to deliberate well, recognize when more information is needed, make good judgments, and carry out good decisions in service of the common good. The steward is one who has the privilege and responsibility of caring for the goods and property of another. I am suggesting that the best way forward involves creatively retrieving elements from the past that have been pushed aside. The manager as office executive is very much the product, not just of industrialization and capitalism, but also of print culture, especially as it reached its peak at the end of the 19th century and the first decades of the 20th century. To what extent is the culture of the "bureau," that is, the office or the desk, reaching a saturation point during the rapid shift that is occurring from print culture to electronic digitalization? When social authority based on the manager as office executive is pushed to the limits of its potential, what might it reverse into?

The possibility of a transformation in the character of the manager seems to be accelerated by features of the information age. The manager as office executive seems tied to a passing era: industrialization, the manufacturing economy, and the culture of writing on paper – especially written policies and the authority of the office so characteristic of the *ethos* of the 19th and 20th centuries. The information age, with its more highly educated workforce, decentralized decision-making, digital and electronic technologies as complements to oral and written communication, deeper awareness of the quest for work that is worthwhile, and increased desire to balance employment with other parts of a meaningful human life, might provide an opportunity for transforming the character of the manager, from office executive toward wise steward.

1
The Dreams of Future Managers

We need a better way to conceive of the manager. Future managers often conceive of their work in very different terms than future physicians. Rather than seeing their future in terms of helping others, future managers tend to conceive of their work in terms of quantifiable success, especially financial success. Our contemporary context invites a transformation in the character of the manager. With regard to the character of the manager, our culture is in a state of confused transition. Young adults drawn to careers in business administration are given relatively little support to conceive of their career ambitions as service to others. Might the dreams of future managers involve not only making a good life for themselves, but also wisely acting as stewards to advance the common good?

The difference came into focus on a typical Tuesday afternoon. A chance convergence helped me notice something initially hidden but later rather obvious: students pursuing a career in business, for the most part, have very different dreams and aspirations regarding the moral and social significance of their futures than do those going into medicine.

Upon reflection, it's not so clear to me that they should.

My purpose in this book is to provoke reflection, discussion, and hopefully a transformation. What is the task of moral philosophers with regard to management? Can moral philosophy play a role in transforming the self-understanding of managers regarding the ethical and communal purposes of their work? My goal is to bring about a change in the way we conceive of the character of the manager.

Let me turn to the events of that Tuesday afternoon. It was more than a decade ago. As a philosophy professor, I had been assigned to serve on a committee that evaluates students from our university who plan to apply for medical school. I teach at an institution in the United States that describes itself as "a Catholic, Jesuit university ranked among the top research institutions in the nation."[1] As an institution, our university has an outstanding record, among other things, of preparing undergraduate students for professional careers in health care, law, business, and engineering while placing a strong emphasis on the liberal arts. For undergraduate students hoping to become physicians, we try to do as much as we can to help our pre-med students increase their chances in the highly competitive application process for medical school. My task on the committee included interviewing a dozen or so pre-med third-year students annually as part of their application for medical school. The students already had cleared several hurdles before being assigned to me for an interview. My job involved asking questions about motivation, academic competence, intellectual maturity, interpersonal skills, and other abilities. At the end of each interview, I was charged with writing an evaluation of the student's promise as a physician. The report eventually became part of the student's medical school application file. Inevitably, this involved me asking those dreaming of entering medical practice, "Why do you want to become a physician?" I was conducting such an interview on that day.

Several years before, when I was new to this task, I was amazed by my first such interview. As I expected, he showed up well dressed and neat. That's not what impressed me. Rather, I marveled as he recounted a long list of experiences volunteering in various health care settings. His talent and his dreams struck me. He told me, "I was always the smartest kid in the class, and I especially liked science. I want to use my abilities to help people." He had begun volunteering at his doctor's office when he was 14 years old. Over the next six years, this student had served in a wide variety of health care settings: emergency rooms, nursing homes, the cancer floor of a hospital, even a stint at a health clinic in a third-world country. I had access to this student's grades. He was bright; his academic record merited him the interview. But he had more than a good mind; his record of volunteering seemed to show he had a big heart.

As it turned out, the next student I interviewed was impressive in very similar ways. In fact, almost every subsequent student assigned to me had a similar story with comparable credentials. Granted, some were slightly more extraordinary than others. The office staff screened the students before assigning them to me, so I only saw those who were on the higher end academically. In addition, these students knew not only how to dress and speak well; each evinced a commitment to "helping others."

Young people seeking to pursue the life of medicine have been encouraged from childhood to develop a habit of seeing their future in terms of helping others, reaching out and transcending their own interests. Of course, this isn't completely unusual. Almost every child who is brought up well is encouraged from a very young age to dream of becoming a "community helper." Who are the community helpers? Firefighters, police officers, nurses, teachers, and physicians. Consider a typical picture book written for young children, *I Want to Be a Doctor*. It contains colorful pictures of doctors who are happy in their work. The book invites children to dream of a meaningful career. "Doctors help you stay healthy. When you're not well, they help you feel better."

In a similar way, the pre-med students I interviewed, still a couple years away from medical school, had been encouraged to take on aspects of the character of the physician-as-community-helper. Almost every single student I interviewed had volunteered and served in the community in various ways: assisting in hospitals, tutoring children in reading or mathematics, helping in soup kitchens, and doing a wide variety of community service. The Catholic, Jesuit character of our university certainly contributes to this *ethos* of service. In addition to our commitment to academic excellence, we have a special commitment to educating "the whole person" and helping our students acquire a formation whereby each learns to make sound judgments by coming to see the world as a wondrous opportunity for growth and good works. Our campus has multiple offices with full-time staff that coordinate student volunteer service activities. Of course we are not alone in these efforts: many colleges and universities, including most secular and government-run schools, share this goal, especially for students preparing for careers in health care.

I served on that committee for several years, and after a while, I came to expect that each student I interviewed would have remarkable stories to prove his or her motivation. Again and again, I asked, "Why do you want to become a physician?" I filled a notebook full of responses. Over time, the answers became routine.

"I want to help people."

"I want to make the world a better place."

"I want to serve God by serving my neighbors in need."

"I like helping people, and I think going to medical school and becoming a physician would be a way for me to help people even more."

"I believe each person is given talents to use for others, and I think the practice of medicine would allow me to develop my talents while helping others."

Dulled now by the repetition of these interviews, I must have been feeling a bit grumpy on that particular Tuesday. I was trying to squeeze in one more such appointment before my afternoon class. Here was another aspiring physician, not yet 21 years old, who had a very long list of ways in which he had used his abilities to help others. So, I pointed out to this chipper young man, "There are other ways that you can help people, you know. I mean, you don't have to become a physician. Have you ever thought about becoming a nurse? Or how about a teacher?" I pointed out that, at that time, there was a need for more schoolteachers, especially teaching science or mathematics in inner cities and rural areas.

The student responded by explaining how his intelligence and skills were particularly suited to life as a physician. So, I suggested that it might be possible that he is drawn to the prestige and pay that physicians generally receive. "Perhaps you are really motivated by these things. Doctors are paid well, after all."

This seemed like a revelation to him. "Oh, no. I'm not really interested in the money at all. Of course, I'd like to have enough to pay my medical school bills and to raise a family. But most of all, I want to help people."

Time had gotten away from me, and I had to rush off to teach a class. So, I brought the interview to a close and shuffled across campus to teach a section of "Business Ethics." While I began teaching that afternoon's class, the earlier conversation from the interview lingered in my memory. On a whim, I asked the students, mostly business majors, the same sort of motivational questions.

"Why do you want to go into business?"

"We want to make money."

I countered, "Why not go to medical school? After all, won't most physicians make more money than many of you who are pursuing a career in business?"

I began to see the divergent tendencies in the self-understandings of pre-med students and business students: while pre-med students tend to articulate the purpose of their future careers and of their lives as community service in which they will use their talents to help others, business students frequently understand their work, and perhaps their lives, primarily in terms of self-interest, seeing any public benefit as an unintended consequence. This understanding of business activity seems deeply ingrained, not just in students who aspire to a career in business, but also throughout the culture of advanced capitalism, even among professors, especially in those of us who teach the humanistic disciplines. For more than a generation, business as profit maximization has become the default assumption.[2] This fits with a widespread theory of the firm where the purpose, existence, size, and boundaries of business organizations are accounted for in market terms: business firms exist to reduce transaction costs while maximizing profit. Viewed this way, businesses exist for efficiency and effectiveness. The goal is success, especially financial success. Even many not-for-profits have adopted a version of this approach where the purpose of the organization and aim of the manager is a specific, quantifiable outcome subject to measurement, such as moving up in a ratings system. From this perspective, it seems natural and sensible for one pursuing a degree in business administration to think of the purpose of one's career, and perhaps of one's life, in terms of quantifiable success such as "making money." Isn't that every business manager's goal?

When pressed, the students in my business ethics class recognized that "money-making" is not adequate as an expression of their own personal life goals. When asked whether money-making is a worthwhile goal, several of the students recognized that money-making is a means to other personal goals. Several business students spoke of their personal motivations, expressing a desire to support a family and raise children, to provide for their future children a good home and a secure life, and to be able to give something back to their community.

One way to move toward a reevaluation of the purpose of business administration is to notice a distinction between entrepreneurs and managers. The entrepreneur, as a character, is both well known and quite attractive to us. Steve Jobs, the cofounder of Apple, personified the entrepreneurial type. A lover of beauty, he was applauded for innovative insight and creative risk-taking while possessing an almost intuitive gift for sensing hidden possibilities while identifying and seizing new opportunities. Energized by the joy of fresh ideas, the entrepreneur is motivated not by money, but by the possibility of bringing about social change.

In contrast, most of the students in my business ethics class were pursuing degrees in business administration; they were not going to become entrepreneurs. Most would become managers of one sort or another. As managers, they would come to find themselves charged with staffing, arranging, planning, and monitoring various organizations. In some organizations, a single individual carries out both roles: the entrepreneur with a new idea later "changes hats" to become the manager who organizes the group and executes the plan. However, it more frequently happens that separate people play these two roles. In my classroom, the students as future managers I taught a decade ago have gone on to find themselves working in a vast range of positions: some in publicly traded companies, others in private firms, and many in nonprofit organizations. Indeed, managers work in many social groups: at various levels of government, in health care and various social services, in NGOs and civil society groups, in retail and hospitality services, in transportation and delivery, in athletic and cultural endeavors, in churches and religious institutions. Managers are needed just about everywhere that people work together.

Future managers who aspire to make a lot of money might seem to have good reasons for their hopes. Having been brought up in a consumer culture where wealth is glamorized (sometimes almost idolized as the highest good), it's not unusual to hear of top executives demanding rock star compensation that equals or exceeds the fortunes of superstar athletes and Hollywood celebrities. In advanced economies, the salaries and compensation packages of CEOs has risen rapidly, far outpacing both the rate of inflation and stock values, even as almost everyone else is seeing incomes stagnate or slip. For students majoring in business administration whose stated motivation is "to make money," perhaps their inspiration is the highly paid top office executive.

I asked my business students to consider another question. "Over the last hundred years, which did more to benefit society and make everyday life better: medicine or business?"

At first blush, almost everyone might think that medicine has done more good than business, but with more reflection, the complexity of the question emerges. Consider all of the ways life has improved because of business and the work organized by managers — the improved buildings in which we live; the heating and cooling systems on which we rely; electricity and communications; better transportation, food and clothing; and innumerable luxury and entertainment items. Of course, we have greatly benefited from medicine as well, but most of us make use of medical advances less often, perhaps only on a few dramatic occasions in life. Besides, health care is increasingly part of the business sector drawing on and sometimes dominated by values of efficiency and effectiveness. Quite a few idealistic pre-med students later come to find themselves making decisions about their own career – about medical specializations, residency options, and employment opportunities – while having to balance a genuine desire to promote health with business concerns attuned to financial realities.

I asked the students to think back over the past century. "Trace back your family's history as far as you can, or do what you can to imagine what life was like 100 years ago. Then, ask yourself, which has done more 'to help people,' the health care sector or the business sector?"

When I focus on my own family, this question is not easy to answer. While the health care sector certainly has helped me and my family, the impact of the business sector has been perhaps even more direct and more tremendous. A hundred years ago, my grandparents lived without electricity or indoor plumbing. My father, who was born in 1931, once wrote me a letter in which he described the impact of modernization on his childhood home. "I remember the excitement and anticipation of the arrival of electricity on the farm as something that paralleled the joy we shared at the end of World War II. When I hear biblical passages about coming out of darkness into light, I recall the sharp contrast between finding your way to bed with a kerosene lamp versus the illumination of the miracle of electricity."

The business sector has helped people in countless ways.[3] When I contrast in my imagination the descriptions from my father of the farmhouse where he was born (without running water or electricity) and compare it with the house where he lives now, his current dwelling might seem almost like a castle. Countless families could tell the same story. While millions of people do not enjoy the benefits of living in an advanced economy, for those of us who do, the last century brought untold improvements: in construction, plumbing, electricity, transportation, communication, etc. My point is straightforward. When we ask about the social improvements brought about by the health care sector compared with the business sector, it is not easy to decide which has done more over the last century to "help others."

When pressed in this way, the students in my business ethics class began to articulate deeper motivational reasons: "I'd like to be able to support a family." "I want to have a good life."

With regard to the character of the manager, our culture is in a state of confused transition. Young adults who find themselves drawn to careers in business administration are given relatively little social and cultural support to conceive of managerial activity as part of a good life involving service to others – especially compared with pre-med students. We rarely encourage young children to become managers.[4] Why the difference? Why did the aspiring physicians explain their motivations in terms of "helping others" while the business students answered in terms of instrumental rationality and self-interested materialism – even though such an answer was inadequate to capture the complexity and depth of their own desires?

We need a better way to conceive of the manager.

As my argument unfolds, I examine in detail the character of the manager that dominates advanced economies. When we encounter this character in contemporary fictional narratives, we recognize almost instantly the type: one charged with the task of organizing a group using various procedures to accomplish efficiently a given measurable result. Certainly we meet this character in modern stories – novels, movies, television programs, plays – but the character is even more familiar in the drama of contemporary social life. As Peter Drucker famously put it, the manager's task is "to make work productive and the worker effective."[5] As such, the manager is expected to accomplish specified goals, meet quotas, raise ratings, or show increased profits. More than a century ago, Frederick Taylor, the father of scientific management, summarized the modern understanding of the manager's task: to know "exactly what you want men to do, and then seeing that they do it in the best and cheapest way."[6]

Later, I examine the moral philosophy embodied in this sort of manager.

It goes without saying that this character is familiar to those preparing to become future managers. It's also well known that those who are good at this role can expect an above average salary and, when quarterly or annual goals are met or exceeded, managers get even more in the way of bonuses and raises, sometimes in very large amounts. Many CEOs receive extraordinarily high compensation packages, and this certainly reinforces the notion that the simple and single goal of the manager is reducible to cash. When the students in my business ethics class told me that they are studying business "to make money," perhaps they hoped that they would one day hit that Fortune 500 CEO jackpot, even though most of them very likely will not. Most managers are not part of the top one per cent of income earners. In fact, managers typically make less than physicians, though some obviously make very much more.

Increasingly, we hear voices asking whether our conception of the character of the manager is flawed. Gary Hamel, the contemporary management writer, laments that while modern management "has helped to make businesses dramatically more efficient, there's little evidence that it has made them more ethical."[7] For that reason, Hamel urges his readers to "strive to transcend the seemingly unavoidable trade-offs that have been the unhappy legacy of modern management."[8] Our conception of the manager developed during the age of industrialization. Does our conception of the manager constrict the moral vision and moral imagination[9] of those drawn to become managers? Why have so many business executives, including those who have graduated from top business programs, become involved in business scandals seemingly motivated by greed? The list of culprits practicing cowboy capitalism is long: Robert Vesco's 1970s mutual fund scam; Ivan Boesky and the insider trading scandal of the 1980s; Michael Milkin, the "junk bond king" of the 1980s; the Savings and Loan crisis of the late 1980s and early 1990s; Enron; Tyco; WorldCom; Adelphia; corrupt hedge funds managers, especially Bernie Madoff's Ponzi scheme, and so on. In many of these cases, bystanders were hurt while executives who made millions got off with relatively minor penalties. Success in business seems to mean padding the bottom line without attending to the common good.

With each ethical failure in the business sector, calls are voiced stressing the need for business ethics. Courses and programs have been developed to teach how to apply moral principles and theories to corporate contexts and the business environment.

The situation seems to have reached a turning point in 2008. What went wrong in the global economic near meltdown of that time? The financial crisis and the ongoing economic turmoil were not caused by a failure in business ethics; it is not that we needed new ethics programs, better codes of ethics, better principles, or better moral theories. While there obviously were some instances of dishonesty, greed, and even illegal economic activity in the events leading up to the crisis, the underlying causes are widely recognized as being more profound.[10]

Increasingly, we hear various calls to rethink business, management, and the education of future managers. In *Rethinking the MBA*, a group of Harvard business professors called for a transformation in business education with regard to basic questions of purpose; a recent Carnegie study, *Rethinking Undergraduate Business Education*, makes a similar call for a new kind of education for business students, one that focuses less on narrow technical expertise and more on good judgment and enhanced social contribution. A growing call to integrate more fully the humanistic concerns of the liberal arts with business education is expressed also in several recent books, including *Humanism in Business* and *Humanistic Management in Practice*.[11]

At my own university, a "Service Leadership" program has been recently developed for business students. (This new program was not yet in place for the students who told me they were studying business "to make money.") The "Service Leadership" program parallels the very successful health care service opportunities that have become a virtually expected part of the culture and medical school application process for future physicians. Business students who choose to participate in the "Service Leadership" program give 300 hours of community service. From a long list of service sites in the urban neighborhoods near our campus, business students now volunteer in various roles. As the program's literature states, this sort of service offers "a unique opportunity to gain meaningful leadership experience and make personal connections that can last a lifetime." The program, which has quickly come to be perceived as attractive to both business students and to employers, boasts that students give time, serve the underprivileged, practice vital leadership skills, and work with others toward a common goal.

Is it realistic to think that future managers should think of themselves as servant leaders?[12] An objector might insist that the sole purpose of business is profits, and that business executives are motivated by self-interested money-making. In response, we should note that neither altruism nor egoism quite capture the complexity of human activity. Most human actions involve both self-interest and self-transcendence; we can transcend ourselves to benefit others even as we remain bound to our own interests.[13] Is there a way of conceiving of the activities of the manager as a matter of doing something for someone else? Might those whose talents make them natural leaders become motivated to pursue something other than profits or power? In addition to the standards of success external to the activities of the manager, are there excellences internal to the very activity of managing? If so, are there character traits that can be acquired and which would enable one to pursue those excellences? Might managerial activity in a market economy be more attentive to treating humans as persons endowed with a capacity for intelligence and self-determining freedom who can make choices and form habits ordered toward the common good?[14] If so, how?

These issues are subtle and complex. On the one hand, it is worthwhile for those of us in the humanities to unmask the ambitions of the young. There is something right about raising suspicions with regard to future physicians who go through the motions of "helping others" just so they can gain acceptance into medical school in order to become wealthy. No one wants to encourage a similar kind of self-deception among managers. I am certainly not interested in giving cover to self-deceived managers. Further, the character of the doctor, especially as conceived by young people applying to medical school, might seem idealized and dated. That idealism too frequently fades after the stress of medical school, a residency that's underpaid and grueling, the pressures of educational debt, and the realities of specialization. The result for some is a sense that contemporary medical practice produces a character (and a set of character traits) quite different from the ideal of the physician-as-community-helper.[15]

On the other hand, I want to hold out a challenge to moral philosophers, moral theologians, and others in the humanities. We have a chorus of voices criticizing the self-interested materialism of those in business. Without in any way encouraging self-interest or crass materialism, isn't it possible that we could do more to articulate and build up a conception of the character of the manager such that "helping others" is integral? Can we do more to make managing, administering, and executive leadership compatible with the life of virtue? Is it possible to reconceive what it means to be a manager so that the dreams of those who pursue such careers might move beyond mere self-interest to think of one's activities in terms of helping others and serving the community?

As I hold out this proposal, that those of us in the humanities can do more to build up in aspiring managers and in the broader culture a conception of organizational leadership in terms of helping others and promoting the common good, and that managing is an activity with its own standards of excellence, I need to acknowledge immediately an objection. Certainly the long list of corrupt business leaders has infected our conception of what it means to be a manager, but those of us in the humanities frequently play into these vices. The current state of the humanities (and moral philosophy in particular), as practiced at contemporary research universities, is not particularly conducive to the sort of reflection and reasoning that I am encouraging. Specifically, a good bit of contemporary academic philosophy aims toward narrow but intense research on topics of concern primarily to other specialists (and to graduate students seeking to become professional academics). In order to respond to the objection that humanists are partly to blame for encouraging a conception of the business manager as motivated solely by profits, I draw from alternative ways of engaging in the practice of moral philosophy, building on the recent revival in virtue ethics (along with narrative ethics and literary criticism), retrieving seemingly forgotten forms of argumentation from great moral thinkers of the past, and recovering ancient insights for our social context – all while moving back and forth between periods of detailed focus and other moments that aim at a larger, holistic standpoint that is more interdisciplinary in character.

Jeffrey Cornwall and Michael Naughton, addressing themselves to entrepreneurs, ask a question that is fundamentally similar to the sort of inquiry that I am proposing: they ask, "Who is the good entrepreneur?"[16] In framing their question this way, as a "who-question" about a character, they encourage the same sort of inquiry that I think is worthy of significantly deeper reflection, and I affirm their focus on questions of vocation and virtue. At the same time, their emphasis is different from mine in two ways. They focus on the character of the entrepreneur and the unique problems that entrepreneurs face, especially the challenges that come when a new enterprise goes through a period of rapid expansion and growth: their aim is to investigate how a good entrepreneur passes on those excellences of original intent (innovation, flexibility, supportiveness, and a care for both customers and employees) without devolving into a bureaucratic, unresponsive system unconcerned with realizing genuine human goods.

In contrast, I focus on the character of the manager.

Cornwall and Naughton write as moral theologians. (In contrast, I see myself as a moral philosopher.) They draw fruitfully from the contemporary social encyclicals of the Vatican to advance an account of the good entrepreneur that aims to synthesize the concerns of business with the life of virtue. In a similar way, the essays collected in the book *Human Development in Business* draw from theological resources to advance a similar concern to engage questions about business leadership in light of a "new humanistic synthesis."[17] These writers bring into focus both criticisms (of shortsighted, profit-driven selfishness, consumerism, and materialism) and a positive proposal, an alternative vision of a sort of manager who is wise, honest, and responsible. Doing so gives rise to a question.

Is it possible to be a good manager and to practice the virtues?

Those of us who want to answer "yes" are faced with a significant challenge if we take seriously the account of the virtues developed by Alasdair MacIntyre.[18] MacIntyre sees in the manager an amoral character entirely unconcerned with and unable to embody the virtues. His criticisms problematize the manager as a character. In later chapters, I examine MacIntyre's arguments in detail; doing so provides a deeper diagnosis of contemporary inadequacies while pointing to our need for a better way to conceive of the manager and a better way to understand the role of moral philosophy in contributing to our notion of the character of the manager. MacIntyre's work provides a beginning, but we need to go further. I propose that one way forward involves a creative retrieval of an older, deeper conception of the humanistic role of philosophy in the process of character transformation. My hope is that, just as those who now dream of becoming physicians quite naturally seek to develop intellectual excellence and habits of service as they conceive of their future work in terms of making a good life for themselves while helping others and serving the common good, dawning on the horizon is a time when future managers do so as well.

2
Moral Philosophy and the Manager

We need a better way to understand the role of moral philosophy in contributing to our notion of the character of the manager. A Socratic approach to moral philosophy, which stands in contrast to a more widespread view of the professional philosopher, is proposed. One who uses a Socratic approach understands the philosopher's tasks in terms of pursuing wisdom and cultivating virtues needed to pursue excellence in one's social roles and as a human being. Alasdair MacIntyre takes this sort of Socratic approach. The book's purpose is to apply this approach to moral philosophy to engage, criticize, and extend MacIntyre's work on the manager as a character.

When an executive, administrator, or manager asks the question, "What does it mean to manage a social group?" or "What is management?" – the inquiry is, most likely, either a preliminary question (to help novices learn to become managers) or part of the formal training of those who are already practitioners. It may be an occasion to draw back and consider one's activities from a different perspective. In any case, when managers ask and try to answer such questions, they are not engaging in management.

In contrast, when a philosopher asks, "What does it mean to do philosophy?" or "What is philosophy?" – these are not preliminary questions. Asking and trying to answer those questions is right at the heart of the practice of philosophy.

However, when a philosopher, especially a moral philosopher following the example of Socrates, asks "What is management?" or "What is the character of the manager?" – it might not be quite as clear just what is being asked. Such questions can be understood in several ways.

It is quite reasonable for inquiry into the nature of management to seem like a sort of preliminary explanation of a complicated form of activity, akin to the kind of discussion one has when learning to play a game. Raising questions about what it means to be a manager might seem to presume that the one asking is uninformed or lacks basic information. "Before we start, please explain the object of the game and the rules." Indeed, most management textbooks used in business schools begin with such a chapter.

In contrast, when a moral philosopher who follows the example of Socrates asks about the nature of management, the question is raised for very different purposes. In ancient Athens, obviously there were no modern managers. What Athens did have was a new class of "knowledge workers," people who claimed that their craft involved the persuasive use of words. In the golden age of ancient Greece, with the rise of democracy, specialists in public speaking were able to merchandise their skills by claiming they knew how to navigate life in a democracy to gain power, money, and prestige. In the warrior culture that preceded the ascendancy of Athens, power and goods were frequently acquired through physical battles. By fighting with one's limbs, warriors such as Odysseus exercised cleverness and courage to secure a good life.[1] As Athens adopted democratic forms of governance, success in public life increasingly came not from the skills of the warrior, but from successful persuasive speaking. In such a context, it was possible to acquire wealth through attacking and defending, not on the battlefield with one's limbs using weapons, but in courtrooms and public assemblies with one's tongue using language. Success in public life relied on the power to secure victories in court or to convince majorities by advancing candidates and policies that protect and advance one's interests. In that cultural setting, experts in rhetoric presented themselves as masters of a skill that was crucial for leadership success in public life.

Plato repeatedly warns his reader that it is dangerous to commit one's soul to such teachers.

When Socrates conversed with Protagoras or Gorgias, the aim of his questions about the nature of rhetoric and the character of the sophist was not to understand the rules of their game, but to transcend them and to put them into a different light. Socrates' questions were so basic that they sometimes confused his interlocutors. In our day, were Socrates to ask, "What is management?" or "What is the character of the manager?" – he would be inquiring not to learn the rules of the game, but to call the game into question and to inspire his interlocutor (and others) to take up an attitude of wonder about the hidden assumptions within contemporary social practices.

The task of the philosopher, understood this way, can be compared with that of the poet, for both are concerned with wonder. Like the lover or the one who prays from the depth of one's heart a cry of thanksgiving or praise, the poet and the Socratic philosopher take up a stance that is a bit alien to the world of everyday concerns. Philosophers, like poets, lovers, and those who pray, have concerns that, in a sense, are incommensurable with those of the business world and public life as these are typically conceived. The Socratic moral philosopher stands off to the side and asks questions from the margins.

The everyday world of business operates with a set of concerns that are well known. The daily activity of attending and responding to consumer desires involves exercising intelligence, creativity, and labor by producing and merchandising goods and services for which there is a market. As a social system, the business world aims to relieve life's troubles. Experts of almost every sort offer to solve life's problems, or at least to ease the tensions, burdens, and boredoms of contemporary life – for a fee. Because human life requires cooperating with others in groups, organizations need leaders charged with the function of planning and leading. The manager, it would seem, is the one with such expertise.

So, when a philosopher asks, "What is it to be a manager?" – the question is not based on a lack of information about how office executives and those in administrative roles fit as functionaries in the contemporary social system. Instead, the question aims to rise above the here and now by viewing things from a perspective that transcends current assumptions. Wondering about the status quo and putting it to question allows the issue to disclose itself in a different light.

When Socrates asked his contemporaries to explain the meaning of their terms and the nature of their activities, it was not because Socrates lacked information about the way those terms were used in the Athens of his day. His analysis of language pointed beyond words, transcending the immediate concerns of the here-and-now in order to gain an illuminated perspective for inquiring into social life and provoking dialogue with one's contemporaries in pursuit of truth about how to live well together. The goal of Socrates was to sting his contemporaries by awakening them to contradictions and confusions implicit within the form of social life they practiced. Once the interlocutor is awakened, the Socratic goal is to transcend the limitations of one's constricted confusions by rising to an alternative framework where things might reveal themselves in a clearer light.

It is easy to misunderstand the purposes of the Socratic moral philoso- pher. Socrates seemed to many of his contemporaries as a head-in-the- clouds wanderer dwelling in detached pure thought, a "stranger to the world" who "falls into wells, and many other embarrassments, too."[2] However, that misinterprets the Socratic task. The moral philosopher journeys toward transcendence not to escape the darkness of the here- and-now, but to gain a clearer and more beautiful insight into the truth and thereby to promote the common good.

What is this alternative perspective that is sought by the Socratic moral philosopher? At times, it helps for the philosopher to take up a stance on the margins of one's culture. The philosopher longs to get out of the cave to see things as they are in the light of day; in this way, the moral philosopher is similar to the prophet who retreats into the desert or up to the mountaintop to gain a divine perspective on one's community.[3] At other times, a deepened perspective can be gained by immersing oneself intensively into the social life of one's contemporaries.[4]

Inspired by Socrates, I see myself engaging in the practice of moral philosophy in a way that has this sort of ancient pedigree. While I am certainly not alone in trying to bring this way of doing moral philos- ophy to bear upon business and management, my approach differs from the way that moral philosophy is most typically practiced, both among professional philosophers generally and in the contemporary literature of business ethics. In the English-speaking world, moral philosophers who have applied themselves to issues of professional ethics have tended to proceed with a complex but discernable set of standards regarding their tasks, methods, and questions to be investigated.[5] Richard Hare, the Oxford philosopher and business ethicist, expressed a widely held view when, writing about business and professional ethics, he asked, "So what is philosophy, and what good does it do?" Hare responded by explaining that, in his view, philosophy "is the study of *arguments* to find a way of telling good from bad ones. In short, philosophy, broadly speaking, is *Logic*."[6] Next, Hare noted that this leads immediately to the study of language. "You cannot study arguments without studying the meanings of words, and the logic that that meaning generates. All study of arguments leads us to the study of the language."[7] As Hare's essay unfolds, it becomes plain that he thinks that the task of moral philosophy is to analyze language in order to justify theories and prin- ciples, and to sort out problems that arise when those are applied in particular contexts such as business.[8]

This conception of moral philosophy, expressed quite clearly by Hare and widespread among contemporary professional ethicists, stands in rather sharp contrast with the ancient Socratic understanding of moral philosophy as an "art of character" in which the philosopher's task is to awaken, transform, and build up a set of character traits crucial for living well in a way that beautifully and truthfully integrates one's various social roles. This is not to say that Hare was unconcerned with building up virtue and encouraging people to act with good principles. Hare wrote, "The best advice I can give is that everybody in a particular walk of life, be they doctors or lawyers or business people, would be sensible if, first of all, they cultivated sound *moral* principles."[9] However, Hare did not think it was his task, as a moral philosopher, to do the cultivating. His work was "resolving the conflicts" and "justifying the principles" that arise at a second-order level.[10] With regard to cultivating virtues, that's not his department. He hoped that his reader, as he put it, had been "well brought up,"[11] but Hare seemed to leave the task of building up virtue and character to those who are charged with tending for the children.[12]

Hare's account of the philosopher's task fits with a notion of the professional ethicist that emerged in recent decades. The moral philosopher who specializes in business or professional ethics claims to be an expert credentialed with advanced training in logical and linguistic analysis, proficient in "ethical theory" (or more likely, "ethical theories") that purportedly provide the means to solve hard cases. As such, the ethicist as specialist brings expertise in resolving conflicts that arise from linguistic or logical confusion while justifying principles that bring side constraints to the activities and practices of organizational firms. Such constraints are purported to insure that the policies of a firm accord with morality.

In our service economy, where there seems to be a service professional for every consumer need, it turns out that there is a rather lucrative market for professional ethicists. Gordon Marino, suspicious of this new market for professional ethicists, tells the story of a financial consulting firm that hired an ethics consultant. The salesmen were taking clients to "gentlemen's clubs," and the female associates were becoming disgruntled as clients were transferring their accounts to their male counterparts. Upper management saw a court case forming, so they brought in an ethics expert. The advice? "Put a halt to the practice of entertaining clients at strip joints."[13] As Marino notes, it is ridiculous to think that hiring a professional ethicist is necessary in order to reach a sound judgment in this kind of case. The issue does not call for expertise in academic philosophy such as Kantian deontology, the utilitarianism of John Stuart Mill, or any other ethical theory. What's needed is a bit of flat-footed common sense along with good habits of character that allow one to possess a decent moral sensibility and a bit of fortitude and temperance.

Our need to recover the virtues while being wary of "ethics experts" is a recurring theme in the writings of Alasdair MacIntyre. As I argue in the next chapter, MacIntyre is a sort of Socratic moral philosopher for our day. He has helped shift the focus in ethics away from a debate about competing moral principles to retrieve a concern for virtues, habits of character, narrative, tradition, and cultivating the traits that allow us to become excellent in our various roles while considering more deeply how these roles fit together in our own life stories.

In certain ways, MacIntyre's approach to philosophy shares several features with both the philosopher Richard Rorty and the "Frankfort School" of German critical theorists. Rorty famously distinguished between philosophers who are "systematic" and those whose aim is to "edify".[14] On Rorty's account, systematic philosophers dominate the professionalized mainstream of the discipline; they see the task of philosophy in terms of advancing toward an eternally valid system that accurately represents reality. In contrast, edifying philosophers have a very different purpose; they call into question the central presuppositions of both contemporary culture and philosophy. Their task is to "keep space open for the sense of wonder"[15] while withstanding the tendency of their contemporaries to close off conversation by claiming to justify a complete and finished system of thought. Because the philosopher's task (as understood by edifying thinkers) seems peripheral and a direct challenge to those in the professionalized mainstream, Rorty notes that such thinkers are frequently accused of not really being philosophers.[16] However, this charge misunderstands or ignores their conception of the tasks of philosophy. "One way of thinking of wisdom as something of which the love is not the same as that of argument, and of which the achievement does not consist in finding the correct vocabulary for representing essence, is to think of it as the practical wisdom necessary to participate in a conversation."[17] The edifying philosopher sees in the poet and novelist allies whose aim is to advance social dialogue while inspiring a vision of a more humanistic world.

In *Achieving Our Country*, Rorty extends his program of edifying philosophy by offering a critique of his contemporaries. His charge is directed against the fashionable hopelessness of despairing Heideggerians, gloomy Foucaultians, and 20th-century western European Marxists such as the critical theorists of the Frankfurt School.[18] Despite Rorty's jab at the critical theorists, his approach to philosophy shares their concern with concrete social engagement. Max Horkheimer (1895–1973), one of the founders of the Frankfurt School, described philosophy's task as follows.

> The real social function of philosophy lies in its criticism of what is prevalent. That does not mean superficial fault-finding with individual ideas or conditions, as though a philosopher were a crank. Nor does it mean that the philosopher complains about this or that isolated condition and suggests remedies. The chief aim of such criticism is to prevent mankind from losing itself in those ideas and activities which the existing organization of society instills into its members.[19]

Horkheimer and his colleagues in the Frankfurt School were critical especially of a modern character, the "bourgeois individual," the modern property owner with middle-class values who views reason as an instrument to pursue individual aims. The bourgeois individual is cunning and clever in the pursuit of ends, but lacks a rational way to evaluate whether the goal pursued is worthwhile or humane. Part of philosophy's task, according to the Frankfurt School critical theorists and others, is to pillory this modern character.[20]

As my argument unfolds, I show that this understanding of philosophy's task does not go far enough. Plato and Aristotle certainly aimed to criticize the sophistical rhetoricians of their day, but they also advanced transformative arguments that aimed to change the social understanding of these social roles. The task of the philosopher is not merely to criticize what is prevalent, but also to build up an alternative "character" along with the corresponding dispositions while carving out a space for civil conversation regarding questions of deep purpose.

Let me anticipate and respond to several likely objections.

Some readers might ask, "Is this book's argument a scholarly analysis aimed at advancing the state of the debate among academics whose research focuses on business ethics, or is it merely a sermon aimed at inspiration?" At times it may seem to be one or the other without really being either. In this way, one source of initial protest might come from readers who find that, as my argument unfolds, it seemingly becomes at times too scholarly and bookish. It is well known that academics tend to presume in their readers familiarity with terms, figures, texts, techniques of conceptual analysis, and debates about topics that are of interest primarily to fellow specialists. In virtually every field, the move toward specialization results in a vocabulary that both increases precision and narrows the scope of the conversation's participants; only those with a similar training are inclined to participate in discussions that employ discipline-specific approaches and jargon. I try to withstand this tendency. After all, the moral and social questions that concern the character of the manager have significance well beyond specialists in humanities departments in the academy. I have deep sympathy with those who protest against the tendency in the world of professional scholarship to become insulated and irrelevant to broader moral and social matters. At the same time, it is worth noting that the tendency toward specialization, while it can result in a vice of narrowness and a fascination with peripheral details, arises out of a desire for precision and clarity that is both genuine and, in its proper context, quite praiseworthy. So, my hope is to communicate in a manner that draws on the resources of the academy, especially a humanistic approach to moral philosophy, without succumbing to undesirable vices.

In order to get my argument off the ground, I need to call upon a set of dispositions in my reader. As I have said, my goal is to cultivate and grow a transformed conception of the character of the manager. I need to appeal to a sort of trust in my reader to remain focused amidst sections that seem demanding, to remain patient through apparent digressions, and to remain persistent as my argument unfolds. I have provided references, not only to indicate the source of quotations and material that has shaped my thinking and writing, but also to guide those who seek more background material.

Another very different sort of objection might come from those steeped in the world of professional scholarship. To some, it might seem that my purpose is not sufficiently "theoretical" or "scholarly" – or that it is not really an argument. After all, my goal is to bring about a transformation. In response, I reply that the sort of scholarship in which I understand myself to be engaged involves retrieving a sense of the moral philosopher as a thinker who aims to transform and build up a set of dispositions in one's reader, one's culture, and oneself.

As such, my scholarship involves both describing previous instances of this form of philosophical writing[21] and attempting to enact such an effort. For readers who are inclined to protest initially against this type of transformative argument, I again need to call upon a parallel set of dispositions, including trust, patience, and persistence. I want to leave space for my reader, as a flesh-and-blood person, to affirm or reject the transformation that I propose. I am inviting my reader to follow along with the transformation at the level of one's imagination, and I am hoping to leave space for critical reflection and personal participation in the flesh-and-blood existence of those attracted to the argument and the transformation I recommend.

What do I mean by a "transformative" argument? To bring an answer into focus, it might help to contrast the philosophical approach of Richard Hare, as referenced earlier, with that of Pierre Hadot. In his book, *Philosophy as a Way of Life*, Hadot reminds his readers that, for the ancient Greeks, philosophy involved a concrete manner of living, "both in its exercise and effort to achieve wisdom, and in its goal, wisdom itself. For real wisdom does not merely cause us to know: it makes us 'be' in a different way."[22] Hadot brings into focus a range of thinkers – ancient, medieval, modern, and postmodern – who share this conception of philosophy as a transformative practice. Hadot artfully traces a continuity of purpose in the intellectual activities of a range of thinkers, from Socrates through Epicurus, Marcus Aurelius, Ignatius of Loyola, Goethe, and even including the postmodern Michel Foucault. Each engaged in intellectual practices in order to bring about a change, a transformation from unawareness through a set of "spiritual exercises" to a changed way of life. Hadot traces this approach while skillfully examining the differences between the competing ways of life that these and others proposed. Along the way, Hadot's argument is both a criticism of the professionalized character of contemporary academic philosophy and a call to retrieve the ancient sense of philosophy as the love of wisdom.

In certain ways, Hadot's argument about the practice of philosophy and the social role of the moral philosopher, while indebted to Plato, does not go as far as the approach that emerges from a deep reading of Plato's dialogues. In criticizing those who see philosophy as intellectual problem-solving disconnected from a way of life, Hadot underemphasizes the way that the ancient Greeks aimed to shape culture by transforming other social characters in addition to those whose central life activities involve teaching and researching in the practice and discipline of philosophy. As Whitehead famously quipped, philosophy is "a series of footnotes to Plato."[23] For that reason, returning to the dialogues of Plato is a constant source of refreshment for moral philosophers. Gerald Press, in his guide to reading Plato's dialogues, emphasizes not only arguments and debates, but also the characters in the dialogues who advance various positions and lines of reasoning along with attention to narrative, plot, perspective, irony, and the relationship that Plato as writer cultivates with his reader. "Disciplinary divisions and specialization in higher education lead students to suppose that philosophy, whatever it is, is something different and distinct from literature."[24] Press convincingly shows that there are profound shortcomings in trying to separate the "philosophical doctrines" of Plato from the literary qualities of the dialogues. As Press argues, approaching Plato's writings with this sort of disciplinary fragmentation is anachronistic and unwise.[25]

The practice and discipline of philosophy involves cultivating attentiveness to both the logic of arguments and the literary and dramatic qualities of the sorts of speech in which those arguments are embedded. Press notes that Plato comingles argumentation within a subtle narrative context, so perceptive readers need to attend to more than logical arguments detached from a specific set of characters and circumstances. "The most important single point – something readers should always observe – is the difference between what happens in the dialogue and what effects Plato means this to have on the audience."[26] Not only did Plato invent the dialogue "as a distinctly philosophic medium."[27] He also invented philosophy as a "discrete form of intellectual activity."[28] Attending to arguments about character is inseparable from attending to the characters that make those arguments.

Through his writing, Plato and the characters in his dialogues engage with and debate a wide range of roles and social practices. In particular, these include rhetoric (the practice of giving persuasive speeches), dramatic narrative (the practice of telling stories with a setting, characters, and a plot), as well as the activities of sophists (who claim expertise in teaching virtue, seducing students by merchandising knowledge with their claims of wisdom about the art of successful living) and statesmen (who lead communities). Plato's dialogues certainly propose philosophy as a way of life – as Hadot emphasizes. However, they do more. The dialogues also open up reflection on the story of one's life and the multiple roles one plays. In various dialogues, Socrates converses with teachers, writers, public speakers, statesmen, a priest, and characters that play various roles in their families and as citizens. Plato's dialogues encourage reflection on what it means to excel at a range of social practices: hunting and fishing; tending plants and raising animals; gymnastics and athletics; music and drama; medicine and engineering; making contracts and presenting cases in court; merchandising and retailing; the activities of the priest and the statesman; and many other social activities.[29] By presenting us with a range of characters, roles, and dramatic narratives, Plato encourages his reader to consider the traits exemplified in each character's way of life.

For example, we meet in one dialogue the young priest Euthyphro, who is prosecuting his father on a questionable charge. The setting, characters, and plot of the dialogue give rise to a set of questions in the reflective reader. Is Euthyphro's willingness to prosecute his father on questionable charges the mark of filial piety? What does one owe in piety to one's parents or one's elders? Or consider Meno, who implicitly questions whether his teacher, Gorgias, is taking advantage of him by charging for lessons in the art of successful living. This gives rise to a range of questions. Can virtue be taught? What is virtue? What are the qualities of a good student? Is Meno a good student? Are the qualities required to be a good student distinct from the qualities needed to live a good life? What is a good human life?

By opening up a space for shared reflection on these sorts of questions, Plato's dialogues provoke us to go beyond Hadot's question (about what it is to undertake philosophy as a way of life). The dialogues also encourage the reader to call into question given assumptions about social roles while taking up a quest to understand more deeply excellence in a range of roles and character states.

The dialogues of Plato encourage reflective readers to wonder: what qualities of character are required to become excellent in one's various social roles, as a citizen, a member of a family, and in one's livelihood. Plato seems to suggest that the quest to pursue understanding about such questions is part of the task of appropriating the character traits needed to do any of these well. Considered this way, the task of the philosopher involves not only pursuing wisdom as a way of life, but also creating the conditions in which other members of one's community can reflect more deeply about the character of their lives and the transformation needed to pursue excellence in their roles in the community.

I suggest that, in our time, we do well to take up this task by first listening carefully to the warnings of Alasdair MacIntyre – and especially to his account of the manager as a character. Widely regarded as one of the most important moral philosophers of our day, I propose that MacIntyre is an important gadfly for us. His writing has been influential in fields beyond moral philosophy. By engaging with, criticizing, and extending MacIntyre's treatment of the manager as a character, my purpose is both to provoke – awakening us to the limitations and contradictions implicit in current accounts – and to cultivate a transformed understanding of the character of the manager.

3
MacIntyre, Our Gadfly

Alasdair MacIntyre's work has been called "striking" and "stunning." MacIntyre's exceptional strength as a philosopher is his sting. We lack, he argues, both a shared conception of what it means to live well together and a way to engage one another rationally in a common pursuit of excellent living. Having convinced ourselves that there is no rational way to converse about our common quest for lives that are excellent and meaningful, we are lost – to a degree that may be unprecedented. In MacIntyre's writing, the manager emerges as a central character. The manager MacIntyre describes seems stuck with the motivational pursuit of success and unable to pursue human excellence for its own sake. Engaging, criticizing, and extending MacIntyre's arguments is difficult but worthwhile.

The philosophical writings of Alasdair MacIntyre have received unusually high praise. Consider a few comments about MacIntyre:

"One of the foremost moral philosophers in the English speaking world."

Newsweek[1]

"The most interesting, influential, and provocative figure in moral philosophy today."

Jonathan Wolff[2] (University College London)

"Alasdair MacIntyre is one of the most important philosophers of our time."

Stanley Hauerwas[3] (Duke University)

"One of the foremost ethicists of the last half century."

Choice[4]

Why has MacIntyre's writing been praised in such strong terms? The answer, in part, is that his prose, while sometimes demanding, is comparatively accessible and nontechnical (in contrast to the jargon-laden style of so many academic philosophers of his generation) while his insights are rich and thoughtful. More significantly, MacIntyre's writings possess these qualities while also being controversial and provocative. His moral philosophy is challenging and compelling; some have called MacIntyre's work "striking" and "stunning."[5] I want to propose that we should engage MacIntyre's work precisely because his writing aims to strike and stun us; he is our gadfly.

As is well known, Plato tells us that Socrates used this metaphor in his defense speech at his trial. Socrates compared his irritating questions to the activity of "a sort of gadfly."[6] The story, as recounted by Plato, is that the impetuous Chaerephon, a friend of Socrates, went to the Pythian prophetess to inquire from the oracle whether there was anyone wiser than Socrates. When Socrates was informed of the oracle's message, that there is "none wiser than Socrates," he interpreted it as a challenge to take up a quest for wisdom by seeking someone wiser than himself. His pestering, by unmasking those who claim to know what they do not, was inspired by this divine mission to seek wisdom and thereby to serve Athens. Socrates compared the city to a horse, a great steed that had become sluggish. His strategy – to strike and stun – was not motivated by malice. While his stinging attacks seemed a nuisance, his aim was to awaken and arouse. Socrates defended his annoying philosophical questioning by indicating that his goal was medicinal; his purpose was to exhort his fellow citizens to share his quest for virtue, and by practicing the virtues, to thereby stir up a better form of life.

MacIntyre does not claim the same comparison for himself. He never intimates a personal sense of mission, especially not a religious call comparable to Socrates's inspiration. I am not aware of any place in his writing that MacIntyre calls himself a gadfly. But I want to do so for him.

Let's be more specific about the strengths and weaknesses of MacIntyre's work. What qualities merit the admiration his writing has received? As Thomas D'Andrea put it, "Part of what has made MacIntyre's thought so attractive and influential across the humanities is his sustained critical engagement with a wide variety of standpoints and intellectual styles."[7] Early in his career, MacIntyre published articles on the forefront of analytic philosophy in ethical theory, action theory, philosophy of science, and philosophy of religion. He has written on and engaged Marxism, psychoanalysis, the existentialist movement, continental philosophy, sociology, the classical metaphysical tradition, and countless figures from the history of philosophy. In various moments, his writing embodies some of the best elements of both Anglo-American analytic philosophy (precision, logical rigor, detailed conceptual analysis) and continental philosophy (depth, social relevance, and historical attentiveness).

The most notable achievement of MacIntyre's career has been the 1981 publication of *After Virtue*. While that book was part of a larger trend in academic philosophy – the revival of virtue ethics in the secular, English-speaking academy – its impact has been significant, influencing the way many engage in moral philosophy. *After Virtue* is a book that was written in the middle of MacIntyre's career, and several of the themes in *After Virtue* are anticipated in essays and books that MacIntyre published prior to 1981. Nonetheless, *After Virtue* marks a shift in the direction of MacIntyre's project as a career author, and much of his later writing is a development of the new path he outlined in that now-classic text.

After Virtue begins and ends with MacIntyre sounding an alarm. He warns his reader that contemporary moral philosophy and contemporary culture are both in crisis. The depth of the disorder is hidden because of the state of the new Babel. In the biblical story of Babel, confusion entered social life because of the proliferation of languages. In the new Babel, language is confused, not by a profusion of particular languages, but because the same words are unwittingly used to mean different things. Our moral discourse is disordered, warns MacIntyre, because it is drawn from fragments that now lack the contexts from which their significance derived. Disagreement about the central moral issues of our time – abortion, war, the allocation of resources for health care – is a symptom of a deeper disorder. Unless properly diagnosed and treated, the new Babel will result in interminable debates. The way forward, proposes MacIntyre, is to retrieve insights from a culture somewhat alien to the contemporary world, e.g., the ancient medieval tradition of the virtues. The sting of MacIntyre the gadfly carries a message: During our slumber, the barbarians have been ruling us for quite some time. What is needed is a new St Benedict who will cultivate local forms of community within which civility and the intellectual and moral life can be sustained.

Of course, MacIntyre has had his critics, often deservedly so. He is prone to two recurrent flaws: sweeping Hegelian moments of overstated grand-theorizing and idiosyncratic interpretations of texts from the history of philosophy involving readings that cannot withstand critical scrutiny. At the heart of the first vice is MacIntyre's occasional desire for a totalizing and tidy system – a yearning that is in tension with his better mode, that of cultivator of the virtues. The other vice, more pronounced in the early part of his career, is his propensity at times to overreach his expertise as an expositor and interpreter of the history of philosophy.[8] As a systematician, MacIntyre is not extraordinary; as a historian of philosophy, he is sloppy at times. It is worth noting that MacIntyre occasionally confesses such vices; he has sought to correct them in his published work.[9] Despite such occasional shortcomings, MacIntyre's writing rewards serious engagement.[10]

MacIntyre's strength as a philosopher – his best trait – is his sting. "Wake up," he is warning. Amidst the comforts and conveniences of consumer culture, we find ourselves in a fragmented society, too often unaware that we have lost our bearings, and we have forgotten how to engage in civic and rational discourse about issues of deep purpose. We lack both a shared conception of what it means to live well together and a way to engage one another rationally in a common pursuit of excellent living. The accoutrements of material success have lulled us into a hazy unawareness that the contemporary world is racing toward aimlessness. Having convinced ourselves that there is no rational way to converse about our common quest for lives that are excellent and meaningful, we are lost – to a degree that may be unprecedented. One writer calls MacIntyre a contemporary "intransigent prophet" and a "robe-ripping Savanarola" preaching against the moral corruption of the elites of the day.[11] In a related manner, I propose that Alasdair MacIntyre is our gadfly, our provocateur, the one who busies himself by raising questions that the culture of consumption considers a nuisance.

A central way in which MacIntyre has stung the contemporary world is through his identification of the bureaucratic manager as the anti-hero of our age. In MacIntyre's writing, the manager emerges as a central character, perhaps the key villain in his account of the drama of contemporary social life, the protagonist in his criticism of modern, enlightenment rationality. MacIntyre condemns this villainous character, not only in *After Virtue*,[12] but also in many other parts of his authorship.[13]

For more than 50 years, MacIntyre's writing has provoked and stunned. As a career author, his work draws on a wide range of sources and includes several significant shifts. Because of these complexities, it will help to approach MacIntyre's account of the *character* of the manager from multiple angles. My central axis will be *After Virtue*, especially Chapter 3 of that book. It is in that chapter that MacIntyre provides his most detailed account of the character of the manager. The sort of manager that MacIntyre has in mind is an office executive, that is, a bureaucrat of the kind described by the early-20th-century German sociologist, Max Weber. Weber described the manager as the epitome of modern leadership. However, where Weber saw the manager as the embodiment of progress in efficient, rational organization, MacIntyre sees a character who is both hollow and dangerous.

As should be clear by now, I am coming at these issues as a moral philosopher, as one educated in the humanities, and as one who sees himself as influenced by a Socratic approach. While I have had a long-standing interest in business ethics generally, including issues at the intersection of the moral–cultural sphere and the sphere of market economics, my formal education is in theology and the history of philosophy. In contrast to so many philosophers in the English-speaking world whose training is primarily in the analytic approach that dominates the Anglo-American academy, my own philosophical education is comparatively somewhat idiosyncratic. I have spent most of the last 35 years, as a student and a professor, at Jesuit universities. Other than a semester in Rome and a year in New York, I have studied and taught in the Midwestern region of the United States (in Chicago, Milwaukee, and Saint Louis).

Consider a point made by MacIntyre in his Gifford lectures: published under the title, *Three Rival Versions of Moral Inquiry*, MacIntyre famously described three competing intellectual frameworks. He skewers 1) enlightenment liberalism and 2) postmodernity, and he praises and calls for a revival of 3) the Aristotelian–Thomistic tradition.[14] My intellectual formation occurred precisely within that tradition; the influence of Greek philosophy and the medieval tradition has been constant, and constantly attractive, for me. While the approach to education at the contemporary Jesuit universities with which I am familiar is quite pluralistic,[15] the Aristotelian–Thomistic stress on the virtues remains present, and it engaged and influenced me well before I immersed myself in MacIntyre's work.

Shaped by this tradition, I was taught that in order to do philosophy well, one must learn the history of philosophy with care and attentiveness. In particular, this involves learning to understand texts written in a language other than one's own while attending to the cultural assumptions presumed in the text. It was impressed upon me that transmitting ideas and arguments through the medium of writing is demanding work, both for the writer and for the reader. In short, I learned that the practice of reading philosophy contains its own excellences. To become an active participant in the conversation of the tradition, I learned that it is necessary to acquire and cultivate a rather unique set of interconnected intellectual and moral habits.

As part of this formation, I learned to treat philosophy books as gems, that is, as invitations to enter a dialogue, sometimes friendly, sometimes combative, but always aimed at taking up a shared quest for understanding. Considered this way, reading a philosophy book is akin to forming a relationship with an author, where the author is a potential friend. One's task as a reader is to become properly disposed so that one might both follow the movement suggested by the author and at the same time maintain a critical distance so that one is not manipulated either to accept an unwarranted conclusion or to become disposed in a way that one does not want. Philosophy, understood this way, is a meta-disposition, that is, a disposition toward a disposition, a longing to acquire a personal quality that one does not currently possess in its entirety. According to this approach, there are two different sorts of arguments involved in reading philosophy. On the one hand, one must attend to arguments at the level of logical analysis, asking whether the premises are true and the reasoning is valid in order to evaluate whether the content is transmitted seamlessly from the premises to the conclusion. On the other hand, one must attend to the relationship between reader and author in order to evaluate whether the content is, or should be, transmitted from author to reader. Further, through the activity of engaging with the thoughts and arguments of another, that very activity folds back upon oneself, shaping one's character and intellect in a manner either toward integration or fragmentation. Understood this way, the activity of the moral philosopher involves learning to be disposed properly to the activity of moral philosophy. Because so much of the writing of moral philosophers aims to cultivate a particular set of dispositions, one's task as a reader involves both cultivating and critically questioning the dispositions that make for a good life.[16]

MacIntyre's account of the virtues, while complicated, is drawn especially from Aristotle and St Thomas Aquinas. Within this tradition, each of the virtues is understood as a *hexis* or *habitus*, that is, an acquired personal quality or dispositional trait.[17] The virtues are those traits of character and intellect that allow us to flourish in social practices, as individual persons, as members of various communities, and as human animals subject to various vulnerabilities. The virtues include, for example, patience, honesty, persistence, and justice.[18] The one who has acquired such traits has the thoughts, feelings, desires, and relations characterized by a virtuous person. For example, the person who has acquired the trait of persistence is able to withstand difficulties by thinking the right sort of thoughts, feeling confident amidst challenges, withstanding temptations and distractions, and relating to others and the world with resolve that is at once both impassioned and serious.

MacIntyre's virtue ethics is "neo-Aristotelian" in the following sense. In *After Virtue*, he develops an account of the virtues without relying on Aristotle's "metaphysical biology."[19] While MacIntyre never explains precisely what he means by this, I take it that he thinks he can proceed without employing the function (*ergon*) argument of Book I, Chapter 7 from Aristotle's *Nicomachean Ethics*,[20] and without entering into the question as to whether human beings are animals distinguished by a unique rational nature. Rather than drawing from the function argument, MacIntyre emphasizes a distinction that Aristotle makes between two kinds of goods.

Aristotle draws this distinction in the beginning paragraph of Book I of the *Nicomachean Ethics*. In the book's first sentences, Aristotle asserts that goodness has the quality of an end, that is, goodness is desirable, choice-worthy, and the object of purposive human pursuits.[21] Next, Aristotle draws this crucial distinction: "A certain difference is found among ends; some are activities, others are products apart from the activities that produce them."[22] In other words, while there are goods that are products *external* to a particular activity, there are other goods that can only be achieved while engaging *in* an activity. Carpenters build for the sake of a house; musicians play for the sake of the symphony. The house is a product that is *external* to the activity of building, but the symphony is not a product in this sense; the symphony is, in a way, the activity of the musicians. The central activity that Aristotle has in mind when pointing to what is done for its own sake is active participation in a community. The distinction between internal and external activities, which permeates Aristotle's moral and political philosophy, is central to MacIntyre's virtue ethics.

It is always difficult to tell which parts of a philosopher's work will be studied in the future, but it seems likely that for generations, scholars will continue to discuss MacIntyre's story of the "chess-playing-child."[23] The story is MacIntyre's effort to illustrate Aristotle's distinction between external and internal ends. As my argument unfolds, I repeatedly reference this story.

Consider the example of a highly intelligent seven-year-old child whom I wish to teach to play chess, although the child has no particular desire to learn the game. The child does, however, have a very strong desire for candy and little chance of obtaining it. I therefore tell the child that if the child will play chess with me once a week I will give the child 50 cents worth of candy; moreover I tell the child that I will always play in such a way that it will be difficult, but not impossible, for the child to win, and that, if the child wins, the child will receive an extra 50 cents worth of candy. Thus motivated the child plays to win.[24]

The story traces a transformation in the child. At first, the child is not interested in chess. Then, once the offer of money-for-candy is made, the child undergoes a change. Now, the child is willing to learn; the youngster becomes motivated both to play and to win. MacIntyre goes on to make this point: "Notice however that, so long as it is the candy alone which provides the child with a good reason for playing chess, the child has no reason not to cheat and every reason to cheat, provided he or she can do so successfully."[25] In this circumstance, were the adult called away from the chess table, it would be in the child's rational self-interest to cheat.

In the next part of the story, the child undergoes another transformation. MacIntyre asks us to imagine a scene perhaps several weeks later. The child has now learned to play chess, and the weekly chess games have become a matter of routine. Imagine a visit in which one's pockets are empty. Suppose one tells the child, "It's no use for us to play chess this week. I didn't bring any money." As MacIntyre writes, one can hope that

> there will come a time when the child will find in those goods specific to chess, in the achievement of a certain highly particular kind of analytical skill, strategic imagination and competitive intensity, a new set of reasons, reasons now not just for winning on particular occasions, but for trying to excel in whatever way the game of chess demands.[26]

After this transformation, how might the child now respond to the offer to play chess without the motivation of money-for-candy? Now transformed, the child comes to recognize that there are excellences internal to the practice of chess, and that these excellences are worth pursuing for their own sake. Given the offer to play now, the child might well respond, "I don't care about the money or the candy. Let's just play."

Notice that with this change in motivation, the temptation to cheat is reduced or obliterated. "Now if the child cheats, he or she will be defeating not me, but himself or herself."[27]

MacIntyre uses the example of the chess-playing child to show several transformations. Originally motivated by money-for-candy, the child agrees to take up the activity of chess-playing. After becoming initiated into the practice of chess, the child moves through an apprenticeship (perhaps unwittingly) and comes to learn that there are excellences internal to the practice of chess (apart from the money-for-candy that results as per the agreement). In discovering the excellences internal to the practice, the child undergoes a change in motivation. Rather than being motivated primarily by the goods that come with the pursuit of success, the child comes to be motivated by the excellences integral to the practice.

The only way to pursue the excellences internal to the practice of chess – that special kind of analytical skill required in chess along with the strategic imagination and competitive intensity that are part of the game – is to engage in the practice. In contrast, there are many ways that one can acquire 50 cents or candy other than winning at chess.

The acquisition and development of a set of traits is crucial to pursue the excellences internal to a social practice such as chess. As MacIntyre claims, "it is not difficult to show for a whole range of key virtues that without them the goods internal to practices are barred to us."[28] The virtues are central to the moral life precisely because it is those dispositions that make possible the pursuit of those excellences internal to social practices.[29]

Reviewers and critics have raised many challenges to MacIntyre's project.[30] While responding to his critics, MacIntyre sometimes clarifies his points (when he thinks the criticisms are based on misunderstanding due in part to his own lack of clarity), and at other times, MacIntyre has later modified his position. For more than half a century, MacIntyre's thinking, as expressed in his published work, has been evolving and developing; part of the reason that MacIntyre's thought has undergone change has to do with MacIntyre's capacity for acknowledging the insights of his critics. Many reviewers of *After Virtue* charged MacIntyre with over-emphasizing social practices in a way that left him with an ethic that was susceptible to a form of relativism.[31] One objection appeals to the example of Adolf Eichmann, the so-called architect of the Holocaust.[32] In order to carry out the plan of Hitler's Nazi regime, Eichmann directed the deportation and execution of thousands of Jewish people. To accomplish this, Eichmann seemed to exhibit many virtues: loyalty, reliability, trustworthiness, etc. Does a virtue ethic that focuses on character-traits-needed-to-excel-in-social-practices leave us susceptible to blind obedience and without the ability to criticize social practices and traditions other than our own?[33]

MacIntyre developed a variety of sophisticated responses to this challenge.[34] In 1999, he conceded that a virtue ethic that is not attentive to human biology is inadequate. Responding to his critics, MacIntyre adjusted his account of the virtues:

> In *After Virtue*, I had attempted to give an account of the place of the virtues, understood as Aristotle had understood them, within social practices, the lives of individuals and the lives of communities, while making that account independent on what I called Aristotle's "meta-physical biology." Although there is indeed good reason to repudiate important elements in Aristotle's biology, I now judge that I was in error in supposing an ethics independent of biology to be possible – and I am grateful to those critics who argued this case against me.[35]

So, MacIntyre's considered account of the virtues is more complicated than that which he presented in *After Virtue*.[36] (In acknowledging that our biology as human animals is morally significant, MacIntyre points to the need to develop a set of virtues that flow from acknowledging our shared animality; this includes the virtues of "just-generosity," including sympathy toward those who are sick or disabled and hospitality toward strangers, unexpected guests, and those outside one's limited community. By drawing on the virtues of acknowledged dependence, MacIntyre has the resources to respond to the challenge raised by the example of Eichmann. MacIntyre considers his later work on the virtues to be "reconsiderations" and "extensions" of the *After Virtue* project. Despite these, MacIntyre wrote in 2007, "I have as yet found no reasons for abandoning the major contentions of *After Virtue*."[37]

MacIntyre's virtue ethics is part of a larger criticism of 1) the moral culture of modernity, 2) enlightenment rationality, 3) modern moral philosophy, 4) the philosophy of emotivism, and 5) the acquisitiveness of contemporary consumer society. We live in a culture in which the goods of success, especially as measured in economic terms, have crowded out a concern for 1) those excellences internal to practices, 2) the traditions through which those practices are transmitted, and 3) the virtues that enable the pursuit of excellence. These points of criticism converge in MacIntyre's disparagement of the character of the manager.

As I have indicated, as my argument unfolds, I point to shortcomings in MacIntyre's social criticism by retrieving a fuller sense of the tasks of moral philosophy. My charge is that, perhaps because MacIntyre operates primarily in the mode of gadfly with regard to the manager, he has left unfinished and underdeveloped the task of building up an alternative conception of this character. However, before I turn to that part of my argument, it is worthwhile to draw out in detail MacIntyre's stinging attack on the character of the manager.

4
The Manager as Office Executive: Emotivism Embodied in a Character

MacIntyre's account of the manager focuses on the office executive, that is, the bureaucrat. MacIntyre has in mind the career professional, appointed on the basis of certifiable qualifications and compensated accordingly, charged with managing a specific, limited area according to written policies and rules, and applying those in an impersonal manner within a hierarchical structure. To understand more deeply MacIntyre's conception of this character, three of the sources that most influence his account of the bureaucratic manager are investigated: Marxism, British analytic philosophy, and the sociology of Max Weber. This character, criticized by MacIntyre, is virtually identical to the sort of executive praised by Milton Friedman in his famous article, "The Social Responsibility of Business Is to Increase Profits."

In Chapter 3 of *After Virtue*, MacIntyre famously focuses on three characters: 1) the aesthete, 2) the therapist, and 3) the manager. Each of these characters aims at a goal that is given, and each uses rationality as an instrument to determine the most efficient way to accomplish the agreed-upon end. The manager works typically in an organization with a bureaucratic structure, whether a private corporation or a government agency, in a context of competitive struggle for scarce resources with the responsibility of directing human and non-human resources as effectively as possible toward predetermined ends.[1] The character type that MacIntyre has in mind is well known. One particularly clear description of this character is provided in a British newspaper article from World War II about Albert Speer, the infamous Minister of Armaments and War Production for the Third Reich. The account describes Speer as very much the successful average man, well-dressed, civil, noncorrupt, very middle class in his style of life ... [Speer] symbolises a type which is becoming increasingly important ... the pure technician, the class-less bright young man without background, with no other original aim than to make his way in the world and no other means than his technical and managerial ability. It is the lack of psychological and spiritual ballast, and the ease with which he handles the terrifying technical and organizational machinery of our age, which makes this type go extremely far nowadays. This is their age; the Hitlers, the Himmlers we may get rid of, but the Speers, whatever happens to this particular special man, will long be with us.[2]

With rhetorical understatement, MacIntyre declares that this sort of manager is not a "marginal figure" in the social drama of the present age.[3]

During the same period immediately after World War II, Herbert Simon famously referenced the "administrative man"[4] who uses an outcome calculus to optimize efficiency. Simon noted that the administrative man "satisfices" rather than maximizes; the best administrative decision or policy is the one that suffices to satisfy the minimum requirements needed to meet a measurable objective in light of time constraints and limited information.[5]

This sort of character is easily recognizable, not only in high-profile figures such as CEOs and CFOs, but also in countless vice presidents and administrators, middle managers, even first-line managers. The modern bureaucratic manager, although first developed in the context of industrial manufacturing, can now be found in virtually every social organization. In addition to the business sector, managers are present in government, health care, education, social services, and in almost every aspect of the developed economies of the industrial and post-industrial world. One widely used management textbook tells students, "once you graduate from college and begin your career, you will either manage or be managed."[6]

Note that MacIntyre's criticism of the bureaucratic manager is not the same as the standard distaste for bureaucratic inefficiency. For example, MacIntyre's criticisms of the bureaucrat are different from those of Ludwig von Mises.[7] Mises wanted his readers to recognize the power of bureaucracies – sometimes fruitful and other times destructive – and then to frame that power within the bounds of constitutional democracy, leaving room for entrepreneurial managers who are not bureaucrats.[8] As Mises put it, "The terms bureaucrat, bureaucratic, and bureaucracy are clearly invectives."[9] They connote not only inefficiency, but an inhuman

loss of dignity, a learned inability of office clerks, an acquired habit of refusing to make common-sense decisions. Understood this way, the term *bureaucrat* is "always applied with an opprobrious connotation."[10]
    The heart of MacIntyre's criticism of the bureaucratic manager lies elsewhere. Because MacIntyre's description of the character of the manager (and his criticisms of this character) are prominent in *After Virtue*, that will be my focus. To draw out certain themes from the argument of *After Virtue*, I point to three sources that inform MacIntyre's conception of the character of the manager: Marxism, British analytic philosophy, and the sociology of Max Weber. Let's examine each in turn.

MacIntyre and Marx

Long before writing about the bureaucratic manager as a "character," MacIntyre had been critical of bureaucracy, most notably in his writings on Marxism. As is well known, MacIntyre was, in his youth, a member of the Communist Party.[11] His first book, *Marxism: An Interpretation* (1953), was published when he was in his early twenties. (It is worth noting that the youthful MacIntyre was critical of certain features of Marxism; he aspired to be both a Christian and a Marxist, as much as both were possible.) Fifteen years later, he published a significantly revised version of this book with a new title, *Marxism and Christianity* (1968), and he wrote many essays on Marx and Marxism during that period.[12] By the time that *After Virtue* was published (1981), MacIntyre's views on Marxism had shifted again. MacIntyre refers to Marx in *After Virtue* only a handful of times; in those instances when he agrees with Marx, he states that he does so "for non-Marxist reasons."[13] Nonetheless, elements of MacIntyre's criticism of the bureaucratic manager found in *After Virtue* are already present in seminal form in MacIntyre's earliest publications, especially in his Marxist writings.
    In his early writings on Marxism, MacIntyre expresses a desire to learn from both Marxism and Christianity. From the Christian gospels, MacIntyre is attracted to the prophetic command to show mercy, particularly as it is expressed in the parable of the last judgment, the story in which the shepherd gathers all the nations to separate the sheep from the goats. "Then the righteous will answer him and say, 'Lord, when did we see you hungry and feed you, or thirsty and give you drink? When did we see you a stranger and welcome you, or naked and clothe you? When did we see you ill or in prison, and visit you?' And the king will say to them in reply, 'Amen, I say to you, whatever you did for

one of these least brothers of mine, you did for me.'"[14] MacIntyre finds, implicit within this parable, five principles.

1) Redemption is not simply a matter for individuals; "all the nations will be assembled" for judgment and the possibility of redemption.
2) Secular social structures, permeated by sinfulness, are subject to eternal judgment for the ways they embody distortions and fail to measure up to the transcendent order.
3) The task of eternal judgment, separating the sheep from the goats, i.e., the righteous from the sinful, belongs to God alone, and is not for humans to presume.
4) Humans have the task of showing mercy, especially to the poor and the outcast.
5) We meet God, who is transcendent, in the immanent context of time and space when we encounter those in need, and we are frequently unaware of this.[15]

MacIntyre was attracted to Marx and the project of communism precisely because he thought that Marxism took up the prophetic challenge of Christianity more faithfully than Christians. MacIntyre advanced three criticisms against Christians.

1) Orthodox Protestants, emphasizing individual salvation and other-worldly concerns, have tended to be passive concerning the injustices of this world.
2) Liberal Protestants, engaging in activism, tend to disregard the reality that the redeemed are also infected by sin and in need of continual redemption, and
3) Traditional Christians tend to assume that they know the identity of the righteous based on acts of religious observance.[16]

The young MacIntyre was attracted to the prophetic voice in Karl Marx, in Marx's call to create a just social order. However, by the time that his book on Marx was revised in 1968, MacIntyre, while still attracted to the "radical criticism of the secular present,"[17] seems more wary about the promise of Marxism, and is openly critical of Stalinism.[18]

Important features of MacIntyre's engagement with Marxism[19] are captured in an important two-part essay, "Notes from the Moral Wilderness," that MacIntyre published in the late 1950s.[20] MacIntyre takes it as given both that modern liberal capitalism (which he sees as the endless pursuit of more and more money) is morally empty and that the bureaucratic means–end rationality of Stalinism is morally corrupt. He presents his criticism of bureaucratic rationality primarily against Stalinism, and he does so from a position that he describes as a "moral wilderness," for he openly questions whether he and his fellow Marxists have an adequate account of the moral life. The key sort of bureaucratic manager that MacIntyre has in mind during the early part of his authorship is not the Harvard MBA, but the Stalinist bureaucrat who uses authority from above, making things official by marking them with his rubber stamp. Of course, as it turns out, MacIntyre later comes to think that there is little difference between the Stalinist bureaucrat and the capitalist executive who runs a company of workers he has never met to produce goods or services about which he knows almost nothing.

MacIntyre's criticism of Stalinism is presented as a sort of *reductio*. His argument goes like this. Within Marxism, there is a commitment to both scientific determinism (in the inexorable march of history) and the freedom of self-determination (in the confidence of revolutionaries that their actions can change the world). When this conflict between determinism and determination arises, it results in a kind of deification; Stalin is deified, or the party is deified.[21] MacIntyre then claims that Marx would have been critical of Stalin at this point. Stalinism did not result in the classless society that Marx and Engels promised: it resulted in "bureaucratic state capitalism."

MacIntyre does not provide a detailed explanation of this phrase. In fact, he concedes that, "on the positive characterization of bureaucracy specifically, Marxist analyzes have been notably weak."[22] He faults Marxism for failing to provide an adequate account of bureaucracy.[23]

So, MacIntyre's treatment of Marxism contains a criticism of bureaucracy, even if he has not provided a detailed account of bureaucracy. Implicit in this criticism of bureaucracy is an anticipation of the bureaucratic manager. Just under the surface, in both Marx and MacIntyre, there is a yearning, perhaps almost romantic, for a community of self-regulated laborers who are happy in their work and able to guide their activities without the need for bureaucratic policies and regulations. Consider MacIntyre's example of the fishing crew "whose members may well have initially joined for the sake of their wage or other share of the catch, but who have acquired from the rest of the crew an understanding of and devotion to excellence in fishing and to excellence in playing one's part as a member of such a crew."[24] On MacIntyre's telling, when the members of such a fishing crew face a difficulty, for example, if one member of the crew were to die at sea, then "fellow crew members, their families and the rest of the fishing community will share a common affliction and common responsibilities."[25] One senses that MacIntyre shares the romantic ideal of Marx on this score: such a community of workers doesn't need a set of bureaucratic policies to plan a funeral. The workers, by virtue of their own self-direction as exercised within their shared community, can make their own decisions about how to order their lives together. It is this humanistic side of Marx that is attractive to MacIntyre, and he uses this humanism as part of his criticism of the bureaucratic state capitalism of Stalinism.

Two other aspects that MacIntyre finds attractive in the philosophy of Marx are worth noting. First, Marx is a philosopher of *praxis*. He is concerned with the way that ideas impact social practices. In discussing the tension between freedom as a contemporary goal and the suffering conditions of many, MacIntyre states that such questions "demand action" and involve "the transformation of philosophy into an instrument of action."[26] Throughout his writings on Marxism, we find in MacIntyre a deep sympathy for the notion that philosophical ideas should and do become embodied in concrete social practices. We can feel in MacIntyre's writings on Marxism his criticism of "Oxford armchair style" philosophy. "The notion that the moral philosopher can study the concepts of morality merely by reflecting ... on what he or she and those around him or her say and do is barren."[27] This contrast between the Hegelian and Marxist concern with the way that ideas shape social life compared with the anti-Hegelian style of British analytic detachment is particularly acute if we recall that at the same time that he was writing as a Marxist, he was a student and then a young professor trained in and surrounded by the Oxford analytic style.

A third feature of MacIntyre's Marxist writings anticipate his account of the manager. The young MacIntyre was particularly attracted to the Marxist criticism of liberalism. Capitalism, on MacIntyre's way of understanding the world, is the social embodiment of liberalism in the economic sphere, and utilitarianism is the moral philosophy that corresponds with capitalism. Throughout his early writings on Marxism, MacIntyre sees himself as "committed to a radical critique of the existing social order."[28] What is the precise nature of this radical critique? What is its object? MacIntyre answers by pointing to "the liberal belief that facts are one thing, values another – and that the two realms are logically independent of each other."[29] In his early Marxist writings, MacIntyre states, "For the liberal, the individual being the source of all value necessarily legislates for himself in matters of value; his autonomy is only preserved if he is regarded as choosing his own ultimate principles, unconstrained by an external consideration."[30] As we will see, it is precisely this strict fact/value distinction that MacIntyre identifies with the enlightenment liberalism that he criticizes in *After Virtue* and which he sees as embodied in the character of the manager.

The manager and the embodiment of emotivism

Next, let's focus on the way that MacIntyre engages British analytic philosophy in his characterization of the manager. Recall the setting and context of Chapter 3 in *After Virtue* where the character of the manager makes his first appearance. In Chapter 1 of *After Virtue*, MacIntyre begins with a disquieting suggestion, a thought experiment drawn from Walter Miller's novel, *A Canticle for Leibowitz* that aims to awaken us to the contemporary crisis in moral philosophy and culture. In the future world that MacIntyre imagines, a series of environmental disasters are blamed on the activities of scientists. Violent riots result in book burnings and the destruction of laboratories; the community of scientists is systematically murdered or imprisoned. Generations later, there is an effort to revive the practice of science, but expressions such as "neutrino," "mass," "specific gravity," and "atomic weight," torn from their natural home, come to be used in arbitrary and competing ways as many of the beliefs that made those expressions meaningful in their original contexts had been lost.

MacIntyre suggests that modern moral philosophy is currently in this kind of disordered state. It is made up of fragments that lack the contexts from which their significance derived. For those unfamiliar with this diagnosis of modernity, it is startling, and it raises an obvious objection: if a catastrophe sufficient to throw the language and practice of morality into grave disorder had occurred, surely we should all know about it. In response, MacIntyre claims our culture is in a state so disastrous that we are blind to its problems and there are no large remedies for it.

MacIntyre claims that the most striking feature of contemporary moral discourse is that so much of it is used to express disagreements, and these disagreements appear interminable. Contemporary moral debates are interminable, according to MacIntyre, in several senses: they seem to go on without any end in sight; they have no clear terminus, that is, no clear goal that the disputants are aiming at together; and they rest on a conceptual incommensurability such that each side presents arguments that are valid, but does so while employing concepts and premises not shared by opposing disputants.

Next, MacIntyre considers another objection: Is not this standoff between competing moral grammars a feature of any historical situation where there is more than one way of understanding how to live a good life? In response, MacIntyre writes, "One philosophical theory which this challenge specifically invites us to confront is emotivism."[31] He describes emotivism as "the doctrine that all evaluative judgments and more specifically all moral judgments are nothing but expressions of preference, expressions of attitude or feeling, insofar as they are moral or evaluative in character.[32]

In short, emotivism is the philosophy that states that, with regard to morality and values, each person is entitled to his or her own feelings; we should tolerate the individual choices of others insofar as they are merely expressions of private or personal value.

In order to understand the connection between the character of the manager and the philosophy of emotivism for MacIntyre, we can get an important clue by tracing the roots of MacIntyre's thinking, beginning with his college days when he attended A. J. Ayer's lectures on ethics. Ayer's moral philosophy is expressed succinctly in a book that has become a classic of British analytic philosophy:

> The presence of an ethical symbol in a proposition adds nothing to its factual content. Thus if I say to someone, "You acted wrongly in stealing that money," I am not stating anything more than if I had simply said, "You stole that money." In adding that this action is wrong I am not making any further statement about it. I am simply evincing my moral disapproval of it.[33]

During MacIntyre's formative years, this sort of moral philosophy predominated in British universities. Philosophers saw it as their task to analyze the meaning of the terms used in moral discourse, and then, assuming a strict fact/value distinction, moral judgments were thought to be nothing more than expressions of value, that is, personal feeling. Under the presumption of a sharp split between facts and values, statements of *fact* are limited to mathematics and the natural sciences, and all other statements are considered expressions of emotion, i.e., personal *values*. This philosophy of emotivism is generally identified with modern British thought and usually traced to David Hume (1711–76) and G. E. Moore (1873–1958). This sort of emotivism was in vogue among British philosophers while MacIntyre was a student.

From his youth, MacIntyre has been critical of the emotivism advanced by his teachers, elders, and fellows. (In Chapter 8, I focus on MacIntyre's criticisms of the character of the manager, and these are tightly connected with his criticism of emotivism. In this chapter, my goal is to understand

MacIntyre's conception of the manager more deeply; a central aspect of that involves understanding the philosophy of emotivism, which MacIntyre thinks is embodied in the manager.) After attending Ayer's lectures, he later wrote a master's thesis, completed in the early 1950s, in which he criticized both the philosophy of G. E. Moore and the emotivism of C. L. Stevenson. From the MA thesis onward, MacIntyre was "gripped by a sense of the inadequacy of the dominant styles of English-speaking ethical theory, and working primarily with the idiom of Oxford ordinary language philosophy, he is attempting to formulate an alternative to supplant these."[34]

Over the 30-year period between MacIntyre's days as a student and the publication of *After Virtue*, he established deep and persistent criticisms of emotivism. The heart of MacIntyre's criticism is drawn from Wittgenstein. It is based on the distinction between meaning and use. He faults analytic philosophers with evaluating emotivism as a theory of meaning while disregarding it in terms of use. MacIntyre notes that many later analytic philosophers rejected emotivism on the grounds that it failed as a theory of meaning. He mentions John Rawls, Alan Donagan, Bernard Gert, and Alan Gewirth as examples.[35] (These, of course, are the leading moral philosophers within analytic philosophy at the time that MacIntyre was writing *After Virtue*.) Each argued, contra emotivism, that morality is based on some rational principle; it is not a matter of nonrational feelings. However, MacIntyre thinks his fellow analytic moral philosophers have overlooked the success of emotivism with regard to use.[36] Drawing upon Wittgenstein's distinction between meaning and use, MacIntyre claims that moral philosophers should do more than analyze utterances and meanings; moral philosophers should turn to concrete social practices in order to understand the way that ideas are embodied.

MacIntyre asserts that every moral philosophy includes claims about the way its account of reasons, motives, intentions, and actions "are embodied or at least can be in the real social world."[37] He points out that, from the time of Plato and Aristotle, most moral philosophers saw it as part of their task to spell out the way their ideas could be socially *embodied*. Stanley Hauerwas describes MacIntyre's project this way:

> A philosopher, [MacIntyre] insists, should try to express the concepts embedded in the practices of our lives in order to help us live morally worthy lives. The professionalization of philosophy into a technical field – what might be called the academic captivity of philosophy – reflects (and serves to legitimate) the compartmentalization of the

advanced capitalistic social orders that produce our culture of experts, those strange creatures of authority in modernity.[38]

MacIntyre chides his teachers and his contemporaries (especially the English-speaking philosophers of the analytic school), suggesting that the "dominant narrow conception of moral philosophy" results in a predictable outcome. It insures that moral philosophers ignore the task of spelling out the way that their philosophy might be embodied. "We therefore must perform it for them."[39]

Before turning to the three modern characters who embody the philosophy of emotivism, MacIntyre asks, "What is the key to the social content of emotivism?"[40] His answer is that "emotivism entails the obliteration of any genuine distinction between manipulative and non-manipulative social relations."[41] His argument is straightforward. As emotivism asserts that evaluative judgments are nothing but expressions of individual preference, it follows that there is no principled way to say that relating to others in a non-manipulative manner should be preferred to manipulative modes. "For evaluative utterance can in the end have no point or use but the expression of my own feelings or attitudes and the transformation of the feelings and attitudes of others."[42]

According to MacIntyre, the social content of emotivism is embodied in the aesthete, the therapist, and the manager. Each of these characters aims at a goal that is given, and each uses rationality as an instrument to determine the most efficient way to accomplish the agreed-upon end. For the aesthete (a rich young man), his goal is to live a life that is constantly interesting; he wants to be endlessly engaged. And as he has a large supply of economic resources at his disposal, he can do almost anything he wants to pursue his interests. For the therapist, the client sets the goal. MacIntyre follows Phillip Rieff's description from *The Triumph of the Therapeutic*, where Rieff shows that in the therapeutic mode, techniques are used to transform neurotic symptoms or maladjustments, but the client's ends are accepted as given, and evaluating the worth of an individual's purpose is considered outside of the therapist's professional scope. The rich aesthete typically has deep pockets and is unconcerned about scarce resources. In contrast, the manager finds himself or herself "engaged in a competitive struggle for scarce resources" and aiming at "predetermined ends."[43] "It is therefore a central responsibility of managers to direct and redirect their organizations' available resources, both human and non-human, as effectively as possible toward those ends."[44] In this way, a central feature of MacIntyre's interest in the character of the manager has to do with his insight that the character embodies a moral philosophy. "Emotivism is a theory embodied in characters. ... The manager treats ends as given, as outside his scope; his concern is only with technique, with effectiveness in transforming raw materials into final products, unskilled labor into skilled labor, investment into profits."[45]

MacIntyre's description of this character is drawn from the sociologist Max Weber (1864–1920).[46] So, let's spend some time recalling Weber's sociology and his account of bureaucratic organization.

Max Weber and the bureaucratic manager

Max Weber detailed the bureaucratic structure required to implement the modern manager's concern with control, precision, efficiency, and reliability. In *The Theory of Social and Economic Organization,* Max Weber aimed to understand social and economic life as it was embodied in his time and place, that is, in Germany at the beginning of the 20th century. Contemporary manager writer Gary Hamel states, managers are "still working on Taylor-type puzzles and living in Weber-type organizations."[47] Weber was critical of the sociological approaches dominant among his German contemporaries, so his project involved developing a new methodology to study society and social organization. In particular, Weber developed an "ideal-type" theory.[48]

Weber's ideal-type theory is an effort to respond to a problem faced in the social sciences. Should the sociologist aim to understand social life in terms of very general, abstract ideas or by way of specific historical examples? Each has deficiencies. The more abstract and theoretical approach ends up disconnected from the flux of lived experience; a focus solely on concrete particulars and historical instances results in an endless description of discrete individuals. To overcome these problems, Weber approached the task of understanding societies through ideal types. "An ideal type is formed by the one-sided accentuation of one or more points of view and by the synthesis of a great many diffuse, discrete, more or less present and occasionally absent concrete individual phenomena, which are arranged according to those one-sidedly emphasized viewpoints into a unified analytical construct."[49] Weber's goal as a sociologist included understanding the German society of his day. To do so, he focused on social authority and legitimacy by identifying three characters, that is, three ideal authority types: traditional, charismatic, and bureaucratic.

Leaders in *traditional* societies – and here, Weber uses ancient China and Egypt frequently as examples – have authority and legitimacy based on a sense of the sanctity of the traditional social order: it has always been this way.[50] According to Weber, authority is legitimated in a traditional society when it rests on "an established belief in the sanctity of immemorial traditions and the legitimacy of the status of those exercising authority under them."[51]

In contrast, the *charismatic* leader acts authoritatively by virtue of a "gift of grace," not by appealing to precedent, but by operating in the prophetic mode and proposing a new social order.[52] Charismatic leaders are deemed legitimate by their followers, according to Weber, when their authority is perceived as "resting on devotion to the specific and exceptional sanctity, heroism or exemplary character of an individual person, and of the normative patterns or order revealed or ordained by him."[53]

These two characters, the traditional elder and the charismatic prophet, are both ideal types in Weber's methodology, representative figures who capture the form of social organization in specific historic settings. Weber argues – and here he thinks that he is making a "scientific" argument – that these two ideal types inevitably give way to a new mode of social organization: modern *bureaucratic* rationality.

What is it about bureaucratic forms of authority and legitimacy that, according to Weber, necessitates their dominance? In order to answer this question, it will help to recall Weber's understanding of bureaucracy. The term "bureaucracy" has a French etymology, *bureau*, that is, a writing desk. By extension, a "bureau" is an office where policies are written and institutionalized. At the heart of a bureaucracy is an office executive, one who establishes, maintains, and implements policy. Weber asserts, as an empirical claim open for verification, that bureaucratic organizations tend to outperform societies with traditional or charismatic leaders. Further, he claims that traditional and charismatic modes tend to transform into bureaucratic modes. Charismatic leaders have the ability to call the given social order into question, but they must become transformed in order to have long-term social impact.

> If [the charismatic prophet] is not to remain a purely transitory phenomenon, but to take on the character of a permanent relationship forming a stable community of disciples or a band of followers or a party organization or any sort of political or hierocratic organization, it is necessary for the character of charismatic authority to become radically changed. Indeed, in its pure form charismatic authority may be said to exist only in the process of originating. It cannot remain stable, but becomes either traditionalized or rationalized, or a combination of both.[54]

Because of this, Weber thinks that the question of social dominance results in a choice between tradition and bureaucracy, and given these alternatives, bureaucratic organizations tend to prevail.

What are the features of bureaucratic organizations, according to Weber, and why do they tend to prevail over traditional social orders? Let's consider these two questions.

In his description of the character of the "bureaucratic administrative staff," Weber points to a series of mutually interdependent ideas that must be accepted in order for social authority to be considered legitimate. He assembles several lists of interconnected ideas and "fundamental categories." The first such list has to do with the fundamental categories of "rational legal authority."

1) Management is by rules and policies.
2) Organization is by specialty; authority is limited to a particular sphere of competence.
3) Offices are arranged according to a formal hierarchy with clear areas of control and a system for appealing grievances.
4) Employment is based on technical qualifications that are certifiably demonstrated.
5) The "office" and its policies are strictly separated from ownership and personal life.
6) Conduct is judged in objective terms without concern for subjective appropriation.
7) Managerial policies and decisions are recorded in writing.[55]

Next, Weber assembles a list of fundamental categories of "pure legal authority." The administration and its staff are:

1) subject to the impersonal obligations of the office but otherwise personally free,
2) organized according to a hierarchy of offices,
3) arranged in clearly defined spheres of competence,
4) filled by a free contractual relationship with free selection,
5) selected based on technical qualifications,
6) remunerated by fixed salaries with a right to pensions,
7) treated as full-time employees, that is, as a full-time occupation,
8) constituted as a career, with opportunities for promotion according to seniority or achievement,
9) separated in terms of appropriation; staff members do not own or become their positions,

10) subject to strict and systematic discipline and control in the conduct
     of the office.[56]

In summary, the ideal type of the bureaucratic manager, according
to Weber, is *an office executive, a career professional, appointed on the
basis of certifiable qualifications and compensated accordingly, charged with
managing a specific, limited area according to written policies and rules and
applying those in an impersonal manner within a hierarchical structure while
being subject to a hierarchical chain.*

Why, according to Weber, is the bureaucratic manager such a powerful
character type in the modern world? Why do bureaucratic organizations tend to prevail over traditional social orders? At the beginning of
the 20th century, when Weber was writing, many of the key features
of bureaucratic organization seemed attractive. During the transition
from an agricultural economy to an industrial economy, it made sense
to think that organizations led by educated career professionals (rather
than those who gained authority by virtue of birth or charisma) would
make better leadership decisions. An organization structured in a hierarchical manner with a clear system of responsibility was thought to
be more successful in terms of social control than traditional forms
of social life. The model of bureaucratic management produces more
consistency and reduces arbitrary judgments and the tendency to
make decisions based on concerns not central to the purpose of the
organization. The organization could be structured more easily to
serve its purposes efficiently and effectively. Dividing the organization
into subunits allows top management to place middle managers with
expertise in the functions in charge of their subunits, thus promising
greater expertise, accountability, and control. The emphasis on impar-
tiality increases objectivity and equality, which is presumed to reduce
the tendency toward poor decisions swayed by concerns irrelevant to
the organization. Finally, when leadership roles are filled according to
certifiable technical qualifications, arbitrary decisions with regard to
hiring and firing are reduced and the chances are vastly improved for
putting in place the most qualified person rather than one who benefits by family, ethnic, religious, or class membership. For these reasons,
Weber concluded that the bureaucratic type of administrative organization is, "from a purely technical point of view, capable of attaining the
highest degree of efficiency and in this sense formally the most rational
known means of exercising authority over human beings."[57] Indeed,
Weber's claim is stronger. Not only does he think that organizations
structured in accord with the fundamental categories of bureaucracies

are more efficient, he suggests that they are virtually inevitable. "When those subject to bureaucratic control seek to escape the influence of the existing bureaucratic apparatus, this is normally possible only by creating an organization of their own which is equally subject to the process of bureaucraticization."[58] At this point, Weber makes an off-handed remark that anticipates a central theme in MacIntyre's virtue ethics: "Only by reversion in every field – political, religious, economic, etc. – to small scale organization would it be possible to any consider-able extent to escape its influence."[59]

Conclusion: MacIntyre (and Friedman) on the manager

Let me call attention to one more feature of this character. Although MacIntyre is highly critical of the manager – (I outline his criticisms in Chapter 8) – this character might be either criticized as a villain or praised as a hero. For example, the bureaucratic manager described by MacIntyre seems to me to be virtually identical to the character praised by Milton Friedman in his famous 1970 article in the *New York Times Magazine*, "The Social Responsibility of Business is to Increase Profits."[60] As Friedman's title made plain, he argued against the claim that managers and corporate executives, in their roles as executives, have social respon-sibilities to the community in which their corporations do business. To make his argument, Friedman draws a sharp distinction between the responsibilities that one has as an "executive" and the responsibilities one has "as a person." (Writing in 1970, Friedman made no effort to use gender-neutral language.) "As a person, he may have many other responsibilities that he recognizes or assumes voluntarily – to his family, his conscience, his feelings of charity, his church, his clubs, his city, his country." As Friedman makes clear, these responsibilities are private and individual. On this score, Friedman is expressing the heart of modern liberalism: the corporation has no business telling the executive which church or religious community he should belong to, if any, and recipro-cally, the executive should not impose his personal moral preferences onto his professional decision-making role. In his life outside the corpo-ration, he may feel obliged in certain areas, and "He may feel impelled by these responsibilities to devote part of his income to causes he regards as worthy," but Friedman claims that it is a violation of his role as execu-tive to bring his personal moral concerns into his role as corporate exec-utive. Friedman presumes that the corporate executive will have moral concerns in his role as parent, congregant, or citizen, but "they are the social responsibilities of individuals, not of business."

Friedman states that the responsibilities of the executive are the same whether one works for a profit-driven corporation, a hospital, a school, or a charitable group. The organization has a stated purpose, and the executive is charged with organizing people and resources in an efficient manner to accomplish that given purpose. In business, the executive's role is to aim at increased profits. Based on this conception of the role of executive, Friedman draws his conclusion: "there is one and only one social responsibility of business – to use its resources and engage in activities designed to increase its profits so long as it stays within the rules of the game, which is to say, engages in open and free competition without deception or fraud."[61]

MacIntyre and Friedman have very different assessments of the manager as corporate executive, but each describes the same character. For Friedman, the corporate executive is a central hero in the exercise of the free-enterprise system; MacIntyre sees the very same manager as a villain. Despite this difference in assessment, Friedman's description of the corporate executive helps bring some of the features of this character into sharper focus: the manager MacIntyre has in mind is an office executive who is charged with managing the resources of a specific social organization by implementing, executing, and enforcing policies to efficiently and effectively accomplish a given end. Before turning to MacIntyre's criticisms of the manager (in Chapter 8), it will help to deepen our understanding of several key concepts. I now turn to consider, from several angles, the manager as office executive in terms of character, plot, perspective, and setting.

5
Strengths and Weaknesses of Treating the Manager as a Stock Character

MacIntyre identifies the manager as a stock character in the social drama of the present age. What are the strengths and weaknesses of conceiving of the manager in these terms? Stock characters are distinguished from other sorts of characters, especially protagonists with more complexity that undergo a transformation. MacIntyre treats the manager as a stock character in order to sound an alarm: he wants to awaken his reader to a Faustian bargain where one trades increased pay, power, and prestige that managers typically receive in exchange for a life that is morally hollow, lacking virtue, and without purpose when considered in terms of the human quest for an integrated and meaningful life. MacIntyre's social criticism is subjected to several objections.

MacIntyre describes the manager as stock character in "the social drama of the present age."[1] He uses the word "character" because of the way it links dramatic and moral associations. What does it mean to treat the manager as a stock character? What are the strengths and weaknesses of treating the manager as a stock character? Throughout his writing, MacIntyre frequently italicizes the word *character*, signaling that he is using the term in a distinctive manner. MacIntyre links Max Weber's sociology of "ideal types" with the notion of character types as these appear in both moral philosophy and dramatic literature.[2] Drawing an analogy between contemporary social life and the sort of character one meets in medieval morality plays, MacIntyre claims that the manager is a stock character. What does this mean?

The character of the manager is for MacIntyre an abstraction; it is a type, not a particular human person. MacIntyre writes, "Characters are the masks worn by moral philosophies."[3] Philosophies enter social life in various ways. The most direct ways are through lectures, books, sermons, and conversations. Less directly, moral and metaphysical ideas can enter social life through literature and the arts. MacIntyre is encouraging us to look beyond formal arguments to notice other ways that a philosophy can be embodied and transmitted into social life. He draws a connection between a philosophy as it is presented in a literary character and its analogue: the embodiment of a philosophy in a social role. In this sense, a character is a type in the life of a society who embodies, perhaps implicitly, a moral philosophy. For the one who inhabits the role, the character acts to guide, structure, and constrain action. For others who encounter this character, it is crucial to be able to recognize and interpret the intentions of such characters. Those who encounter the character define themselves in part by the way of response.[4]

MacIntyre doesn't trace the history of stock characters from the ancient Greek stage through medieval morality plays to contemporary culture. Doing so, even briefly, will deepen our understanding of MacIntye's purpose and the type of manager he describes.

Aristotle provides a rich collection of compressed character descriptions in his moral philosophy, his *Poetics*, and throughout his writing.[5] In his description of the virtues, Aristotle glides easily from a discussion of character traits to a description of stock characters, even stating, "It makes no difference whether we examine the disposition or the person corresponding to the disposition."[6] The *Nicomachean Ethics* provides a virtual "field guide" to many stock characters: the coward, the courageous person, the rash person, the self-indulgent person, the moderate person, the wasteful person, the generous person, the greedy person, the vulgar tasteless person, the generous bountiful person, the shabby person, the conceited person, the excellent person who has an appropriate sense of one's excellence, the small-souled person who underestimates one's worth, the inordinate lover of honor, the one foolishly indifferent to honor, the hot-headed and explosively angry person, the bitter person, the gentle person, the spinelessly indifferent person, the boaster, the truthful person, the self-deprecating ironist, the buffoon, the witty one, the boor, the fawning obsequious servile person, the friendly person, the contentious person, the person with no sense of shame, the young person with a proper sense of shame, the mature person who does not act in a shameless manner and who has thus outgrown shame, the just person, the person of practical wisdom, the good friend, and the contemplative person.

Multiple ancient and medieval texts provide similar "field guides" to stock characters.[7] For example, *Tractatus Coislinianus*, the treatise on comedy that corresponds to the account of tragedy that Aristotle provides in the *Poetics*, includes a list of character sketches,[8] as does the book by Aristotle's student, Theophrastus, titled *Characters*.[9] The character studies of Theophrastus were circulated and extended in medieval Europe and during the renaissance, especially through a 1614 text by Sir Thomas Overby that includes descriptions of many stock characters.[10] Medieval morality plays involved Avaricia, Beauty, Death, Discretion, Fellowship, Knowledge, Strength, and Vice.

The "Vice" is worthy of special attention. "Whatever else the Vice may be, he is always the chief comic character."[11] Sometimes he is a clown or jester, but other times, he is a villain. The medieval *villanus* was a serf bound to the soil of the *villa*; he lacked the chivalrous character of the knight. The remnants of this type are found in the character, "the Joker," from Batman. Bruce Wayne (and his alter ego, the Batman) are faced with the ongoing task of bringing order to Gotham, often by facing his central nemesis, the Joker, who appears in various versions of Batman, from the comic book and Cesar Romero's television interpretation ("Egads. What sorcery is this?") to the darker versions of Hollywood films as played by Jack Nicholson and Heath Ledger. Ledger's depiction of the Joker in the 2008 Batman film, "The Dark Knight," is particularly nihilistic. The Joker, who has become the leader of a group of bank manager–mobsters, double crosses them and unmasks their clownish quest for capital. "You and your kind, all you care about is money. This city deserves a better class of criminal. And I'm gonna give it to them." Left with the scar of a permanent smile, the Joker narrates repeated tales of failed love; his character calls into question the established social order, suggesting that wisdom is found in realizing that beneath every moral convention, expression of love, or claim to truth, there is disorder. "The only sensible way to live in this world is without rules!"

The Vice also appears as a stock character in Ingmar Bergman's great film, *The Seventh Seal*, in the character Skat, the clownish troubadour. As the other troubadours perform a silly animal song that celebrates the meaninglessness of life, Skat slips backstage where an attractive woman lures him with the prospect of feasting and drinking. Attracted by his excited appetites for food and drink, she then begins to nibble on his ear. With his appetite for sexual gratification aroused, he gives in to her seduction as together they hide behind a hedge to frolic. The plot is advanced through the actions of this character and his interactions with others. Later, when the husband of the seductress confronts Skat, he relies on a comic ruse to escape peril. Near the end of the film, Skat finds himself in trouble again. He is trapped on a tree limb by Death, and he once again tries his clownish strategy, but his tactic is to no avail in the face of Death.

> *Skat*: Hey, you scurvy knave, what are you doing with my tree? You
>   might at least answer. Who are you?
> *Death*: I'm felling your tree. Your time is up.
> *Skat*: You can't. I haven't time.
> *Death*: So you haven't time?
> *Skat*: No. My performance –
> *Death*: Cancelled – because of Death.

MacIntyre treats the manager as a villainous stock character analogous in certain ways to the role of Skat in Bergman's film, the Joker, or the Vice in medieval morality plays. Each of these characters is used to show audiences that jesting intemperance is unsuccessful when considered under the aspect of eternity. MacIntyre wants to show his reader in an analogous way that the manager lacks a virtuous character when considered in light of the quest for a complete and integrated human life.[12]

MacIntyre blends this literary notion of a "stock character" with Max Weber's sociological notion of the "pure ideal type." Weber developed the notion of an ideal type in response to the problem of developing a method that could claim to yield scientific knowledge of social groups. Weber was faced with a deep and ancient metaphysical challenge: the problem of the one and the many. How can the sociologist achieve unified comprehension out of the many instances that make up social life? Sociologists are concerned with understanding the meaning of social groups, and every human social group is made up of individual human beings. The sociologist wants both 1) to understand the subjective meaning of human action in social contexts and 2) to recognize that the social world is characterized by apparently infinite complexity, discrete individual particularities, and events beyond our ability to study in a controlled laboratory environment. Can the sociologist provide a unity that organizes the manifold of experience? If the focus of the sociologist remains at the level of "the given concrete case of a particular actor" or even "a given plurality of actors," then the sociologist can never move beyond particularities to achieve unified understanding of social life.[13] In that case, sociology can never become "a science which attempts the interpretive understanding of social action."[14]

To overcome this problem, Weber proposed that sociologists focus on "the theoretically conceived pure type."[15] Out of the multiplicity and details of social experience, Weber sought to integrate the parts into an ordered pattern at an abstract level that picks out generalized common-alities producing a "pure ideal type."[16] What is a "pure ideal type"? It is an abstraction – not a concrete reality – but this generalized abstraction was supposed by Weber to make possible a scientific understanding of social groups in terms by focusing on *types*. Weber conceded that "it is probably seldom if ever that a real phenomenon can be found which corresponds exactly to one of these ideally constructed pure types."[17]

This "analysis in terms of sociological types"[18] is the methodological key to Weber's conception of three characters: the traditional patriarch, the charismatic prophet, and the bureaucratic manager. Each of these characters is a type, that is, an abstraction that we never encounter directly. As an ideal, this character is constructed from experiences with many individuals. The sociologist makes use of *types* because of their "usefulness," especially for the purpose of "systematic analysis."[19]

MacIntyre, in a similar way, makes use of the methodology of "ideal types," but he does so for a very different reason from Max Weber. MacIntyre, as a moral philosopher, identifies three modern characters (the aesthete, the therapist, and especially the bureaucratic manager) in order to engage in criticism of the culture of modernity. His main target is the modern self: criterionless, disengaged, "able to stand back from any and every situation in which one is involved, from any and every characteristic that one may possess, and to pass judgment on it from a purely universal and abstract point of view that is totally detached from all social particularity."[20] For the modern self, questions of purpose are matters of taste, that is, matters of individual preference. MacIntyre uses several names to describe this philosophy: enlightenment ration-ality, liberalism, and modernism. Enlightened secular liberal modernity proceeds as if there is no (public) rational criterion to determine that one goal is better than another. The expertise of the manager, then, has no place for evaluating whether a particular goal is worthwhile; instead, the manager is the "efficiency expert," the one who can determine the most efficient means to organize products and people to accomplish a given end.

What are the strengths and weaknesses of this conception of a *character* as a type in a social drama? On the one hand, MacIntyre very help-fully moves moral philosophy beyond disputes internal to those expert in logical analysis into the realm of social life. "If we listen to much contemporary discussion of ethics, we might conclude that ethics is principally or only a matter of arguments."[21] In his effort to turn away from the armchair style of philosophy that he saw practiced by the professional academics that were his teachers and which characterized much of academic moral philosophy in the 20th century, MacIntyre aims to understand *character* in terms of "use" by turning to social life. Further, by drawing an analogy between literature and social life (as a drama), MacIntyre's conception of the manager as a *character* involves retrieving (in certain ways) an ancient and very rich way of engaging in the practice of moral philosophy.

MacIntyre's contribution to moral philosophy is part of a larger trend in the late 20th century: the rediscovery of the centrality of narrative. MacIntyre's central contribution in this area is his argument that human action is intelligible only in narrative form.[22] He uses an analytic-style argument to show that the conception of action widely used in both analytic philosophy and Sartrean existentialism, where each action is construed as a discreet event, is unintelligible. From this, MacIntyre draws several conclusions. Each action is intelligible only as part of a narrative. We are storytelling animals. Each human life has a narrative shape with a plot: a beginning, middle, and an end. We find ourselves always in the middle of such a narrative. Further, each action in every individual life has a setting. "We enter upon a stage which we did not design and we find ourselves part of an action that was not of our making."[23] While each of us is the central character (and in some ways, the author) in the story of our own lives, we also are characters in the lives of others, and we are members of communities that have a narrative shape. "We enter human society, that is, with one or more imputed characters – roles into which we have been drafted – and we have to learn what they are in order to be able to understand how others respond to us and how our responses to them are apt to be construed."[24] In order to learn to make one's way in a community, one needs to learn a set of stock roles. One needs to learn what a child and what a parent is, and many other stock characters: "wicked step-mothers, lost children, good but misguided kings, wolves that suckle twin boys,"[25] and countless other types. "The telling of stories has a key part in educating us into the virtues."[26] Narratives shape our lives individually and as members of communities that have histories. The tradition of each community is the story of the arguments and conflicts through which the community has been and continues to be shaped. A tradition, then, is a "historically extended, socially embodied argument, and an argument precisely in part about the goods which constitute that tradition."[27]

As characters in a narrative, we live in light of a possible future. Shaped by the traditions and communities in which we are set, we advance the plot by making choices in the present in light of some conception, however dim, of expected goals and purposes. In this sense, each human action is intelligible only as part of a search. The notion of life as a "quest" is central in MacIntyre's narrative account of human action. As each action is intelligible only in terms of a larger narrative, it turns out that the whole of a human life is a single narrative: it is the story of a quest, that is, a journey or a search.[28] It is only in the course of the quest that the journey's goal becomes clear.

Despite these important strengths, MacIntyre's conception of the manager as a *character* is susceptible to several challenges.

First, in treating the manager as a "type," MacIntyre invites a charge that "centers on his use of broad generalizations."[29] Do managers – as particular flesh-and-blood persons – actually operate as if their sole purpose is to accomplish a given end in the most efficient manner possible? Are all managers educated and enculturated in a manner that encourages them to bracket questions of purpose from rational evaluation? Does the *type* that MacIntyre describes, the character of the bureaucratic manager, in fact correspond with the way that managers actually speak and act? Might attending to the activities of managers reveal norms of excellence internal to the activity of managing well?

On this score, Thomas Whetstone has suggested that ethics researchers need to listen to managers and the way they use virtue language. Whetstone has challenged ethics researchers "to increase their understanding of extant virtue language as the basis for a renewed development of virtue ethics."[30] Whetstone proposes a research program that involves "listening to what managers themselves say when discussing excellent managers and their behaviors."[31]

A further criticism of MacIntyre's approach comes into focus when we consider the difference between his approach and with the slightly different approach used by Robert Bellah and his colleagues in *Habits of the Heart*.[32] Bellah's work is deeply influenced by MacIntyre's *After Virtue*, but there are several important differences in approach. *Habits of the Heart* begins by introducing us to four middle-class Americans: Brian Palmer, Joe Gorman, Margaret Oldham, and Wayne Bauer. On the one hand, each of these is presented as concretely existing human beings. We learn something about the particularity of these four Americans, but Bellah also shows how these people (perhaps unwittingly) are shaped and constrained by the character types each embodies. For example, Brian Palmer is a manager, and Margaret Oldham is a therapist.[33] As such, we come to feel a tension between thinking of someone as a concretely existing human person and construing someone as a mere type, as with MacIntyre.

Note one other important difference between Bellah's *Habits* and MacIntyre's *After Virtue*. Bellah and his colleagues suggest that Americans (like Palmer and Oldham) tend to speak using the grammar of modern individualism even though they engage in social practices that rely on older and more substantive moral grammars. The first story recounted in *Habits* concerns Brian Palmer, a Silicon Valley manager who had a very successful life in material terms, and then faced a major life change when his wife divorced him.[34] This forced Brian to evaluate his life, to begin listening to classical music and to reflect on what was important in life. Eventually, he remarried, and he found that true joy comes in being able to give himself to others, especially in his family. Bellah points out that Brian Palmer lacked an ability to articulate why his new life is better than his old life; he lacks a moral grammar and a sense of rationality that certain purposes (e.g., living to give oneself) is better than another form of life (e.g., living to acquire things). Bellah shows that, although many Americans have become habituated to speak using the modern grammar of individualism, in many cases, their lives are shaped by a set of practices drawn from older grammars.

I suspect that MacIntyre's use of the manager as a *type* results too often in two other deficiencies. 1) For those who work in the world of business, one might effortlessly deflect MacIntyre's criticism. "Oh yes, I know the type." Because the manager is a stock character, it seems perhaps too easy for flesh-and-blood managers to deflect MacIntyre's criticisms. 2) For those of us who work in the humanities, MacIntyre's approach seems to reinforce a familiar condescending attitude that humanities professors hold toward those who are charged with making managerial decisions. In doing so, we may "unwittingly collaborate as a chorus in the theatre of the present."[35] In treating the manager as a mere stock character, there might be a tendency to disregard the complexity of concrete flesh-and-blood managers or to ignore the possibility that the inner life of particular managers might be morally significant, reflective, or deep.

MacIntyre's turn to narrative (and his concern with the literary associations tied to character) is part of his criticism of doing moral philosophy solely by way of the analysis of arguments. The turn to narrative is a reenactment of the criticism made by early-19th-century romantics against the rational formalism of the enlightenment.[36] The romantics were, like MacIntyre, not only moral and social philosophers, but also social critics alarmed at the hollow formalism of enlightenment modernity. Note this difference, however. Many of the romantics also were artists. In particular, they were poets, playwrights, and writers of literature. Because they were attentive to fiction writing as a craft, they were attuned to a different set of questions about "character." As social critics, they wanted to build up a set of character traits in their readers. As writers, they were faced with the challenge of telling stories with good plots and compelling characters.

In developing excellence in the craft of fiction writing, those who seek to add to the body of literature must become schooled in the practice of storytelling. Consider for a moment the sort of advice that writers of fiction are given: "Develop memorable characters. Your characters must have depth. They should not be one-dimensional." Aspiring writers are told that characters should "invoke strong emotion in us; we want to be just like them or we want to be completely opposite."[37] Character and plot are inextricably interconnected. A fictional character is memorable, deep, and multi-dimensional as the character's traits and personality are revealed through the plot. A well-told tale has a character arc that "shows the changes a character goes through during a story. Every great protagonist learns and grows from her experiences within a story."[38] Those who compose narratives are advised to develop a central character that emerges "at the end of your story as a new person who has learned something from her journey."[39]

In works of literature, the "character arc" may be either a growth or a diminution. Dorothy visits Oz and learns that Kansas is not so bad after all: "There's no place like home." Anakin Skywalker (in the prequel *Star Wars* trilogy) begins as protector of the Old Republic and is corrupted by Palpatine to eventually become Darth Vader: "Give yourself to the Dark Side." In tales where the protagonist is a young noble, the plot invariably unfolds so that the princely character must act in a way that shapes him to become a beneficent king or a tyrannical dictator. Not every Dorothy is a maiden who emerges matured through her coming-of-age story; consider Shakespeare's Juliet compared with Nabokov's Lolita.

As Aristotle made clear in his *Poetics*, plot always involves some change in a central character.[40] In an excellent plot, the change entails both a reversal and a recognition.[41] For example, in *Oedipus Rex*, the news from the messenger (that Oedipus is the son of Polybus) is supposed to cheer him. Instead, the messenger's news has the reverse effect; Oedipus recognizes that he has murdered his father and married his mother. MacIntyre's story of the chess-playing child, with a well-drawn character arc, is a tale with similar plot features. The child undergoes a reversal. Early in the story, the child is uninterested in chess and willing to cheat in order to gain money for candy. As the plot unfolds, the child comes to recognize the excellences internal to the practice of chess: strategic imagination, analytic thinking and competitive intensity.

MacIntyre's story of the chess-playing child compresses in a few swift lines a development that takes weeks or months, from outsider to a social practice, to apprentice, and then toward becoming a journeyman on the way to mastery. During the journey toward mastering a discipline or practice, one comes to recognize goals and excellences in activities that were first undertaken for instrumental purposes. Malcom Gladwell famously suggests that mastery of a discipline requires following the "10,000 hour rule."[42] The child in MacIntyre's chess story does not seem to have played chess for 10,000 hours, but he has played long enough to discover that there are excellences in the activity of playing chess that go beyond money for candy. This reverses the child's inclinations. The child learns that the best way to proceed is by turning away from the temptation to cheat and toward the habit of honesty.

The narrative approach has been most influential, at least with regard to applied ethics, in the health care context.[43] That may stem in part from the resources available through fiction; countless compelling literary characters are physicians, and these are not typically stock characters.[44] Literature provides many stories of physicians who have become transformed through the practice of medicine. The characters in these stories face various challenges including fears, temptations, doubts, guilt, misguided perceptions, or feelings of disconnectedness, imbalance, and aimlessness. After countless hours of practicing medicine, physician characters show us that it is possible to discover the excellences in the activities of a practice; the transformed physician excels in observation, diagnosis, and proposing appropriate cures while taking delight in doing these well, even as these excellences improve the physician's ability to pursue the good of health for one's patients.[45]

In contrast, we seem to encounter significantly fewer protagonists who are manager characters in literature, drama, cinema, or television. Can a manager undergo a kind of moral transformation analogous to that of the chess-playing child? Is it possible for a manager to go through a reversal and recognition while engaging in the activities of managing? Are there literary resources for an examination of this kind of transformation in the character of a manager?

Casting about for fictional examples of managers, we might think of Michael Scott, the fictional manager of Dunder-Mifflin Paper Company in the popular television sitcom, *The Office*, or Gordon Gekko, portrayed by Michael Douglas in the 1987 film *Wall Street*, or his inverse shadow, Mr. Twimble from the Broadway musical *How to Succeed in Business*

Without Really Trying. The smiling Twimble has found the secret to corporate success: "I do it the company way. Executive policy is by me OK." Each in their own way, these characters are hollow and shallow embodiments of the Weberian bureaucrat who accepts organizational purposes as given and then arranges means to accomplish set goals. Charles Dickens gave us Scrooge, the personification of a shriveled man hardened to life and love by his greed. Sinclair Lewis gave us Babbitt, a fictional real estate businessman in the 1920s. Babbitt is perhaps less well known and more complicated than Scrooge, but he embodies a similar moral hollowness. He appears to be a middle-class man, but he worships at the altar of the market. "What we need first, last, and all the time, is a good, sound, business administration."[46] Not accomplished in any practice, "neither butter nor shoes nor poetry," Babbitt conceives of his "calling" in real estate in terms of his ability to make money by "selling houses for more than people could afford to pay."

We don't need to look far to find such characters in the social drama of contemporary life. They abound in the sub-prime lending meltdown, the leveraged buyout destroyers of Wall Street that have been dubbed the "Barbarians at the Gate,"[47] or the "Smartest Guys in the Room" at Enron.[48] Are there any managers who, in contrast, are more complicated and who have more moral depth? Where can we turn to find an exemplar of a person who engages in the work of organizing social groups, leading, and planning while being guided by more than the quest for larger profits? Can we turn to novels or film[49] in the hopes of finding a manager character with a character arc akin to the chess-playing child, that is, one who learns to pursue internal excellences? Fiction writers haven't provided us with many resources in this regard; there seem to be comparatively few central characters who are managers.[50]

Joseph Badaracco is one of the few writers working in business ethics that has turned to literature to help executives reflect on character. His book, *Questions of Character*, flows out of a decade-long teaching experiment at the Harvard Business School. Badaracco describes his approach to business ethics in terms of discussing literature and facilitating discussions of plot and character. This "invites readers to learn about leadership and about themselves."[51]

The philosopher Dennis Samson has suggested that the kind of character that I am seeking – a manager from literature who undergoes a transformation and discovers the excellences internal to the practice of managing well and the virtues needed to pursue those excellences – can be found in the character of Konstantin Levin in Tolstoy's *Anna Karenina*.[52] In Book VIII, Chapters 9 and 10 of the massive Russian novel,

Tolstoy describes Levin's transformation from an urbane philosophizer driven to despair from reading Spinoza and Schopenhauer to one who finds meaning in his work as a manager. Levin discovers that thinking in the ways suggested by the philosophers he was reading had the result that he could find no answers, and he felt reduced to despair. With this recognition, Levin undergoes a reversal by returning to his work as a manager. "The management of the estate, his relations with the workers and his neighbors, the care of his household, the management of his sister's and brother's property, of which he had the direction ... all filled his time."[53] Levin found this work deeply satisfying. Tolstoy describes it as "something new in his soul," something to be "joyfully tested."[54] When Levin asked himself what it is that he had discovered that now gives him such a sense of meaningful purpose and which now makes him so glad, he answers, "I have discovered nothing. I have only found out what I knew."[55] Levin undergoes a reversal and a recognition; he is transformed through his participation in the activity of managing the estate well and in seeing how that activity can be properly ordered in relation to the moral and spiritual excellences of a good life. Tolstoy describes the new habits of character that Levin developed in his work: his ability to deliberate, make fair and prudent judgments, and execute; his ability to treat those under his care with concern and honesty; his ability to stand firm amidst the difficulties that come with the work.[56]

Can a manager develop these traits while engaging in the activity of managing – as Levin seemed to do? Or is the setting (on an agricultural estate) required for this transformation? Tolstoy poetically uses this setting when he writes that Levin "cut more and more deeply into the soil like a plough, so that he could not be drawn out without turning aside the furrow."[57] Was Levin changed through the activities of farming and coming to understand his identity in terms of the tasks associated with forming and sustaining a family and a community? But aren't the tasks of managing well, organizing people and products for a common purpose, integral to the task of farming just as they are to any other setting where managers work?

Returning for a moment to MacIntyre and narrative, we can draw several conclusions. On the one hand, MacIntyre has provided a very helpful account of human action by which he shows that actions are intelligible only when considered in the larger context of the narrative of a life. In doing so, he uses resources from and allusions to literature. At the same time, I want to suggest that he has not gone as far as he might to draw from the resources of literature. Implicit in his story of the chess-playing child, MacIntyre makes use of a character who is more than a type or a stock character. Through the plot, we observe a character arc. In a well-told tale, literary characters undergo a change, from one set of traits or dispositions to another. MacIntyre uses the manager as a stock character to criticize a set of dispositions and a role that is too common in our consumptive culture. I am suggesting that those of us concerned with the virtues could do more to draw from literature a character arc whereby the character of the manager might be transformed.

To summarize, MacIntyre treats the manager as a stock character in order to show his reader that one who takes up this role is destined for a Faustian bargain, accepting the material goods of money, power, and prestige while trading away what is more worthwhile: the pursuit of an excellent, integrated human life ordered toward meaningful and worthwhile common goods. In treating the manager as a stock character, MacIntyre's approach is subject to several criticisms. His approach tends to disregard the lived experience of flesh-and-blood managers. Treating the manager as a stock character may make it too easy for managers (and future managers) to deflect his criticisms; after all, the criticisms seem aimed at abstract "others." Further, by treating the manager as a "type" and a "stock character," MacIntyre's criticisms may unwittingly reinforce the very hollowness they aim to censure. In doing so, treating the manager as a stock character seems to disregard the complexity of the decisions faced by concrete flesh-and-blood managers without offering resources for managers who genuinely seek to act in a reflective manner while promoting the common good.

What traits might this transformed character embody? Before we can answer this question, we will need to consider other aspects of the concept of character. Let's turn next to the notion of character traits and the question of how such traits, especially excellent traits, are acquired.

6

Plot and Perspective: Character Traits and Their Cultivation

Is it possible to detect a story or set of stories that characterize the development of individual managers? If so, from whose perspective will that story be told? What is a virtue? What is a vice? How are virtues acquired and developed? MacIntyre's answers to these questions are contrasted with those of Aristotle and Thomas Aquinas. The development of the virtues involves a second-person relationship between teacher and learner with a certain level of intimacy, trust, and a sort of friendship. Moral philosophers and managers are encouraged to move beyond treating one another as stock characters to develop a shared concern for deliberative reflection on managerial activities and the dispositions integral to excellence in both managerial practice and human activity.

As MacIntyre's work unfolds, he invites us to focus less on "character types" and more on "character traits." Considering the character traits of the manager in greater detail brings into focus questions about plot and perspective. Is it possible to detect a story or set of stories that characterize the development of individual managers? If so, from whose perspective will that story be told? In order to circle around these questions, let's contrast MacIntyre's understanding of character traits with the account presented in Aristotle and Thomas Aquinas. Both in the later chapters of *After Virtue* and especially in his publications to follow, MacIntyre's work points to and is an important contribution to a retrieval of the virtue tradition.[1] In particular, MacIntyre draws from Aristotle and Thomas Aquinas to emphasize the centrality of character traits in the moral life. MacIntyre describes the virtues as dispositions that "sustain practices and achieve the goods internal to practices."[2] In the story of the chess-playing child, the child learns that honesty makes possible the pursuit of those excellences that are internal to chess. What does it mean to call a virtue, such as honesty, a disposition or character trait? What makes some dispositions virtues and others vices? How might excellent character traits be acquired and developed? Is it possible for the manager-as-office-executive to practice the virtues? My purpose in this chapter is to address these issues, investigating in greater detail the notions of virtue and vice, to understand MacIntyre's view that the manager-as-office-executive becomes blocked from practicing the virtues.

As I have indicated,[3] MacIntyre's account of the virtues is drawn especially from Aristotle. In the *Nicomachean Ethics*, Aristotle begins his account of the virtues by seeking to identify the general category to which the virtues belong. Aristotle invites us to consider whether a virtue is a feeling (*pathé*), a capacity (*dunameis*), or a dispositional trait (*hexis*).[4] After presenting arguments to rule out the first two, Aristotle settles on the conclusion that a virtue is a *hexis*.[5] Translators have used a wide range of terms to capture Aristotle's meaning. The Greek etymology of this noun is related to the verb "*eichon*," which means "to have." Accordingly, a "*hexis*" is a trait one "has." For this reason, the medievals translated this term as "*habitus*,"[6] (making a noun out of the Latin verb, *habere* – to have). In English, *hexis* is frequently but perhaps unhelpfully translated as habit. A *hexis*, as Aristotle understands it, is a trait that has been confirmed and consolidated by conscious, deliberate choices such that the disposition becomes second nature. The English term "habit" seems to connote instead a routine, unconscious pattern. Not only is a *hexis* a deliberate disposition, it is a firmly established quality that is lasting, abiding in character, and difficult to displace.[7] It is a trait that one has in an enduring way. So, rather than thinking of *hexis* as a stable habit, it is better to think of it as one's character. A human being's character is shaped in part by one's temperamental traits and social environment, and these certainly become part of one's character, but only as they are appropriated and embodied in one's deliberate actions. As such, *hexis* and *habitus* have been translated as "state of character," "trait," "tendency," "quality," "condition," "characteristic," or "disposition."

As a stable, enduring dispositional state, a *hexis* is distinct from a physical trait.

An individual person might be described in terms of physical appearance by calling attention to a physical trait such as hair color, skin pigmentation, body structure, height, and so forth. In contrast, a *hexis* is revealed not in one's physical appearance, but in one's actions. A *hexis* is the sort of disposition that shapes one's thoughts, feelings, desires, and relationships and reveals itself through the actions of a person.

Aristotle draws a distinction between a "*hexis*" and a "*diathesis*," both of which are sometimes translated as disposition.[8] The differences are that a *hexis* is 1) consciously chosen, and in comparison with a *diathesis*, is 2) more lasting, and 3) more firmly established. An example might clear up the distinction between these two sorts of dispositions. Imagine the difference between a rookie athlete and a seasoned veteran. Both are teammates about to engage in an athletic contest that they see as important and difficult. To face this challenge, each will need to be disposed in the right sort of way. The situation demands a sort of focused perseverance. For the veteran, this state of character is firmly established; the veteran has been in such situations before and knows what is required. In order to bring about this state in the rookie, it may be necessary for the coach to deliver a fiery speech and to play music that excites the passions and promotes focus. In this emotional state, the rookie becomes disposed to think that the challenge ahead can be surmounted; but this state, which is brought about primarily as a result of the influence of the moment, is a disposition that is volatile. The coach hopes this state is sustained in the rookie athlete through the duration of the contest. In contrast, such a disposition to focused perseverance may be more deeply habituated in the veteran. So, a "*hexis*" is a firmly established and enduring trait developed through deliberate choices that have been confirmed and consolidated that disposes one to act in a certain way.

What makes a particular disposition a virtue? The answer offered by Aristotelians is not utilitarian: the excellence of a disposition is not based on outcomes. It might help to begin with a list of excellent dispositional traits: patience, perseverance, determination, bravery, humility, sobriety, studiousness, modesty, gentleness, kindness, self-discipline, intelligence, practical wisdom, deliberative ability, ability to make good judgments, ability to execute, resourcefulness, clarity in expression, sharpness of memory, depth, fairness, honesty, truthfulness, punctuality, initiative, attentiveness, integrity, loyalty, friendliness, cooperativeness, civic concern, sensitivity, compassion, creativity, faithfulness, hopefulness, and loving care. What is it about these particular traits that makes each excellent? Why is it good to become a person whose actions, thoughts, feelings, desires, and relationships are characterized by these traits? The answer given in the tradition of the virtues, especially by Aristotle and St Thomas, seems to be different in certain ways from the answer given by MacIntyre in *After Virtue* (though neither points to outcomes as decisive).

For Aristotle and St Thomas, the virtues are those dispositional traits that are integral to one's flourishing as a human. This, of course, gives rise to deep questions: What is it to be human? What kind of animal is the human being? How is the human animal different from other animals? In order to know what makes for an excellent human life, we need to understand, at least in outline, an answer to these questions. Aristotle and Thomas Aquinas both conceive of the human as a rational animal. Each provides a detailed account of our humanity by focusing on human powers of growth, nutrition, reproduction, sensation, attentiveness, emotion, desire, imagination, abstraction, memory, judgment, reason, linguistic capacity, sociality, and so forth. In particular, this account focuses on four central features of our humanity: feelings, desires, relationships, and thoughts. The virtues, then, are traditionally understood to be those dispositional traits that perfect human feeling, desiring, relating, and thinking.

MacIntyre's account of the virtues, which is multilayered, moves in a slightly different direction.[9] The account of the virtues that MacIntyre provides in *After Virtue* seems to reject the Aristotelian/Thomistic schema of conceiving of virtues as character traits that perfect one's humanity. Without fully explaining himself, MacIntyre stated in *After Virtue* that we must reject Aristotle's "metaphysical biology."[10] Almost two decades later, in *Dependent Rational Animals*, MacIntyre admitted (in a qualified way) his error on this score, and he acknowledged this change in his thinking in the 2007 Prologue to the Third Edition of *After Virtue*.[11] In any case, MacIntyre's account of the virtues shares with the traditional Aristotelian/Thomistic accounts an emphasis on dispositional traits, but it differs in the way it qualifies those traits.

The three-stage account from *After Virtue* points to social practices, the lives of individuals, and the history of communities. MacIntyre proposes that character traits are excellent in so far as the possession and exercise of the trait enables the possessor:

1) to achieve those goods internal to social practices;[12]
2) to engage in the quest for self-knowledge and increasing knowledge of the good;[13] and
3) to have an adequate sense of the traditions (which provide both practices and individual lives with their necessary historical context) to which one belongs or which confront one.[14]

In order to illustrate these three layers, let's return for a moment to the example of chess-playing. Is patience, as a dispositional trait, an excellence? In response to this question, the MacIntyrean answer is that patience is a virtue because it enables one to pursue those excellences internal to a practice such as chess, allows one to engage in the quest for self-knowledge and knowledge about the features of a good life, and allows one to have an adequate sense of various traditions, including the tradition of chess, the other traditions out of which chess-playing arose, and the various traditions that might raise challenges to chess as a worthwhile social practice.

Beyond these three layers, MacIntyre revised his account of the virtues in his 1999 book, *Dependent Rational Animals*. He added a fourth layer that flows out of the acknowledgment that human beings are animals. Acknowledging that we are animals brings to light the role of vulnerability and dependence in human life. Our lives begin in a state of radical dependence. Typically, each human depends upon the gracious hospitality of one's mother. Her actions while one is developing *in utero* impact one's life, and the actions that our caregivers directed toward us during infancy and childhood impact us as well. Further, at any given moment of our lives, we are vulnerable to various injuries and diseases in which we may need the support of others. Many of us will reach a chapter of our lives when we rely upon others for care. With these features of our humanity in mind, MacIntyre points to a set of character traits that enable us to flourish as dependent animals. On MacIntyre's considered account, the virtues are acquired dispositional traits integral to excelling in social practices, our individual lives, our shared lives, and our lives as vulnerable, dependent animals.

With this account of the virtues in hand, let's next investigate how excellent dispositional traits might be acquired. Understanding the moral life in terms of developing excellent traits involves a certain kind of pedagogy, where education is understood in its etymological sense of "building up," "drawing out," or helping to form those habits and traits that are integral to an excellent human life.

Notice that virtues, as acquired traits, can be distinguished from traits of temperament. Aristotle wrote of "the temper with which a human is born" as including "certain deep-seated affections."[15] The ancient wisdom traditions, including that of the Greeks, recognized that human beings exhibit early in life various traits and tendencies. Contemporary psychological research points to a similar notion, i.e., that human beings come "hard-wired" with temperamental propensities.[16] Various traits or predispositions can be identified from infancy, especially with regard to "emotional, motor, or attentional reactivity."[17] The virtue tradition teaches that each of us is given different tendencies; contemporary psychological research increasingly confirms this.[18] For example, some people have, in the face of stressors, a more heightened negative effect than others. So, if courage is the acquired character trait of being able to stand firm in the presence of danger without being reckless, it is worth noting that some people are temperamentally disposed to have a heightened attention to distress while others are prone to a kind of fearlessness. Each person comes with his or her own gifts and temperamental tendencies.[19] The virtue of courage differs from a temperamental trait in that it is acquired. Courage is not "given" in the same sense that one's temperamental tendencies are given.

So, granting that there is a distinction between temperamental traits that are given (a kind of first nature) and dispositional traits that are acquired (a kind of second nature), and granting that the virtues are of the second kind, how are such traits acquired? Aristotle's answer is complex. On the one hand, Aristotle states that we acquire the virtues by practicing the virtues. He compares virtue acquisition to learning a skill. "We get the virtues by first exercising them, as also happens in the case of the arts."[20] For example, the way to learn to play the piano is to play the piano. The way to learn to play it well is to play it well. (It's also true that the way to become a sloppy pianist is by being a sloppy pianist.) For this reason, Aristotle writes that "it is through acting as we do in our dealings with human beings that some of us become just and others unjust, and through acting as we do in frightening situations, and through becoming habituated to fearing or being confident, that some of us become courageous and some of us cowardly."[21] Our actions fold back upon us to shape us. We become what we habitually do. Virtues are endorsed, confirmed, and consolidated by the deliberate choices of the one possessing the virtue. Repeated choices shape character.

However, this is only part of the story. Aristotle also holds that humans learn in the first place "by imitation."[22] The human is the most imitative of all the animals, and Aristotle points out that the ability to imitate is one of our central advantages over the other animals. Imitation is primary in learning – both in acquiring skills and in acquiring virtues. Carpenters learn their craft both from watching those more advanced than themselves and by engaging in the activity of building. Musicians learn to play, at least in part, through imitation. The habits required to excel in making something – whether it is building a house, playing a sonata, or making a speech – are learned principally through imitation. An analogous truth applies to those habits of character conducive to living well.

Characters shape character.

To understand this point, let's first recognize how much our picture of human life is clouded by certain habits of modernity and modern conceptions of selfhood. (I want to review this so we can purge ourselves of the worst errors that come with those patterns of thinking.) The modern self, as MacIntyre describes it, conceives of itself as a detached ghost, disengaged from all physical and social particularity.[23] On this account, each human being has at his or her inner core a non-gendered, immaterial *ego*, completely unlike anything in the world of space and time, and capable of taking up a critical stance over and against the world.

On the other hand, this conception of selfhood captures only half the story of the modern ego. Another conception pervades modernity, i.e., the notion of "non-selfhood." This comes in many varieties; it is the belief, frequently unstated, that human beings are nothing more than organisms-in-an-environment, objects like other objects in the world. So, modernity presents two notions of human life: the disengaged theorist and the immersed consumer. (Frequently, these two go together as subject and object.) Each of these flawed views of selfhood gives rise to objections regarding character formation.

When the self is construed as an immaterial *ego* (whether Cartesian, Kantian, or Sartrean, etc.), then, by denying one's facticity, one can try to deny that characters (from stories and from social life) shape one's own character by using the following argument. Characters are social constructs that exist in space and time. The self is immaterial, and hence is outside of space and time. So, the self is and ought to be free in the sense that it should be unencumbered, unrestrained, able to observe whatever one wants, and unconcerned with characters or character formation. (Versions of this argument have been made repeatedly in response to the charge that moral and cultural standards are degraded by certain novels, motion pictures, television programs, video games, Internet pornography, etc. "Those things don't effect me, and I doubt that they really effect other people either. And who are you to tell me what to think or how to live?") When the self is conceived as a disembodied ego, the notion of "character formation" and being "educated into the virtues" is dismissed as one more effort by the space-and-time world to restrain the self's freedom.

At the same time, modernity presents an alternate (and in certain ways, contrary) notion of the human: the nonself. On this account, humans are consumers, organisms-in-an-environment responding to the surroundings in a determinate pattern. Another version of the human as nonself construes humans as mere collections of brain-neurons-firing. When human life is viewed this way, the notion of "character formation" is dismissed for a different reason. Character traits are thus viewed as distracting by-products, convenient perhaps to communicate with uneducated folks, but ultimately meaningless. Just as meteorologists sometimes talk as if hurricanes have "personalities" and distinct traits – "Hurricane Katrina is a ferocious and very unfriendly visitor" – the scientists know that Katrina is not a character at all. On this way of thinking, just as a hurricane is ultimately reducible to a mechanism whereby a low-pressure cyclonic system forms when heat is released as moist air rises over tropical waters, characters and character traits are thought to be ultimately reducible to other more basic realities.

The problem is, as MacIntyre has shown, that when we construe ourselves as pure theorizers (or mere consumers), we cannot account for intelligible human action. This is because "a background has been omitted," namely, "the concept of a story and that kind of unity of character that a story requires."[24] So, integral to the practice of construing human actions as intelligible is the notion that we are characters in a story. On this account, human life is an adventure story, a journey toward a destination only dimly glimpsed and which becomes clearer (occasionally) as the quest unfolds.

I am proposing that we should set aside two widespread and perhaps initially attractive conceptions of the human: the theorist and the consumer. Human beings are persons, endowed with a capacity for intelligence and self-determination, shaped and conditioned by the social structures in which we find ourselves, but also able (in certain ways) to call such conditioning factors into question. Our actions along the way involve two features. On the one hand, each human action is a reaching out toward the destination as it is perceived. On the other hand, each action folds back upon the acting person, so that the habits of the one who acts are shaped by the action.

Recall MacIntyre's claim: "The telling of stories has a key part in educating us into the virtues."[25] In part, this is because the characters that we encounter in stories open up possibilities and aspirations. When we encounter a character, whether in life or in fiction, we can be attracted or repulsed by the traits embodied in that character. "I can become that kind of character." Or, "I would never want to become that kind of person." Characters shape character by appealing to the moral imagination. As one acts on those aspirations, character is formed.

MacIntyre follows Plato and Aristotle in insisting that it takes virtue to aspire to virtue, to acquire virtue, and to practice virtue.[26] So, if we are looking for a formulaic answer to our question – How are excellent dispositional traits acquired? – it might seem that the answer is twofold. 1) Imitate the virtuous. 2) Repeat.

However, the answer is even more complex. The question presupposes that we can begin at the beginning, but this is never the case. By the time that we are concerned with asking about traits and how to acquire excellent dispositional traits, we are always already in the middle of the story, and we already have acquired a set of character traits, some of which will help us on the way toward acquiring further virtues. The family and community in which one was raised, the language and culture in which one was shaped, the music, art, and stories in which one's moral imagination was formed, all play important roles in cultivating character traits. Character formation for those who are able to reflect on character formation is also reflection on one's own character and the character traits that have been instilled and cultivated in oneself. To some extent, we can gain a critical distance from ourselves to call into question the traits that we embody, while at the same time, we remain bound in certain ways to the family, community, and culture in which we have been shaped.

Further, another complexity shows itself with regard to the distinction between traits that are "given" and traits that are "acquired." It may seem, based on the distinction I drew between temperamental traits and acquired dispositional traits, that the distinction is primarily temporal in character. Each of us, it seems, is born with varying gifts, and each of us has the opportunity, in various ways, to make use of those gifts and thereby to acquire various excellences. However, as the primary way that we acquire excellent traits is by imitation, and as imitation involves receiving, it turns out that acquisition is inextricably tied up with giftedness. Socrates makes this point in his conversation with Meno at the end of their dialogue, as recounted by Plato. Their conversation begins with Meno, a scoundrel from Thessaly, asking Socrates a question that implicates Meno's teacher. Meno has been paying money to Gorgias in order to learn how to give bold and persuasive speeches. Along the way, he has learned of the importance of the speaker's ability to present himself as trustworthy, that is, as one who possesses excellence of character and intellect. So, Meno asks Socrates whether he is getting his money's worth. "Can you tell me, Socrates, whether virtue is acquired by teaching or by practice; or if neither by teaching nor by practice, then whether it comes to man by nature, or in some other way?"[27]

As the story unfolds, Socrates seems to indicate that virtue is acquired "some other way." Through the dialogue, Plato is able to show the reader that one must be inquisitive, persistent, self-directed, and self-governed in order to pursue virtue and its nature[28] – despite the fact that Meno obviously lacks these traits. But how does one develop these character traits? The dialogue ends with Socrates suggesting that such traits come to the virtuous as a gift from the divine. It is a blessing and an act of grace to be given the openness to receive and the inquisitiveness to seek virtue. Socrates breaks off his conversation with Meno because he sees that Meno lacks the openness needed to receive the virtues.[29]

Thomas Aquinas and the medieval Christian writers drew a distinction between the natural virtues, which could be acquired through human effort, and the supernatural virtues of faith, hope, and love. The supernatural virtues are given (as divine gifts) rather than acquired. But in a certain sense, the ability to acquire any excellent character trait is itself a gift. For this reason, Thomas Aquinas points out that there is a gift (of the Holy Spirit) that corresponds to each of the (naturally acquired) cardinal virtues.[30] For example, consider courage as a character trait. It is the disposition to curb recklessness and stand firm in the face of fear in accord with right reason. As such, it can be acquired by practice. By developing the habit of restraining fear and backing away from reckless daring, one can make progress in becoming a person who embodies this trait. Yet, there are also senses in which courage can be a gift. St Thomas describes a "connatural mode" by which one is able to stand firm in one's resolve to accomplish a difficult task.[31] An honest hard worker, perhaps unable to articulate this sort of connatural fortitude, might nevertheless embody this trait. Further, consider the example of the person who, in the prime of life, discovers that they have cancer or some other life-threatening disease such that they will have to face difficult medical therapies, suffering, and perhaps an early death. In some cases, we see people who face such difficulties with grace and courage – even a courage that seems to go beyond the natural reserves that had been acquired to that point. Thomas Aquinas seems to have had this kind of case in mind when he described the gift of courage as an infused confidence that expels fear.[32] Considered this way, acquiring the virtues is at once both a "receiving" and a "building up" of excellent character traits. The virtues, then, are acquired dispositional traits that are integral to human excellence, but they are acquired in a peculiar sense such that they are received and built up through the activities of one's life.

A further distinction among the virtues is traditionally drawn between character excellences and intellectual excellences. The relation between these is subtle and complex.[33] With regard to developing the virtues, Plato and Aristotle emphasized first developing balanced dispositions with regard to physiological desires, especially the fight–flight urges and the desires for food, drink, and sexual reproduction.[34] The virtues of courage and moderation, developed through acts of courage and moderation, need to be fairly firmly in place before further reflection on the virtues might be fruitful in refining and developing further virtues crucial for life in a community such as generosity toward others, an ability to moderate one's desire for attention and honor from others, gentleness, truthfulness, wit, and friendliness.

Among the habits of character, the virtue of justice holds a special place, for it is a relational virtue that requires treating others with all the other character virtues. Justice is crucial for those in positions of leadership and responsibility, for the responsibilities of leadership tends to reveal one's character. The just person acts with regard for the good of others. The great teachers of virtue in the wisdom tradition conceived of the pursuit of the virtues as a quest, recognizing that specific qualities of character, especially courage, moderation, and justice, need to be developed before one develops practical wisdom. Once all these habits of character are reasonably in place, teacher and learner can turn together to consider the acquisition of excellence of intellect. With regard to action, the central intellectual virtue is practical wisdom, that is, knowing how to act in the right way at the right time for the right reason toward the right person.[35]

A virtue then is an acquired excellent disposition, the exercise of which is integral to the pursuit of the goods in human activities and life. The story of the development of virtue in each human life is profoundly personal, but the ancient teachers of wisdom traced a common pattern in the journey. This story moves typically from childhood to a succession of roles that require the development of various human excellences.[36] One typical pattern moves from family member, student, athlete, soldier–warrior, productive artisan, citizen–leader, statesman, and then sage. In each chapter of such a story, there is a movement from apprenticeship toward mastery. The plot of any individual life may vary from this specific pattern, but each person's story of the development of human excellence is inextricably tied up with a range of practices and social roles.

Formation in the virtues almost always involves guidance from a mentor who acts with care, a keen eye, a degree of intimacy, and a relationship of trust. With a shared awareness of reciprocated good will, teacher and learner can examine and narrate together from multiple perspectives the journey of the quest for excellence. For the learner engaged in the pursuit of excellence in a social practice, the quest involves the development of one's character along with awareness of oneself and the deliberate decision-making vital to such a quest.

Part of the task of the moral philosopher as moral pedagogue takes place within the dialogue of this sort of narrative relationship. Beyond the moment of awakening one's interlocutor to inconsistencies in one's form of life, this conversation includes developing a relationship of trust where teacher and student together can investigate the excellences vital to one's activities and the dispositions integral to the pursuit of those excellences.

Consider for a moment the perennial question of whether sports build moral character. Countless after-dinner speakers at athletic banquets have extolled the manner in which participating in athletics builds character, dedication, discipline, perseverance, strength, an ability to work well with others, and humility. Of course, not every athlete cultivates such dispositions. Many elite athletes develop an unruly desire for physical prowess, a craving for constant recognition, a wish to dominate others, a taste for risk-taking or brutality, or a willingness to do anything to achieve victory.[37] Athletics can be a school of virtue – or vice. At the elite level, athletics seems in many cases to cultivate egocentric dispositions along with a tendency to focus solely on winning the next big contest while bracketing or ignoring reflection on questions of human purpose. A similar point could be made of soldiers: some become honorable and virtuous while others do not. Indeed, virtually every social practice provides an opportunity to cultivate virtue or vice.

Is this also true of modern management?

MacIntyre encourages his readers to take up a point of view over and against the Weberian bureaucratic manager. We have seen that MacIntyre treats the manager as a stock character, focusing upon and criticizing a set of dangerous traits frequently developed by those who take on the role of the modern manager. Executives who focus solely on given ends develop dispositions similar to athletes who will do anything to win. They become unable to distinguish between manipulative and non-manipulative social relations, refuse to subject given ends to rational evaluation, and treat authority as justified solely in terms of power and achievements.[38] Like a child who agrees to play chess solely for candy, the manager-as-office-executive who conceives of one's task in terms of measurable outcomes such as corporate quarterly profits, government mandated outcomes, or an administratively concocted point system becomes tone deaf to standards of excellence internal to activities. Habituated to see goods solely in terms of quantifiable results, such a character develops all too often the trait of *pleonexia*, the insatiable and ruthless desire to acquire more and more while arrogantly viewing others as mere instruments for one's purposes. The economic crisis of 2008, diagnosed in MacIntyrean terms, is part of a morality tale of vice and greed. "Successful money-men do not—and cannot—take into account the human victims of the collateral damage resulting from market crises. Hence the financial sector is in essence an environment of 'bad character'."[39]

An objector might ask, isn't this overstated? Is it really the case that economic matters and the financial sector inevitably cultivate vice? Might the situation look different if viewed from an alternative point of view, that is, by approaching managers or future managers in a spirit of friendship with a sympathetic desire to understand the perspective and challenges internal to those who engage in management activities? Are managers of every sort effectively prevented from recognizing the goods internal to social practices and formation in the virtues? Isn't it possible that, just as some athletes become egotistical and brutish while others develop qualities of sound character (and it is these that we consider to be more genuinely "athletes"), some managers become hollow in their quest for measurable success while others discover that internal to the activities of planning, organizing, leading, monitoring, correcting, and celebrating there are standards of excellence, such that the story of a manager who takes up a quest to pursue those activities well would involve the cultivation of the virtues? Is it possible for a moral philosopher and a manager (or future manager) to develop a relationship of trust where together they can investigate the qualities of character and intellect that need to be cultivated in order to become excellent at the activities of managing? Is it possible for the character of the manager to be transformed?

In Chapters 14–16, I pursue these questions in more detail. For now, let's turn to a different aspect of the manager as a character by focusing on the issue of "setting" and questions that arise when we attend to the environment of the manager.

7
The Setting: Institutional Social Structures, Success, and Excellence

What is the social setting of the manager as office executive? MacIntyre's essay on moral agency and the "Case of J" provides insights about the setting of the manager. Part of the particularity of the modern manager is the (misguided) belief that one can act in a manner that is devoid of particularity, disengaged from concrete social practices and specific traditions. What character traits are needed to succeed as an office executive? Are these virtues? Raising these questions brings into focus MacIntyre's schema of practices-institutions-goods-and-virtues. Contemporary management literature increasingly has recognized that "soft skills" are needed for managerial success. Reflecting on such traits while asking whether the so-called soft skills are virtues brings into focus the setting of the manager as office executive.

What is the setting of the managerial character that MacIntyre has described? What is this character's background in terms of time and place? How might focusing on setting brings to light subtle features of the character of the manager? To investigate this, let's begin first by examining a lecture that MacIntyre delivered in 1999 to the Royal Institute of Philosophy.[1] MacIntyre asked his listeners to imagine a philosopher's thought experiment. He calls it the "Case of J." "J could be anybody."[2] J had a managerial position in the railways; he was responsible for planning and organizing the schedules of passenger and freight trains, monitoring performance, and coping with breakdowns. In addition to his career as a manager with the railroad, J had other social roles. He was a father, treasurer of his local sports club, and a noncommissioned officer in his nation's military. J had been enculturated by the social structures in which he was raised. He was socialized to think of his responsibilities in terms of duties. J believed that each social role includes obligations with clearly demarcated expectations. His role as father involved obligations distinct from his role as sports club treasurer. J had been raised to believe that a good human being is one who performs one's duties and does not trespass into areas that are not one's concern.

Early in his career with the railway, J had become curious about the freight in the trains he was managing. He asked himself, "What did they carry? Was it commuters or vacationers, iron or cattle?" Upon inquiring, his superiors firmly instructed him that such questions were no concern of his. So, J developed the habit of being a dutiful manager by focusing on planning and efficiency without regard to the content of the trains.

Later in his career, when his nation went to war, J's expertise in efficient planning led to a position in the military. In this social setting, his role required that he organize and plan rail travel for the nation's war effort. Dutifully, he was unaware that the freight of those trains consisted in munitions and Jewish passengers on their way to extermination camps.

After the war, J defended his actions, claiming that he had been following orders and doing his duty.

Having heard the "Case of J," we should recognize that MacIntyre is thinking about Adolf Eichmann. MacIntyre uses this case to draw on widely held intuitions about Eichmann's role in Nazi Germany as the Gestapo Director of the Department for Jewish Affairs and the defense that Eichmann gave at his 1961 trial in Jerusalem. Although MacIntyre's 1999 lecture was delivered to an audience of British analytic philosophers where one is expected to propose thought experiments about people with single letter initials such as J, MacIntyre uses the case to elicit our intuition that moral hollowness such as Eichmann's is malicious. He draws on background knowledge about Eichmann's capture and trial, for example, as vividly described by Hannah Arendt in her 1963 book, *Eichmann in Jerusalem*.[3]

MacIntyre uses the "Case of J" to center on the concept of moral agency. The account of moral agency that MacIntyre develops opens up a space between the standards that are embedded within one's society (along with the social roles immanent within one's group) and the ability to raise criticisms and to call the standards of one's own society into question. He wants to convince his audience that "human beings have by their specific nature a capacity for recognizing that they have good reason to acknowledge the authority of evaluative and normative standards that are independent of those embodied in the institutions of their own particular social and cultural order."[4]

Without going into the details of his argument, I want to push the example of the "Case of J" in a different direction. First, let's examine the social setting of the case. In doing so, we face an immediate question of clarification: Are we examining the social setting of the "Case of J" or that of the "Case of Adolf Eichmann?" In Eichmann's case, as he was an actually existing human being, there is a great deal of particularity that shaped the historical context of his actions. Understanding Eichmann's social setting for us would require the skills of a historian. We would need to inquire, for example, about the social life of Germany in the early part of the 20th century. In contrast, the "Case of J" is a fictional example – a philosopher's thought experiment. At first glance, the "Case of J" almost appears to have no social context at all. However, upon reflection, it becomes apparent that a good bit of history and social particularity is presupposed in the "Case of J."

Part of what is presumed in the "Case of J" is a complicated relationship between MacIntyre and his audience at the Royal Institute of Philosophy. MacIntyre artfully uses the conventions of British analytic philosophy to construct a thought experiment aimed at eliciting an intuition. He presumes that his audience is familiar with this methodological approach. MacIntyre was trained in this idiom, but by the late 1990s when the lecture was delivered and published, MacIntyre had acquired a reputation as one highly critical of this approach.

At first, MacIntyre sounds like one more analytic philosopher. "Imagine first the case of J (who might be anybody, *jemand*)."[5] The listener might very well expect that the "Case of J," where J could be anybody, might be set behind a veil or on a twin earth, and the setting might include a trolley car, a plugged in violinist, a brain in a vat, a man locked in a room receiving messages written in Chinese, or the subjective experiences of one with the neurophysiological constitution of a bat.[6] Instead, as the "Case of J" unfolds, the story culminates in an artful reversal and recognition; the audience realizes that J is not just "anybody." J is someone like Adolf Eichmann. Most contemporary listeners – and British philosophers in particular – share MacIntyre's assessment of Eichmann's shameful actions. Eichmann is the poster child of moral hollowness and the banality of evil. As Hannah Arendt described him at his trial, Eichmann did not appear as a diabolical monster or ruthless villain; he "was not Iago and not Macbeth."[7] Eichmann presented himself as "any man," and thought of himself as a law-abiding citizen, yet he was one who had chief responsibility for implementing the Nazi policy of executing thousands (perhaps millions) of Jewish people. By the standards of efficiency and success, Eichmann was quite accomplished at completing the tasks he was assigned, but as a moral agent with the responsibility to reflect on one's purposes in light of questions about what makes for a good human life, Eichmann was a failure.

Leaving Eichmann aside to focus simply on the "Case of J," what social structures are presupposed in the thought experiment? Because J had both a managerial position in the railways and a position as a noncommissioned officer in his nation's military, we can infer that he is situated in a particular historical context. He dwells in a time and a place where there are railways and nations, that is, in the modern world, especially after the 19th-century period of industrialization.

To make my point, let's imagine a different kind of philosopher's thought experiment. Suppose that we were able to discuss the "Case of J" in a philosopher's realm with ancient or medieval sages in the hopes of benefiting from a dialogue that engages the philosophical acumen of masters from earlier periods. Assume that one could overcome not only the problem of traveling back in time, but also the challenges posed by the need for language translation. The translator would face various challenges. Apart from the simple problems of word matching from the languages of antiquity to a modern idiom, we would face translation difficulties of another sort. There is no equivalent in ancient languages such as Greek or Latin for "railway." In order for our conversation with the ancients and medievals to be meaningful, we would have to explain a great deal, not just about railroads, but about industrialization and modern forms of social and political organization. Here is the point of my thought experiment. Although the "Case of J" might look at first like a simple thought experiment that occurs in a philosopher's realm outside of space and time, the case actually presupposes a social structure, specifically, one that is modern.

What characterizes a specifically modern social structure such as the one presupposed in the "Case of J?" Charles Taylor is the philosopher who has done perhaps more than any of our contemporaries to make explicit the social structures of modernity. In *Sources of the Self*, Taylor aimed to understand the "modern identity" and to show that modernity has its roots in notions of the human good. That project was extended in his more recent book, *A Secular Age*.[8] Taylor's work helps draw into focus several features of modern social life. Modern society 1) prizes the authority of the individual, inwardness, subjectivity, detachment, and radical reflexivity; 2) celebrates the "everyday" and the "ordinary"; 3) is concerned to allow each individual to express his or her innermost nature; 4) celebrates pluralism and diversity; 5) aims at mobility and authenticity; and 6) affirms public secularity where faith traditions that embody conceptions of the good life are problematized such that religious practices, even if they are one's own, are constantly subject to criticism from other traditions and from those who live without practicing a religion.

MacIntyre's "Case of J" is set within this sort of modern society. Because J worked in the railways, we know that he is situated in a modern context. He is a manager. In the ancient and medieval worlds, there were kings and queens, princes and knights, abbots and mother superiors – but no modern managers. The modern self conceives of itself as "able to stand back from any and every situation in which one is involved, from any and every characteristic that one may possess, and to pass judgment from a purely universal and abstract point of view that is totally detached from all social particularity."[9] As such, part of the particularity of the modern manager as a social role is the (misguided) belief that one can act in a manner that is devoid of particularity and disengaged from concrete social practices and specific traditions. How do success and excellence figure into this modern social context?

What character traits are needed to succeed as a modern manager in the sort of setting presupposed by the "Case of J?" Are such character traits virtues? It might help to pause here to examine a distinction that is sometimes drawn at a popular level in the business literature. Isn't there a difference between a "manager" and a "leader?"[10] According to this way of thinking, managers are thought to be like ants: budgeters, organizers, and controllers. In contrast, leaders are big-picture visionaries who use their charisma to change the whole ant farm. However, these two names – manager and leader – are not describing two distinct roles; each is pointing to an aspect of a unified functional role. With regard to emotional overtones and connotations, it might seem more attractive in certain contexts to be called a "leader" than a "manager," but this difference amounts to the same debate about the proper name for the planet Venus: Should we call it the "morning star" or "the evening star?" Both names refer to the same reality. The role in question is the modern office executive that has been our focus. To deepen our understanding of this role, let's turn to two writers concerned with describing managerial functions and activities: Henri Fayol and Henry Mitzenberg.

Writing at the beginning of the 20th century, Henri Fayol developed one of the first and most influential descriptions of the role of the manager. Fayol pointed to a handful of activities associated with the role of the manager: 1) planning, 2) organizing, 3) commanding, 4) coordinating, and 5) controlling.[11] Fayol's account of the manager's role continues to shape the curricula and textbooks of most business schools and courses in management; several widely used texts have reduced these to four functions and then arranged a semester's worth of material in terms of planning, organizing, leading, and controlling.[12]

Henry Mintzberg's approach involves focusing on activities (rather than Fayol's account in terms of functions). In *The Nature of Managerial Work*, Mintzberg's account is based on observations and time studies of the activities performed by managers observing one week in the working life of five chief executives. Mintzberg identified ten distinct but highly interrelated roles: figurehead, leader, liason, monitor, disseminator, spokesperson, entrepreneur, disturbance handler, resource allocator, and negotiator.[13] In *Managing*, Mintzberg revisited, reconceived, and revised his findings based on observations of 29 managers from a wide range of fields.[14]

Fayol and Mintzberg, despite their differences, show that the function and role of the manager is complex. Is the office executive a "leader" or a "manager"? The role involves budgeting, scheduling, hiring, firing, allocating, implementing, monitoring, correcting, and a whole host of activities that we might associate with "administrative or managerial tasks." The role also involves greeting, listening, planning, identifying, solving, communicating, motivating, delegating, mentoring and a whole host of activities that we might associate with "leadership tasks." So, calling the person who takes up this role a "leader" rather than a "manager" doesn't change the tasks, functions, and activities associated with the role in question. The office executive in question has leadership and managerial functions, responsibilities, and roles.

Let's turn now to examine the manager in terms of character traits needed for success in this setting. Are there specific traits that would help such a manager succeed in his or her tasks? To answer this question, I want to group together two sets of literature. On the one hand, there are plenty of books and articles read by managers, ranging from the popular to the specialized, which use the language of traits.[15] The language of traits is familiar and relatively widespread within contemporary management literature. In addition, there is a literature that uses the language of "soft skills."[16] What are these qualities? As it turns out, whether we follow Goleman's language of "emotional intelligence" and "soft skills" or the language of "character-traits-for-success" used by Covey[17] and others, there is fairly wide agreement on the list of qualities needed to succeed as an office executive. These include:

- trustworthiness: the ability to exhibit that one is reliable and dependable
- self-control: the ability to exhibit a calm demeanor

- empathy, likability, adeptness in relationships: the ability to exhibit concern for others
- creativity: the ability to overcome challenges and adapt to novel circumstances
- focused clarity: the ability to multitask and return to task after interruption
- persuasiveness: the ability to motivate
- effectiveness: the ability to execute and get things accomplished.

The business literature, as I have indicated, is full of suggestions about the importance of these (and similar) traits. On the surface, it may appear that focusing on such character traits is a turn toward the virtue tradition. Is it?

If we assume that there are character traits needed to succeed as a manager, we can ask, "Are these traits skills or virtues?" To answer this question, let's return to MacIntyre's account of the virtues, focusing especially on social practices[18] and institutions.[19]

Returning again to MacIntyre's story of the chess-playing child, the tale illuminates a distinction between two different sorts of goods or purposes.[20] At first the child plays for candy, but later he develops a deeper motivation in the pursuit of playing well. MacIntyre's point is Aristotelian in character. All goods have the character of ends or goals. Humans act to pursue ends. However, some ends are products external to activities while other ends are excellences internal to an activity. Goods that are internal to an activity have two qualities: 1) they are specific to the activity, and 2) they can be identified and recognized only by participating in the activity. In contrast, external goods 1) are related to activities contingently, and 2) can be achieved in alternative ways.

In order to explain what he means by standards of excellence that are appropriate to, and partially definitive of, a form of activity, MacIntyre focuses on the experience of entering into a practice. He uses two examples: one from music and one from athletics. "If, on starting to listen to music, I do not accept my own incapacity to judge correctly, I will never learn to hear, let alone to appreciate, Bartok's last quartets. If, on starting to play baseball, I do not accept that others know better than I when to throw a fastball and when not, I will never learn to appreciate good pitching let alone to pitch."[21] MacIntyre's point in drawing from these two examples is to criticize subjectivist and emotivist analyses of judgment and the mistaken notion that any individual can take up a detached point of view to formulate one's own standards based on individual preferences. His argument is phenomenological in character.

MacIntyre invites his reader to consider one's own experience as an apprentice initiated into a practice. In order to learn to appreciate excellence, whether it is found in a movement of Bartok or in a well-pitched game of baseball, one must first be initiated into the practice in question. Doing so involves subordinating one's own (initially poorly formed) judgments and preferences to the authority of the best standards of the practice. Once one has become apprenticed, one can work toward mastery of the practice by engaging in the debates about the goods internal to the practice, for it is precisely these debates that characterize the history and tradition of each practice.[22]

As we have seen, MacIntyre draws a sharp distinction between internal and external goods.[23] External goods are possessions for which humans compete in a zero-sum game. MacIntyre's account here of "practices" differs from Aristotle's notion of *praxis*,[24] even as MacIntyre's approach is neo-Aristotelian in at least two senses. MacIntyre and Aristotle both hold that there is a crucial distinction between goods internal to an activity and goods external to an activity, and both point to internal goods as guiding the activities of one who artfully engages in a practice.

MacIntyre contrasts his notion of a practice with 1) technical skills, and 2) institutions. With regard to technical skills, MacIntyre in *After Virtue* says relatively little, and almost nothing that is positive. He states that a practice "is never just a set of technical skills," but he does relatively little to clarify the connection between skills and virtues. For example, consider the traits that are required to succeed as an outstanding violinist or baseball pitcher. In order to succeed as a violinist, one must develop skills of manual dexterity, a relaxed and controlled bowhold, proper posture, a trained ear, accurate rhythm, and so forth. In a similar way, a baseball pitcher requires skilled mechanics: a balanced stance, a fluid wind-up, a solid leg kick, a powerful push, an accurate release point, a consistent follow-through, and so forth. MacIntyre insists, accurately if perhaps too briefly, that a practice is more than a collection of such skills. The distinguishing feature of a practice, according to MacIntyre, is its own internal goods.

It might have helped if MacIntyre had pressed more firmly to unpack the relationship between skills and virtues, because both seem to be or to involve acquired traits. The relationship between skills and virtues seems to go like this. Skills are acquired traits that allow one to produce those goods external to a practice. Virtues are acquired traits that allow one to pursue those goods internal to a practice. For example, in order for a violinist to produce a sound successfully, a set of skills is required, just as developing skills as a baseball pitcher allows one to throw the baseball in a manner that produces outs. Violin-playing and baseball are each practices, and as such, each have their own set of internal goods. The virtues are acquired character traits that allow one to achieve those excellences internal to each practice. In other words, skills are oriented toward success, while virtues are oriented toward excellence. Drawing this distinction between skills and virtues brings to light a distinction between success and excellence. Success can be measured in terms of the goods external to a practice. Excellence is based on a standard internal to the practice.

Virtues differ from skills in at least one other way. Skills tend to be specific to a particular practice. For example, one may be a skilled master on the violin, but this mastery does not necessarily transfer well to other activities in a human life. In contrast, virtues are character traits that not only allow one to pursue those excellences internal to practices, but the possession and exercise of such traits enables the possessor to engage in the quest for self-knowledge and increasing knowledge of the good and to have an adequate sense of the traditions to which one belongs or which confront one. In other words, the virtues are not specific to a particular practice. For example, consider the persistence that one develops while pursuing the practice of violin-playing or baseball-pitching. Such persistence, once developed, is a trait that can serve one well in the task of living one's life well.

Geoff Moore helpfully has brought into focus MacIntyre's "practice–institution" schema.[25] MacIntyre begins his explanation of the difference between a practice and an institution by citing examples. "Chess, physics and medicine are practices; chess clubs, laboratories, universities and hospitals are institutions."[26] MacIntyre contrasts institutions with practices in terms of the ends sought by each. Practices are distinguished by internal goods and standards of excellence appropriate to the activity. In contrast, institutions are "characteristically and necessarily"[27] concerned with external goods, especially money, power, and status.

The relationship between practices and institutions, in MacIntyre's account, is complicated. To sort this out, let's focus on five features of this relationship mentioned by MacIntyre in *After Virtue*.

1) Practices need institutions in order to be sustained.[28]
2) Institutions are the "bearers" of practices.[29]
3) Practices and institutions are part of the same causal order.[30]
4) Once established, practices and institutions concern themselves with and are attentive to different goods and purposes.[31]

5) The virtues are needed both to pursue the goods internal to the practice and to avoid the temptation to favor external goods to the neglect
of the internal goods.[32]

Implicit in these claims is a theory of the origin of institutions. As
previously noted, MacIntyre's central target is to debunk the claims of
emotivism, especially the notion that each individual can choose his
or her own values. MacIntyre wants to show that the dispositions and
attitudes that go with "choosing one's own values" make it impossible
to pursue excellence. In order to pursue excellence, one must humble
oneself to the standards of a practice and the excellences better known
by those more masterful in the practice than oneself. In order to draw
out the practice–institution schema, let's return again to the example
of chess. In order to pursue the excellences internal to the practice of
chess, an entire social nexus is involved. Fellow practitioners might
agree to form a chess club in order to serve the members. By organizing
classes and tournaments, the members are able to become more excellent practitioners. MacIntyre claims that it would be difficult for practices to survive "for any length of time unsustained by institutions."[33]
So, practices give rise to and depend on institutions. Institutions have
their genesis and origin in social practices.

While the two are intimately related, practices and institutions have
separate goals. Practices aim at excellence while institutions aim at
success. Each is subject to distinct dangers and corrupting tendencies.
Practices (that are not institutionalized) risk unsustainability. However,
once a practice is institutionalized, the practice becomes vulnerable to
the acquisitiveness of the institution. As MacIntyre puts it, institutions
are "characteristically and necessarily" concerned with external goods,
especially money, power, and status. Institutions are thus prone to the
lure of external goods and the neglect of internal goods. MacIntyre
claims, "We should therefore expect that, if in a particular society the
pursuit of external goods were to become dominant, the concept of the
virtues might suffer first attrition and then perhaps something near total
effacement, although simulacra might abound."[34]

MacIntyre's next move is very subtle. After repeating his claim that
making and sustaining a form of human community is a practice,
MacIntyre claims, in an awkward and poorly constructed sentence, that
institutions have "all the characteristics of a practice."[35] Implicit in that
claim (and in the paragraphs that follow[36]) is a distinction between two
different kinds of institutions. Liberal, individualist, modern institutions
(which aim to serve the community by providing the degree of order

needed to allow each individual to pursue his or her own self-chosen conception of the good life) are distinct from ancient/medieval institutions. The difference between these two, according to MacIntyre, has to do with the role of the virtues in the work of sustaining an institution. Within institutions characterized by the ancient/medieval form, the virtues are understood as necessarily exercised "by at least some of the individuals who embody it in their activities."[37] The virtues are understood, at least by some of the institution's members, to be necessary for the sustenance of the institution. In contrast, modern liberal institutions, which purport to produce fair outcomes without relying on the virtues, make no claim to reliance on the virtues. In such a context, the institutional concern for external goods will tend to become dominant and the virtues needed to sustain the institution against consumptive and competitive desires will erode.

Modern theorists from Hobbes and Kant to Rawls have aimed to produce a theoretical justification for modern institutions that rely not on virtue but solely on just procedures to generate fairness out of self-interest. Kant proposed that it is possible to construct a just constitution for a nation of devils. More recently, Alan Greenspan, commenting on the credit crisis of 2008, expressed a similar understanding of modern financial institutions. "I made a mistake in presuming that the self-interests of organizations, specifically banks and others, were such that they were best capable of protecting their own shareholders and their equity in the firms," said Greenspan.[38] Greenspan, like most modern theorizers, thought it possible to form a just institution without any particular members practicing the virtue of justice.

MacIntyre reminds his reader that, although external goods (such as wealth and prestige) can have a corrupting influence, these are in fact goods. Although his tone tends to suggest that external goods are corrupt, that is not MacIntyre's view. Wealth, status, and power are characteristic objects of human desire. Within the tradition of the virtues, justice and generosity pertain to the allocation of these goods. In a similar way, while MacIntyre is critical of modern institutional forms, he is not a critic of institutions. When MacIntyre claims that institutions have all the characteristics of a practice, he is implying that making and sustaining institutions is an activity with its own internal goods.[39]

On MacIntyre's practice–institution schema, practices are concerned with internal goods and standards of excellence appropriate to an activity. In order to be sustained, practices need to be institutionalized. Institutions must be attentive to external goods, especially money, power, and status. Practices without institutionalization risk unsustainability, while institutions are constantly tempted to pursue external goods to the neglect of internal goods. The virtues are needed both for the practitioner to pursue internal goods and for those charged with sustaining institutions to withstand the temptations that frequently accompany external goods.

We are now in a better position to understand the difference between success and excellence that is embedded in the question of whether there is a difference between the character traits that are needed to succeed in one's role as a manager compared to the traits that make for an excellent human life.

Suppose J is applying for a job with a firm, and the firm wants to consider whether J would be a good fit for this position. Assuming that J has all of the technical qualifications required, the firm becomes concerned with J's traits. Cognizant of contemporary literature in organizational development and human resources, the firm has become convinced that the successful applicant will possess these qualities: trustworthiness, a calm demeanor, likability, an ability to multitask and overcome challenges, and an ability to motivate others to get things done. Suppose that J has all of these qualities. Are these traits virtues? In the "Case of J," would it be possible for J to possess each of these qualities of character while dutifully shipping Jewish prisoners to execution? Could Eichmann have possessed these traits?

To answer these questions, I am proposing that it is helpful to follow MacIntyre, not only with regard to the distinction between internal and external goods, but also with regard to a distinction that he makes between virtues and their simulacra. MacIntyre criticizes the account of the virtues found in the writings of Benjamin Franklin and in various forms of utilitarianism. As MacIntyre notes, Franklin's account of the virtues is "framed entirely in terms of external relationships and external goods."[40] Franklin considers frugality a virtue precisely because of its external consequences: a penny saved is a penny earned. But this sort of frugality is merely a "simulacra and semblance" of virtue – a shadow – and not the original. Utilitarians who praise "virtue" because of its consequences are in fact praising traits that tend to success rather than traits that extend human powers and make possible the pursuit of excellence.

A related puzzle arises in the work of Robert Solomon. Using an Aristotelian approach to business ethics, Solomon raised the question of whether there are distinct "business virtues." He proposed "toughness" as one such trait, calling it a "true business virtue" and the "primary business virtue."[41] At the same time, Solomon claims that business virtues are not opposed to the "virtues of civilized life."[42] Are traits such as toughness genuine virtues or are they simply qualities needed for success in a given setting? Later in the argument, I return to this question. For now, it seems clear that the character MacIntyre has in mind is situated in a setting where toughness is a trait occasionally crucial for success, but such a character seems to have no principled way to determine the appropriate limits for such a trait.

This problem brings into focus a tension within the traits required for success as a manager. On the one hand, firms expect managers to develop policies, procedures, and formal routines that can be applied with regularity and which do not depend on particular personalities.[43] Certain traits are required to be successful at designing and implementing such policies: objectivity, neutrality, formality, etc. On the other hand, the manager needs another set of traits in order to respond to contingencies for which there are no policies, including an ability to detect whether or not a particular instance should be treated according to standard procedures. To handle these instances, managers need a different set of traits: flexibility, creativity, attentiveness to the unique particularities of each case, personal concern, informality, etc. So, in order for a manager to succeed, that is, to be able to organize people and resources to accomplish a given task, the manager will need to possess a complicated, and in some ways apparently incompatible set of traits.[44]

In addition, it is worth considering the relationship between the activity of managing and MacIntyre's notion of a practice. On the surface, managing seems to be aimed solely at accomplishing a given, external end. As such, it seems unconcerned with internal goods, and it seems that there are no standards of excellence appropriate to it as such. But this account seems inadequate in at least two ways. MacIntyre distinguishes between modern institutions (unconcerned with internal goods) and traditional institutions (formed in order to sustain a practice). Granting that those who manage institutions unconcerned with internal goods are not engaged in a practice, what about those who are charged with leading, organizing, planning, and administering institutions that house authentic practices? Such "managers" would be different from Weber's bureaucrat in important ways: they would need to be concerned with the practice housed by the institution and the goods internal to that practice. Withstanding the temptations associated with institutions would require the practice of the virtues. Further, because such institutions have "all the characteristics of a practice,"[45] those charged with "managing" such institutions are engaged in a task with its own internal goods. However, the characteristics of such a manager would differ drastically from the Weberian bureaucrat criticized by MacIntyre.

To bring the question full circle, we are now in a better position to understand the social setting of the manager MacIntyre has described and the heart of his criticism. The manager that MacIntyre has in mind operates in a modern social context with large-scale institutions that aim at success as a given end, especially as measured in terms of money, power, and prestige. It may seem over-the-top to charge that there is a moral equivalence between the character of the manager and the character of Adolf Eichmann, but that is the force of MacIntyre's criticism. So long as the manager operates in a modern institution according to a modern account of practical reason, the manager might possess those character traits needed for success in one's role, but such a person will lack the virtues needed to pursue an excellent human life.

Having focused intently on the manager described by MacIntyre in terms of character, plot, perspective, and setting, we are now in a better position to draw out explicitly seven distinct criticisms that MacIntyre lodges against this character.

8
MacIntyre against the Manager

MacIntyre both describes and criticizes a certain type of manager, that is, the modern office executive. Why? What are his precise objections? Seven criticisms are identified and explained. MacIntyre accuses this type of manager of being a manipulator, a sham expert, an amoral technician, a disengaged ghost, a person who is fragmented, a cultivator of acquisitiveness, and a destroyer of communities of virtue. Examining these criticisms gives rise to a series of questions. Can moral philosophy play a role in transforming our understanding of the character of the manager? If so, how? Answering these questions suggests a response that moves beyond "business ethics" or an applied-ethics approach that offers side constraints to an otherwise unbridled pursuit of profit.

Let's pause to summarize what we have learned from MacIntyre about the character of the manager. MacIntyre both describes and criticizes a certain type of manager. Why? What are his precise criticisms?

In the previous chapters, I drew from MacIntyre's writing in order to explore in greater detail the character of the manager he describes in terms of character traits, plot, perspective, and setting. Before turning to MacIntyre's criticisms, let's briefly review and summarize MacIntyre's account of the manager.

On the interpretation that I have suggested, MacIntyre's central purpose as an author is to awaken his readers by sounding an alarm. He is trying to warn us that contemporary culture is in crisis insofar as we lack an ability to engage in rational discourse about questions of human purpose and our pursuit of common goods. Beneath the veneer of debates about social and moral issues, whether those arguments occur in the academy or in the wider public realm, MacIntyre insists that there is a deep disorder, an unrecognized disagreement about the meaning of central moral concepts and an inability to move forward in any nonarbitrary manner. This was the topic of MacIntyre's MA thesis, and this issue has persisted throughout his publishing career.[1] His charge is that the same philosophy that was taught by his teachers and debated by his colleagues – that purposes are nonrational preferences – is embodied in contemporary social life, especially in the *character* of the manager. On the surface, the manager may appear benign: the office executive seems articulate, intelligent, upper-middle class, a modern technician skilled in organizing people to accomplish a given task. To young people facing the decision about a future career and casting about for a way to navigate our age, the material rewards that the manager typically commands might make the prospects of this form of life seem attractive. MacIntyre is warning his reader that these seductions are ultimately unfulfilling. He wants his reader to glimpse the emptiness behind the façade. Skill in organizing groups for the purpose of acquiring wealth, status, and command is an unfruitful power, suggests MacIntyre. In short, with regard to the character of the manager, MacIntyre's central purpose is to reveal to his reader this character's moral hollowness. The bureaucratic manager has no rational way to evaluate the purposes being pursued. Indeed, because of the denial that purposes are subject to rational evaluation, the danger is stronger. Without any rational way to guide organizational effectiveness, the manager's expertise is a perilous weapon. MacIntyre describes this character both to help his reader recognize the worthlessness and barbarism of the manager and to hold up a mirror. By reflecting on the emptiness of this character, MacIntyre hopes that his reader will be inclined to turn away from the fragmentation and self-alienation of this form of life. To summarize:

1) The manager is an embodiment of the philosophy of emotivism, i.e., the claim that goals are nothing but expressions of nonrational preferences; reason is thought to be an instrument for judging the efficiency and effectiveness of various strategies for accomplishing those goals, but reason is considered unable to evaluate the worth of preferences.
2) The manager is a bureaucrat, i.e., an office executive charged with managing the resources of a hierarchical institution according to written policies by implementing, executing, and enforcing those policies in an impersonal manner to efficiently and effectively accomplish a given end.
3) The manager is stock character, i.e., a type in the social drama of the modern world; as a stock character, a) the manager must possess a stable set of traits useful for organizing large social groups, and b) the

manager does not (as a *character*) undergo a personal change to become aware of and realize the goods internal to social practices, the narrative unity of an individual life, or the historically extended, socially embodied argument about the goods that constitute a tradition.

4) The manager, while presuming to be able to stand back from any and every situation and pass judgment from a purely universal and abstract point of view that is totally detached from all social particularity, actually is situated in the social context of the modern world, typically in large-scale projects where the goal is institutional success according to a measurable, external standard and where character traits are prized insofar as each trait is useful for accomplishing that goal.

MacIntyre's criticisms of the manager have been implicit throughout my description of this character. In the last four chapters, his criticisms have been more or less obvious at certain points. Now, let's make those criticisms explicit by examining them in focused detail. Below, I identify seven such criticisms.

The manager as manipulator

When MacIntyre, in Chapter 3 of *After Virtue*, introduces us to the three modern characters who embody emotivism – the aesthete, the therapist, and the manager – he signals almost immediately that he finds each of these, and the manager in particular, to be morally repugnant. MacIntyre states, "The manager represents in his character the obliteration of the distinction between manipulative and nonmanipulative social relations."[2] As MacIntyre puts it, "The manager treats ends as given, as outside his scope; his concern is with technique, with effectiveness in transforming raw materials into final products, unskilled labor into skilled labor, investment into profits."[3] In other words, the manager operates as if there is a sharp distinction between facts and values. Questions of purpose are considered to be nonfactual values. The manager purports to restrict his or her activity "to the realms in which rational agreement is possible – that is, of course from their point of view to the realm of fact, the realm of means, the realm of measurable effectiveness."[4] The manager claims a refusal to engage in moral debate. Unconcerned with purposes, the manager's task, then, is to marshal the resources of an organization to accomplish a given end.

As it turns out, in order for the manager to motivate the members of his or her unit, the manager must act under a guise, pretending that there are good reasons for pursuing specific given ends, but this appeal to reasons that are "good" is a value claim that directly contradicts the manager's value neutrality. Unable to provide reasons for any given ends, managers are left with the problem of cajoling those they lead and manipulating them to accomplish a given end through the lure of external goods. So, despite the pretense of moral neutrality, the bureaucratic manager actually is a manipulator.[5]

The manager as sham expert

MacIntyre develops another criticism of the manager in Chapters 6 and 7 of *After Virtue*: the manager claims to have technical expertise in the organization of large-scale social projects, but this claim to expertise is a façade. MacIntyre argues that there is no such knowledge, and hence the claim to such expertise is a sham.

In digging out the details of this criticism, we face several difficulties. First, MacIntyre does not provide a neat summary of this argument. Instead, it is spread out, appearing in bits and pieces, over two chapters. Second, those chapters of *After Virtue* contain a condensed version of material that had captivated MacIntyre for decades. Prior to the publication of *After Virtue*, MacIntyre had published many articles in the analytic mode in which he developed criticisms of predictive knowledge in the social sciences. (For those seeking a synopsis of these articles, Thomas D'Andrea provides a very helpful summary.)[6] D'Andrea notes that Chapters 6 and 7 of *After Virtue* "provide mostly a streamlined reworking of his previous writing on the explanation of human action."[7] Both of these chapters conclude by applying claims about the unpredictability of human action to bureaucratic management. Without reworking all of the details in and behind these chapters, we can summarize the key points.

In Chapter 6, MacIntyre situates contemporary debates in analytic philosophy about human action in the context of the history of philosophy. By tracing the genealogy of those debates, he aims to show why the enlightenment project left philosophers with a need to account for human action in terms comparable to the mechanism used by moderns in the natural sciences, and why that account failed with regard to human action. Despite the failure of the enlightenment project to produce a law-like explanation of human action, modern managerial practice proceeds as if it possessed such expertise.

In Chapter 7, MacIntyre argues that the social sciences lack any significant predictive power. The heart of his argument rests on the claim that prediction presupposes a mechanistic framework that is static; were humans to act in accord with such a static, law-like model, they would render themselves incapable of responding to novel circumstances. Because human action and social life inevitably entail novel circumstances, following such a program would be a recipe for failure. So, law-like prediction is incompatible with success for social organizations.[8]

Let's draw together MacIntyre's claims from these two chapters of *After Virtue* to summarize this criticism of the bureaucratic manager.

1) The bureaucratic manager claims to be an efficiency expert.
2) The manager further claims to possess knowledge about how to mold organizations.
3) Such (supposed) knowledge would include law-like generalizations about action.
4) If such law-like generalizations about action existed, it would be possible to predict organizational success.
5) Organizational success is incompatible with organizational predictability.
6) So, there is no law-like generalization about how to mold an organization that produces organizational success.
7) So, the manager's claim to expertise is a sham.

In other words, MacIntyre concludes that the authority of the manager rests on a "moral fiction" and turns out to be a "theatre of illusions."[9] MacIntyre's rhetoric at this point is bold: bureaucratic corporations constantly enact a charade. "The most effective bureaucrat is the best actor."[10]

The manager as amoral technician unconcerned with excellence

If we put together MacIntyre's description of the bureaucratic manager with his account of a "practice," it follows that MacIntyre thinks that the activity of the manager is not a practice (in the technical sense developed in *After Virtue*[11]). For the bureaucratic manager, purposes are given and not open for rational deliberation; reason is used as an instrument to transform raw input into profitable output deemed good or desirable according to some external standard. When we put this together with MacIntyre's claim that a practice involves pursuing excellences internal to activities, it follows that he thinks that the modern bureaucratic manager is not engaged in a practice; managers are mere technicians, that is, people trained to apply a set of (*faux*) skills to accomplish a given end, but unconcerned with the excellences internal to their activity and systematically committed to the refusal to evaluate goods in a rational manner. From this, it would follow that the manager is a hollow character. If virtues are character traits that allow one to pursue the goods internal to practices, and if the manager acts solely for external goods, then the manager is an amoral technician prone to vice.

I am not aware of any passage in MacIntyre's writing in which he explicitly asserts, "management is not a practice." However, various texts strongly imply this inference. A debate has emerged in the scholarly literature in response to MacIntyre's implication that management is not a practice, with several scholars responding to MacIntyre, as if this is his claim. For example, in her essay, "Management as a Practice," Kathryn Balstad Brewer takes issue with MacIntyre's characterization of management; she argues that management has its own internal goods. Directly challenging MacIntyre, she concludes, "Management is a practice, and it can be a virtuous one."[12] The terms of this debate have not remained steady; a related topic discussed in the literature questions whether "business" is a practice with its own internal goods.[13] But these questions – whether management (or business) is a practice with its own internal goods – are, in some ways, not quite at the same level as MacIntyre's criticism. MacIntyre's charge is not directed primarily against "management." Instead, MacIntyre's criticism has been directed at the manager as a *character*. "Recall the old joke about an MBA graduate who becomes a consultant to a Philharmonic Orchestra, the punch line to which is that within weeks the orchestra had been downsized to a synthesizer."[14] It is this stock character, the executive with purported technical expertise in social organization who aims at efficiency and effectiveness without regard for internal excellences, that is the object of MacIntyre's derision.

The manager as ghost, detached from "domain-relative" activity

Another feature of MacIntyre's criticism of the manager, one that is implicit in his project as a whole rather than explicitly stated, is more metaphysical in character. It has to do with a tendency, widespread in modernity, to proceed as if abstract rationality, especially in the form of disinterested principles, can be applied to various social realms without attentiveness to local or historical particularities of place and time. The manager is, according to MacIntyre, one embodiment of the emotivist self, that is, the self "able to stand back from any and every situation in which one is involved, from any and every characteristic that one may possess, and to pass judgment from a purely universal and abstract point of view that is totally detached from all social particularity."[15] MacIntyre narrates a history of the modern self, connecting the Cartesian *ego*, disembodied and detached from the world of space and time, to 20th-century emotivism and the bureaucratic manager. Those versed in the history of Western philosophy can hear the echo of DesCartes in the MBA curriculum: "Management science is the application of a scientific approach to solving management problems."[16] Aspiring managers are taught "techniques" for solving problems in a methodical, systematic, logical manner: observe the organization, identify the problem, construct a model that reduces the problem to a set of mathematical relationships, then solve the problem and implement the solution. To become such a manager, one must be "armed" with a set of tools – rational principles (presumed to be neutral) that can be used to methodically identify and solve problems – without the need to bother with the particularities of place or tradition.

MacIntyre aims to unmask the manager who claims domain-neutral expertise. His criticism is directed against the character who, based on a supposed domain-neutral expertise in social organization, claims proficiency that can be applied to anything: increasing agricultural efficiency, making fishing operations more profitable, or knowledge about how to make the trains run on time. He is not saying that the locomotive engineers and switchmen can run the railroad without anyone managing operations; rather, he is critical of the supposition that the manager can develop expert knowledge of an abstract rational method employing supposedly disinterested principles that can be applied to every social domain without regard for the particularities of specific practices and traditions. The force of this criticism seems to be this: the character of the bureaucratic manager rests on a false set of metaphysical assumptions about the self; in pretending to take up a ghostly, detached, disengaged perspective that applies supposedly atemporal principles to particular social contexts, the manager is engaged in a metaphysical self-contradiction.

The manager as fragmented

MacIntyre charges the manager with living a fragmented life. This criticism is stated implicitly in Chapter 15 of *After Virtue*, and much more explicitly in a 1979 essay titled, "Corporate Modernity and Moral Judgment: Are They Mutually Exclusive?"

Before focusing on the details of this criticism, it is worth noting a difference in MacIntyre's tone here. Rather than using a biting and strident manner to awaken his reader to the ways in which managers participate in manipulation and pretension, MacIntyre here expresses a sort of concern for individual human persons who find themselves trapped in a life of self-alienation involving the arbitrary compartmentalization of conflicting roles.

Chapter 15 of *After Virtue* begins by identifying this problem as a central feature of modern social life. "Modernity partitions each human life into a variety of segments, each with its own norms and modes of behavior."[17] Our lives are wrenched into disconnected fragments; we are taught to think and feel according to discreet standards. "Work is divided from leisure, private life from public, the corporate from the personal."[18] In response to this problem, MacIntyre argues in Chapter 15 that modern theories of action (as discreet or disconnected events) are unintelligible without attending to an underlying narrative unity. Human actions are intelligible only within a narrative quest for the good. As we have discussed, he then proposes the second stage in his account of the virtues: Given that human actions are intelligible only within the context of a narrative unity, the virtues are those character traits that sustain us in our quest for the good.

The essay in which MacIntyre developed these themes was part of a University of Notre Dame project involving executives in the electrical power industry. Perhaps for the first time in his professional career, MacIntyre engaged in an empirical study observing and listening to corporate executives. As part of the study, power company executives were asked to respond to various hypothetical scenarios.[19] MacIntyre was struck by the way the executives answered. Instead of thinking of themselves as unified moral agents, they conceived of themselves as beings who splinter morality into disassociated parts.[20] In this essay, MacIntyre identifies two versions of fragmentation.

First, MacIntyre points out that executives in contemporary firms are expected to move between roles in their professional capacity. The corporation places "incompatible and contradictory demands" upon executives. The executive is expected to be meticulous in adhering to routines, diligent in committee work, loyal to superiors, and concerned about accomplishing the goals of the organization. MacIntyre uses the language of virtues to describe the traits of one who would excel at these tasks,[21] but he is quick to point out that the traits required to excel at certain parts of the role of manager are at odds with a different set of traits that contemporary managers also are expected to possess. Because most contemporary corporations conceive of their activities both in terms of profit maximization and in terms of pursuing some public good, corporate executives are expected to have the character traits needed to pursue those goods: "to show initiative, to break rules creatively, to form independent opinions and to act on his or her own."[22] In other words, MacIntyre describes the modern corporation as embodying two incompatible self-understandings directed at two distinct sets of purposes. It is both a profit-maximizing organization (which conceives of itself in morally neutral terms) and a community aimed at public goods (which conceives of itself in positive moral terms). MacIntyre notes that power company executives face this combination of dual purposes in a pronounced way, but this splintering of purposes is not unique to the power industry. As MacIntyre concedes, virtually every for-profit firm conceives of its activities in moral terms, at least in part, as aimed at providing goods or services that promote the public good. Corporate executives then must constantly switch roles, moving back and forth between traits needed for success as measured in terms of profits and traits that allow the pursuit of moral excellence and social goods. MacIntyre concludes that, "the modern corporation is an agency which by its moralizing splinters morality into dissociated parts."[23]

Next, MacIntyre points to a splintering that occurs between the manager's role as profit maximizer and the other roles that the same person may occupy: spouse, parent, neighbor, citizen, etc. MacIntyre writes, "In his capacity of corporate executive, the manager not only has no need to take account of, but *must* not take account of certain types of considerations which he might feel obliged to recognize were he acting as parent, as consumer, or as citizen."[24] So, MacIntyre's charge is that corporate executives are inevitably trapped by the need to draw a sharp boundary between actions suitable to the managerial role as distinct from one's other social roles. In this way, the manager's life is fragmented and lacks narrative unity.

The manager as cultivator of consumptive acquisitiveness

This charge – that the manager promotes the vice of acquisitiveness – appears in several places in MacIntyre's writing. In short, MacIntyre claims that, by aiming at given external goods, especially wealth and power, and by encouraging the workers within one's organization in this pursuit without recourse to internal goods and the virtues acquired in the quest for internal goods, the manager promotes the vice of acquisitiveness.

The details of this criticism can be pieced together from various passages in *After Virtue*. Let's work backwards. Near the end of the book, MacIntyre summarizes his reasoning.

> It must have been clear from earlier parts of my argument that the tradition of the virtues is at variance with central features of the modern economic order and more especially its individualism, its acquisitiveness and its elevation of the values of the market to a central social place. It now becomes clear that it also involves a rejection of the modern political order.[25]

Some of those "earlier parts" of his argument are found in the chapters where MacIntyre discusses the account of the virtues in Athens (Chapter 11) and his interpretation of the philosophy of David Hume (Chapter 16). In both contexts, MacIntyre discusses *pleonexia*, that is, the vice of avarice or greed. His goal is to tell a story that answers this question: How did we undergo a cultural shift such that the ancients and medievals considered greed to be a vice, one of the seven deadly sins, whereas contemporary executives follow the mantra of Gordan Gekko: "Greed is good. Greed works." As MacIntyre puts it, greed, once considered a vice, "is now the driving force of modern productive work."[26] MacIntyre offers a narrative, tracing a decline from 1) the virtues (as conceived by the ancients, especially Aristotle and St Paul), to 2) a Stoic conception of virtue (as disengaged from any particular social context) through 3) a utilitarian transmutation, where the language of the virtues is plucked from its natural home and then subtly altered in meaning so that it comes to be used to describe traits useful for the acquisition of material goods, to 4) our contemporary context, where consumptive acquisitiveness is praised for its utility. For the Athenians, *pleonexia* is the vice of wanting to have more and more, an infinite appetite for finite things. MacIntyre is critical of John Stuart Mill's translation of *pleonexia* ("the desire to engross more than one's share"[27]) because the vice is subtly changed and the sense of a disordered desire for large quantities is lost.[28] Acquisitiveness, warns MacIntyre, is a quality that modern individualism and modern economic activity "does not perceive to be a vice at all."[29]

So, the charge is that the manager must appeal to external goods as motivation to accomplish the organization's given purpose. "The attempt is to get them to regard themselves primarily as consumers whose practical and productive activities are no more than a means to consumption."[30] According to MacIntyre, the manager sanctions and participates in a massive program of miseducation whereby workers are taught that what counts as a good life is the acquisition of consumer goods, i.e., the manager is an unwitting teacher who convinces others that life's purpose is success (in terms of measurable external goods) rather than excellence (in terms of the goods internal to a life well lived).

The manager as large-scale destroyer of small-scale communities of virtue

Thomas D'Andrea points out that "MacIntyre's critique of late industrial capitalism seems finally to rest on a criticism of its scale. It is the very extra-local, international, and now even global nature of advanced capitalism that MacIntyre thinks is the great cause of its systemic flaws."[31] D'Andrea concedes that MacIntyre could have developed his thinking on this topic in greater detail,

> but by all the evidence, he seems to think that it is the entirely instrumental and instrumentalizing rationality enshrined in the managerial culture of today's capitalist societies that makes them unamenable to betterment from within their own framework. When the size of markets expands to the extent that co-ordination and betterment problems become immense, then problems become tractable only through a rationality of means aimed at predetermined – or at any rate determined-from-the-top-by-a-managerial-elite – ends. Both consultation with workers and adequate accountability to them fall out of the deliberative process. The workers' participatory capacity to shape the institutions which are the bearers of the practices in which they labour is thwarted: they are denied the opportunity to employ their own practical reasoning in the deliberations about what shape those institutions should take to serve those practices. Large-scale capitalism so denies them the opportunity for self-education, and alienates them in an important way from their good – that good proper to independent practical reasoners.[32]

MacIntyre concludes *After Virtue* with his famous call for a politics of local resistance and small-scale communities constituted by interlocking practices. With his widely quoted rhetorical flourish, MacIntyre tells us, "We are waiting not for Godot, but for another – doubtless very different – St. Benedict."[33]

As the large-scale civilization of the Roman empire crumbled, St Benedict of Nursia (c. 480–547 AD) established monasteries as small-scale communities of virtue. MacIntyre calls for the retrieval of (doubtless very different) small-scale communities with interlocking practices because he thinks that large-scale institutions lack the resources in terms of practical rationality to overcome the problems they create. Large-scale projects make it all too easy for elites to ignore concrete particularities. The manager is constantly tempted to treat those under one's care as mere cogs in a machine. Further, large-scale social institutions are extremely limited with regard to being seedbeds of virtue. Finally, large institutions are always parasitic upon smaller, local bodies, and yet larger groups tend toward destroying or absorbing those smaller groups.

We have reached a point where we can summarize the argument to this point. MacIntyre describes a particular type of manager, a stock character in the social drama of the present age, an office executive who embodies the philosophy of emotivism whose claim to expertise consists in the ability to organize large social groups to accomplish a given purpose without systematically taking up questions of deep purpose. MacIntyre accuses this type of manager of being a manipulator, a sham expert, an amoral technician, a disengaged ghost, a person who is fragmented, a cultivator of acquisitiveness, and a destroyer of communities of virtue.

MacIntyre's criticisms of the manager as a character type gives rise to a series of questions. How might we challenge this conception of the manager? Can moral philosophy play a role in transforming our understanding of the character of the manager? If so, how? Answering these questions suggests a response that moves beyond "business ethics" or an applied-ethics approach, especially if business ethics is understood merely in terms of a "code of ethics" or set of principles intended to place limits on an otherwise unbridled pursuit of a given end (such as increased profits or moving up in a ratings game). What might be done to cultivate in managers and future managers the characteristics and traits that accord with a holistic, humanistic approach to leadership, planning, and the task of organizing groups?

9

The Virtuous Manager, the Art of Character, and Business Humanities

The standard approach to business ethics has been to apply one or several moral standards, especially as drawn from utilitarianism or Kant's duty ethics, to case studies from the context of modern business. The standard approach is contrasted with virtue ethics. With the contemporary retrieval of virtue ethics, the philosopher's task is reconceived. Moral philosophy involves an "art of character," the activity of making and developing character. After surveying recent literature calling for a humanistic approach to business, the developing field of medical humanities, especially the emphasis on narrative, is described and proposed as a model for developing a "business humanities" approach to advance humanism in business.

What might be done to bring about a change in the social understanding and expectations of the manager's role? What might moral philosophy do to help cultivate in managers and future managers virtuous character traits that accord with a holistic, humanistic approach to management and a concern for the common good? Can philosophers play a role in transforming the self-understanding of managers and future managers? In light of MacIntyre's criticisms of the manager as office executive, what might be done to alter the social understanding of the character of the manager such that we conceive of this role in terms of being a wise steward?

I take up these questions in detail throughout the rest of the book.

For several decades, the central contribution made by moral philosophers concerned with questions about management and business organizations has involved the development of the field of "business ethics." The now standard textbook approach is typified in William H. Shaw's

Business Ethics.[1] Shaw begins with an overview of the nature of morality, describing morality in terms of moral standards. After a schoolbook summary of several such standards (especially utilitarianism and Kant's duty ethics), much of the rest of the text is divided into chapters with cases that arise in modern business contexts. Each case is an occasion to consider disputes about competing standards and their application in the context of contemporary work organizations. Shaw's business ethics textbook, representative of many other such books used for teaching business ethics in college classes, gives almost no consideration to questions of character.

Shaw mentions Aristotle's virtue ethics briefly in a section titled "Morality and Personal Values," but he dismisses questions of character and virtue in two short paragraphs. Shaw notes, "We have an idea of what it is for a person to be an excellent athlete, an excellent manager, or an excellent professor – it is to do well the types of things that athletes, managers, or professors are supposed to do."[2] However, rather than investigating the activities or traits of an excellent manager, Shaw quickly dismisses such concerns to the bin of personal opinion: "excellence is a function of our values."[3]

The rise and stumble of applied ethics generally, and business ethics in particular, has shown that having future managers read textbooks and take courses in applied ethics has not been adequate to shape in managers a stable disposition whereby managers appropriate the sense that responsibility, integrity, and good judgment are integral to management activities. Contemporary universities are quite good at preparing individuals to become professionals with expertise in technical skill for solving problems: physicians, engineers, managers, accountants, lawyers, etc. However, when it comes to teaching such people how to use their technical skills in a manner that makes for a good life for themselves and for others, the record is not so good. Applied ethicists have tried to contribute to this effort, but they have done little more than reproduce interminable disputes, providing a refined vocabulary and new contexts for stale quarrels.[4]

This textbook approach to business ethics stands in significant contrast with the literature of moral philosophy over the last half century. Among moral philosophers working since the time of Elizabeth Anscombe's famous 1958 article, "Modern Moral Philosophy," there has been a significant revival of virtue ethics. As shown in the preceding chapters, MacIntyre is one of several contemporary moral philosophers taking up robust questions of character and moral excellence. Such an approach, rather than focusing on the obligations of agents (as in Kant's duty ethics) or the consequences of actions and policies (as in utilitarianism), brings into focus issues of character. Along with this retrieval of virtue ethics comes a change in understanding of the work of the moral philosopher; the philosopher's task is understood in terms of an "art of character," that is, a work of *poesis*, of poetically making and developing a certain sort of character.

In Plato's *Symposium*, the character Diotima delivers a speech in which she distinguishes between three sorts of *poesis* with regard to how characters can be made: 1) natural "making" occurs through sexual procreation; 2) making one's name in a community involves attaining notable achievement; and 3) poetically forming oneself entails treating one's life as a work of art in which dispositional traits of character and intellect that make for a beautiful life are deliberately chosen and confirmed.[5]

What might be done to consider the character of the manager in such terms? Is it possible to frame questions of management in terms of virtue ethics? How might virtue ethics be applied to questions of management in a manner that moves beyond both the now standard approaches in business ethics (involving interminable debates about the application of disparate moral standards) and MacIntyre's criticisms of the manager as office executive? What is required to move toward a more beautiful and virtuous conception of the manager as a wise steward?

In asking such questions, in addition to recognizing the growing concern with virtue ethics in the business ethics journals, it is worth noting the wealth of resources within the literature of management, including many thinkers concerned to encourage a holistic, humanistic approach to organizational management. For example, in his classic book, *The Human Side of Enterprise*, Douglas McGregor famously distinguished between two approaches to management.[6] He refers to the conventional command-and-control conception of the manager's task as "Theory X." Those who use this approach presume that employees are lazy, disinterested in their work, and motivated only by carrots and sticks, especially money. Suggesting that Theory X is mistaken, McGregor offers an alternative, famously dubbed "Theory Y." In doing so, McGregor draws from the account of human self-actualization developed by Abraham Maslow. According to Maslow's well-known account of the hierarchy of human needs, once basic physiological and safety needs are satisfied, humans seek to satisfy needs for belonging and self-esteem; as those are satisfied, humans seek self-fulfillment by actualizing continued self-development, creativity, and initiative. Accordingly, "Theory Y" leaders view employees as self-motivated whole human persons who find meaning in their work; employees are viewed as whole persons energized when they engage in worthwhile accomplishments. In other words, carrots and sticks don't really motivate people in their work. To be sure, people are unhappy at work if they have low pay, a dismal space to work, stupid rules, or an annoying boss, but removing those doesn't give people a motivation to work harder. People are motivated by challenge, interesting work, and increasing responsibility. According to "Theory Y," the manager's task involves making sure that basic human needs are met and removing obstacles in order to release natural human potential while providing guidance to cultivate the conditions for growth and participation with others in creative self-direction ordered toward common purposes. Rather than management by control, this approach involves what Peter Drucker has called "management by objectives,"[7] that is, building a true team where each member sees their own work as contributing to a meaningful common purpose.

Drucker and McGregor are both humanistic polymaths that draw from psychology, history, sociology, and philosophy. In that sense, a humanistic approach to management is not new. At the same time, it is worthwhile to acknowledge that, in a post-Dilbert period where many have learned to roll their eyes at management fads and buzzwords that come and go (total quality management, reengineering, process management, organizational learning), some might be tempted to dismiss another call for a new humanistic approach to business. In doing so, one might miss the volume and variety of recent calls for a more humanistic approach to business and business education.

In *Academically Adrift: Limited Learning on College Campuses*, Richard Arum and Josipa Roksa offer a devastating assessment of higher education generally, and especially business education. They cite evidence that students concentrating in business coursework report lower levels of time spent reading and writing than students in the liberal arts.[8] Compared with business students, those majoring in liberal arts "demonstrated significantly higher gains in critical thinking, complex reasoning and writing skills over time than students in other fields of study. Students majoring in business, education, social work, and communications had the lowest measurable gains."[9]

Of course, jeremiads lamenting the sorry state of universities are nothing new. In the past, law schools, journalism schools, engineering schools, and the entire university system all have been subjected to severe criticisms, so it may be unsurprising that when the economy is down, there is an appetite for authors criticizing business education. With that said, it is curious that several of the most prominent such recent works call for similar remedies.

In *Rethinking the MBA,* Srikant Datar and his coauthors situate their argument within the 100-year history of the MBA at Harvard Business School. On their telling, business schools such as Harvard's primarily were vocational in character in the early years, with professors drawn from industry. In many cases, early business school teachers were experienced practitioners. From the podium, seasoned veterans dispensed wisdom to the young primarily by telling stories of "what it's like out there." A watershed occurred in 1959 when, in the United States, Carnegie and the Ford Foundation issued reports with deep criticisms of business school research and theory. The proposed solution, which was significantly incentivized by grant money, was to gain academic respectability by conducting empirically based scientific research supported with rigorous statistical analysis. In response to the Carnegie and Ford reports, business education "wisely and appropriately began to introduce greater rigor and disciplinary knowledge into their programs."[10] As business researchers began to focus their studies more narrowly while aiming for greater and greater precision, MBA faculty and the MBA degree increased in stature. However, Datar and his colleagues suggest that the pendulum has swung too far in the direction of the scientific research model. The risk is that business schools might institutionalize their own irrelevance, producing managers unable to see beyond narrow, quantitative studies.

Rethinking the MBA proposes that it is time to rebalance the educational priorities of the business school. While emphasizing quantifiable analyzes and methods, managers found themselves deficient in certain ways. In the MBA curriculum, less time was spent cultivating holistic thinkers capable of creatively reframing contexts nimbly across multiple frameworks, disciplines, and cultural perspectives. Executives found themselves highly proficient in technical analysis, but with few resources for engaging with others in dialogue and discourse about a sense of purpose or identity. *Rethinking the MBA* proposes "the center of gravity of MBA education shifted strongly toward 'knowing' and away from 'doing' and 'being'."[11] For that reason, the authors propose that it is time to "rebalance the scales" by "focusing more attention on issues of accountability, ethics, and social responsibility."[12] Without providing concrete specifics, Datar and his coauthors call for pedagogical and curricular innovations that teach managerial skills while instilling a sense of purpose and identity.

The call for reform is equally pronounced in a recent Carnegie study. *Rethinking Undergraduate Business Education* notes many of the same problems. During their research phase, the authors of the recent Carnegie study visited a range of business schools in the United States. "We were struck by the degree to which undergraduate business students take what they and others call an *instrumental approach* to their studies."[13] Many of the undergraduate business students interviewed in the recent Carnegie study consider required courses in the liberal arts as "requirements to get out of the way" rather than as exciting opportunities for intellectual exploration. In part, these attitudes have been institutionalized; they are "built into the curriculum and the advising system," so that connections between the humanistic concerns of the liberal arts, the personal traits cultivated in such courses, and the importance of those traits as crucially needed to excel in business, are rarely drawn.[14]

The authors of *Rethinking Undergraduate Business Education* propose a remedy that shares a great deal with the recommendations of *Rethinking the MBA*. In particular, the recent Carnegie study proposes an integrative vision of liberal learning for business education. As they put it, "The purpose of liberal learning is to enable students to make sense of the world and their place in it, preparing them to use knowledge and skills as a means to engage responsibly with the life of their times."[15] They articulate this goal in four parts. 1) Analytical thinking: the ability to abstract from particular contexts to produce formal knowledge that is general in nature and subject to methodical investigation. 2) Multiple framing: the awareness that any particular scheme of analytical thinking frames experience in particular ways, and is subject to challenge from different perspectives or points of view that frame the same experience in quite different, apparently incompatible ways. 3) The reflective exploration of meaning: As the traditional heart of liberal education and humanistic learning, it raises questions about "who I am, how I engage the world, and what is reasonable for me to imagine and hope."[16] 4) Practical reasoning: the ability to deliberate and decide on the best course of action in a particular situation. The authors of the recent Carnegie study propose that, "Such thinking is characteristic of professional judgment, including that of business leaders, as well as being a key capacity of citizens and statesmen."[17]

The "Humanistic Management Network" has emerged as a significant group playing a leading role in fostering "the creation and dissemination of actionable knowledge to change business practices towards humanistic ideals."[18] The Network's first book, *Humanism in Business*, is an edited volume of 25 essays that engage philosophical, spiritual, economic, psychological, and organizational arguments drawing from the tradition of humanism to understand and transform business and management. The interdisciplinary projects of the Network have been significantly extended in conferences and global activities bringing together a wide range of people with shared concern for humanistic management as well as the book series,"Humanism in Business."[19]

I see my argument as adding something distinctive to the revived emphasis on a humanistic approach to management. In particular, I write from the vantage point of a moral philosopher in the tradition of the virtues who is concerned with questions of character and narrative. Rather than describing my approach and argument in terms of "business ethics," it seems more appropriate to think of it as a "business humanities" approach. What does this mean?

To provide an overview of a "business humanities" approach, let me begin by drawing a contrast with the development of the field of "medical humanities." The term "medical humanities" can be traced to the 1960s, but the medical humanities movement has expanded significantly in recent decades.[20] As a pedagogical movement, it has a complicated history.[21] Medical humanities developed as a response to shortcomings that were felt as medical culture became increasingly "dominated by scientific, technical and managerial approaches."[22] As physicians and health care professionals have increasingly found themselves buffeted by social and economic pressures, narrowed in their expertise by increased specialization, and feeling at times dehumanized by conceptions of medicine that emphasize analytical detachment, there was a felt need for a more humanistic approach to medicine. In contrast, "business humanities" is still near its infancy.

Medical humanities grew from an effort to cultivate in both medical students and health care practitioners a more profound insight into the human condition. Drawing from the habits of mind and heart that characterize the humanistic disciplines, medical humanities aims at increasing an awareness of human and social concerns, attentiveness to narrative and history, sensitivity toward suffering and the perspectives of those who might sometimes be forgotten, appreciation of creativity, alertness to distinct perspectives, reflection with others on questions of deep purpose, and a commitment to human well-being. While medical humanities draws heavily from narrative literature, it also draws from the other disciplines of the humanities, the social sciences, and the arts.

Because humanistic concerns are widely recognized as essential for humane medical care, many medical schools now offer courses and programs in medical humanities. Degree programs in the field of medical humanities range from an undergraduate interdisciplinary minor to graduate studies culminating in the doctorate. At colleges and universities educating undergraduate students in nursing, pre-medicine, and other health care fields, medical humanities programs are becoming widespread.[23]

The field of medical humanities is interdisciplinary in character. It includes professional associations in North America and Europe with multiple scholarly journals and a growing literature of book-length works. The field is characterized by an ongoing debate as to whether it is a new subdiscipline or a "novel interdisciplinary perspective which sought to reunify the arts and sciences in medicine as a whole and so provide a more rounded and humanitarian approach that rejected the notion of a subdiscipline altogether."[24]

The concerns of literary critics, especially those who focus on narrative, have emerged as central in the developing conversation of medical humanities. By cultivating attentiveness to the rich complexity of setting, character, plot, and perspective, medical humanities encourages health care professionals to use humanistic and integrative approaches. In doing so, the hope is that medical professionals might bring together scientific and technical knowledge appropriate to the medical field with an increased awareness of each patient as a human person.[25] In contrast, the role of narrative literature in business humanities is quite underdeveloped.

At first glance, it might seem that business and the humanities approach the world in fundamentally different ways. Each seemingly has different goals and ideals as well as distinct understandings of the nature of intellectual activity. The activities of those in business frequently focus on organizational success as measured in quantifiable terms, especially profits; in contrast, the humanities involve a quest to understand the quality of human life, in particular by engaging in the activities of language and literature, narrative history, philosophy, theology, and all of those disciplines and practices that yearn to realize more deeply excellences that make our lives more humane and more divine.

Compared to business humanities, the interdisciplinary approach of medical humanities is more developed in terms of professional associations (of which there are several) and scholarly journals (of which there are two dozen). Most of these developed over the last several decades. It is certainly conceivable that in the future, scholarly journals will be launched focusing on business humanities, literature and business, narrative approaches to business, business and the arts, and so forth. Significant work is needed to institutionalize this sort of interdisciplinary synthesis.

It is worth noting that there is a certain attraction that comes with teaching medical humanities that might be lacking in business humanities. Medicine enjoys a strong reputation both in terms of academic rigor and with regard to its moral commitment to helping people. For that reason, it seems rather noble to engage in the work of teaching and research in the area of medical humanities. In contrast, it might seem more difficult to convince teachers of poetry or art history that it is noble to teach future business leaders or to engage in research that brings the concerns of the humanities to bear on matters of business and commerce.

Another concern should be stated with frankness: some of us whose primary work is in humanities departments are surrounded by and may hold attitudes toward business that are, in various ways, suspicious of or condescending toward business students and business faculty. This might be obvious, but it is frequently unstated, and I see these as a source of tension for advancing a new humanistic synthesis and a business humanities approach. It is with some reluctance that I try to describe attitudes that are common in the humanities. I write as a philosopher; my office is in a building that also includes theologians as well as those who work in literature and history. I am aware that there are a wide range of attitudes and tendencies among those in the humanities, and it is difficult to make generalizations about the talented and diverse people with whom I work. With that said, I think it is fair to acknowledge that many of us in the humanities have in various ways tendencies to view business with suspicion or to express at times views that are condescending toward business students and business faculty. Because our disciplines endorse excellences that are internal to intellectual and academic pursuits without measuring such excellence in terms of financial success, it is quite common for us to hold attitudes that might seem condescending toward business. Making such attitudes explicit while also problematizing them is one way to recognize a difficulty in pursuing a business humanities approach.

Several additional steps might help to bridge this gap: recognizing that different disciplines bring with them different sets of values and concerns while acknowledging that many of us in the humanistic disciplines have comparatively limited experience in the business sector. In addition, we might do more to acknowledge that those who work in the business sector find themselves having to make decisions that are quite difficult, even as tenured positions at universities shield faculty in many ways from the risks and difficulties of such decision-making contexts. Acknowledging these and similar points might help reduce a seemingly natural sort of distrust that is rather common between those in business schools and those in the humanities.

Further, current institutional structures that divide business and the humanities into separate schools with distinct faculty and curricula, as well as the climate of hyper-specialization, may raise special challenges (especially compared to medical humanities). My university houses the business school on a different part of campus than the humanities disciplines; each has its own faculty and curriculum, and this seems to be common at many institutions. In a light-hearted way, we might tease that the only thing we share is the same parking lot. But we might also acknowledge that those of us with expertise in the humanities, both in our research and in the courses we have designed and which we teach, presuppose in various ways a set of assumptions that run counter to the educational concerns of those in the business school.

Another aspect of this challenge has to do with a difference that emerges when we contrast medical humanities with the proposed business humanities approach. At many universities, premedical and prehealth programs are housed in the same college or institutional structure as humanities departments. For that reason, undergraduate medical humanities programs face fewer institutional hurdles than might, for example, an undergraduate program in business humanities.

Finally, some parents and students may be suspicious of a business humanities approach with its promise of a long-term investment in the character and attitudes that shape an integrated habit of mind and heart without immediate job prospects in the short term. How might humanists respond to this very genuine concern? After all, it might seem that the current economic difficulties make this an unsuitable time to develop and encourage a business humanities approach, for many students and their parents are quite concerned to make sure that scarce resources are used wisely. To respond to this concern, we might point to the need for students to develop both technical skills (such as those cultivated in the traditional business disciplines) and the habits of mind and heart cultivated in the humanities. The promise of a business humanities approach, it seems to me, rests not in the ability to land that first job, but in more long-term concerns with the character and attitudes that shape an integrated habit of mind and heart. To make this case, we might do more to insure that business students (and their parents) understand the rationale for studying the liberal arts while investigating more intensively, both in our teaching and in our research programs, how the concerns of the humanities can be integrated with business education.

On individual campuses, more can be done to integrate the liberal arts and business curriculum, so that business students might view humanities courses not so much as "requirements to get out of the way" but rather as opportunities to explore and discover the intellectual resources of the humanities. On some campuses, this might be institutionalized into interdisciplinary minors and majors, as has happened with medical humanities. Beyond individual campuses, in order for such a synthesis to flourish, there is a need to develop resources such as databases, shared syllabi, professional associations, and academic journals that encourage scholarship and debate that widens the conversation, beyond philosophy and theology, to bring additional humanistic disciplines to bear on the world of business.

When compared to medical humanities, the state of curriculum development and research in business humanities is comparatively underdeveloped. For example, the New York University School of Medicine maintains a medical humanities Internet site that provides resources for scholars, educators, and students. This now includes a massive database with annotations of works of literature, art, and film relevant to medical humanities focusing on the illness experience, education and medical practice, including works of fiction; poetry; memoir, biography, autobiography; literary, cultural, and social criticism; visual art; film; and drama. The NYU medical humanities Web site includes course syllabi for a wide range of courses on diverse topics: aging, AIDS, death and dying, disability, ethnicity and medicine, film and medicine, gender and medicine, health care policy, the history of medicine, law and medicine, literature and medicine, medical education, medical ethics, medicine and the arts, professionalism, religion and medicine, social issues in medicine, women and medicine, and other topics.

Beyond the business ethics literature, aspects of an intentionally humanistic approach to business and management are suggested in the vast literature that has developed in business and society, corporate social responsibility, micro-finance, worker cooperatives, and other programs and approaches. For example, the Aspen Institute offers seminars for business leaders built around the themes of innovation, reflection, leadership and community with an eye to positive social change.[26] Spiritual writers and theologians from virtually every religious tradition have brought their distinctive resources to bear on questions at the intersection of ethics and economic life.[27] Theological and humanistic reflection on economic questions is particularly well developed within the tradition of Catholic social thought, which includes an extensive literature critical of both laissez-faire capitalism and materialistic

command economies while engaging questions about the proper relation among the political, economic, and moral–cultural spheres in a way
that promotes the dignity of human persons.[28] The tradition of Catholic
social thought is highly interdisciplinary, but compared with medical
humanities, it tends to emphasize interdisciplinarity between philosophy, theology, economics, and political science with less emphasis, as
compared to medical humanities, on narrative literature, film, history,
and the other humanistic disciplines.

Several sources are available for those seeking to bring the concerns
of narrative and literary criticism to bear upon the world of business.
For example, the essays collected in *The Moral Imagination* by Oliver F.
Williams examine a range of ways that literature and film can stimulate
moral reflection in the context of the business world.[29] A colleague of
mine at Saint Louis University teaches a very well-conceived course that
focuses on the way business and commerce are represented in American
film, from the silent film era (Metropolis, Modern Times) through
the postwar decades to more recent films that focus on business and
commerce.[30] In *Questions of Character: Illuminating the Heart of Leadership
through Literature*, Joseph Badaracco artfully shows how fiction and great
literature can be used in business education by approaching a literary
text "like a business school case study."[31] Badaracco begins his book by
describing a class session in which he assigned a little-known short story,
"The Secret Sharer," by Joseph Conrad. It is the tale of a sea captain's first
voyage and his decision to let a stranger come on board after the man
tells him that he has escaped from another ship where he was unjustly
accused of murder. Conrad's short story, according to Badaracco, encourages business students to enter into moral reflection in a wide-ranging
conversation. "Was the new captain ready to take on his responsibilities? What did his actions reveal about his character? How do leaders
learn from their mistakes?"[32] Badaracco shows how literature has the
power to pull people into the story so they can reflect upon their roles
as business leaders and upon their lives.

One might question whether merely adding a larger dose of the liberal
arts to business education is enough to provide the sort of humanistic
synthesis that is needed.[33] After all, the "multiple framing" proposed in
the Carnegie report, among other features, seems perhaps at times to
yield to a sort of undifferentiated pluralism that lacks confidence in the
ability of human persons to take up an authentic search for truth. In a
similar way, it might seem unconvincing that adding more literature
or history to business education will help cultivate good judgment in
future business leaders.

In response to this sort of friendly objection, it is worth noting that the capacity to pose questions and search for the truth implies the rudiments of a response. Certainly it is foolish to think that adding a college course or two in the humanities is all that is needed to produce an integrated life. The increased calls for humanism in business and business education are an opportunity to engage more deeply with a wide array of contributors to a business humanities approach.

In order to add to this conversation, I examine character transformation in the following chapters. My goal in these chapters is to reconsider the role of character transformation in the work of moral philosophers. After that, I turn to examine ways in which moral philosophy might contribute to the transformation of the character of the manager.

10
Character Transformation in the Friendship of Readers and Writers

Contemporary business gurus call for a new understanding of the manager. Gary Hamel has challenged managers to become wise stewards. This chapter focuses on the process of transformation, especially the way that narratives shared in a reader–author friendship can bring about a transformation in the character of the reader. Drawing insights from literary criticism regarding narrative and the friendship between reader and author, the focus turns to the implied narrative, a story of moral transformation intended to occur in the character of the reader. A community of readers can develop a conversation in response to a text, treating authors such as Plato and Aristotle as friends with whom we might engage in an ongoing conversation in order to cultivate the virtue of practical wisdom.

MacIntyre certainly is not alone in his criticisms of the modern manager. In surprising ways, people who might disagree about many other things share the sense that the time is now ripe for a new conception of the character of the manager. For example, protesters in the "Occupy Wall Street" movement and contemporary management gurus both have aimed their criticism at the sort of manager-as-office-executive criticized by MacIntyre in *After Virtue*.

The gap between the literature of contemporary management gurus and that of moral philosophers who work in academic settings in higher education is quite remarkable. The name "guru" is widespread as a term used to describe those who teach managers how to manage. Multiple lists of top management gurus are available from Forbes, Harvard Business Review, and other sources. A guru, of course, is an ancient Sanskrit term for "teacher" or "master." The name points away from the Western canon, even as it has taken on the pejorative connotation as referring to anyone who exploits naiveté to acquire followers. Gary Hamel is frequently included on the list of leading contemporary management gurus. Hamel begins his most recent book with these words: "If you are a leader at any level in any organization, you are a steward – of career, capabilities, resources, the environment, and organizational values. Unfortunately, not every manager is a wise steward."[1] Hamel issues the same sort of call for a new manager in his previous book, *The Future of Management* (2007), where he addresses himself to readers who feel "hog-tied by bureaucracy" and worry that "the system is stifling innovation."[2] Arguing that management is out of date and that current management practices are based on a model that's more than a century old, Hamel invites his reader to envision a new model for management. He points to companies such as Google and Whole Foods as places that have abandoned the command-and-control model of the Weberian bureaucrat. Rather than emphasizing standardization, specialization, goal alignment, hierarchy, planned control, and extrinsic rewards, Hamel argues that the future of management lies in variety, flexibility, activism, meaning, and serendipity.[3]

Other widely read management writers have advanced similar calls to reconceive the character of the manager. Henry Mintzberg, in *Managers, Not MBAs*, criticizes mainstream approaches to management and management education while proposing ways that both could be changed.[4] Mintzberg examines what is wrong with conventional management and proposes a different approach that views management as a practice blending experience-based craft, artistic insight, and scientific analysis. Tom Peters, best known as the coauthor of the 1982 management best seller, *In Search of Excellence*, recently has been called the "Michel Foucault of the management world: a scourge of the rationalist tradition and a celebrant of the creative necessity of chaos and craziness."[5] In *Re-Imagine*, Peters takes on a postmodern voice, writing in short snippets. While fuming about "the failure of organizations invented for another era,"[6] Peters asks his readers to reimagine a new model of organizational leadership. Peter Senge, in his now classic book, *The Fifth Discipline: The Art and Practice of the Learning Organization*, also encourages his readers to envision a *metanoia*, a transformation of the heart and mind with a new vision of organizational leadership.[7] Senge's emphasis on the "learning organization" envisions leaders of new sort who are "designers, stewards, and teachers."[8]

Despite the widespread sense that a new kind of manager is needed, questions remain for those who might bridge the gap among moral philosophy, the insights of the management gurus, and the concerns of Occupy protesters. Moral philosophers can contribute to this conversation in several distinctive ways. For example, more might be done to bring into focus questions about the manager's purpose. Hamel and Peters seem to take it as given that the goal of the new manager is "to win,"[9] but they have done comparatively little to call into question what this means. Who are the winners? How does a winning organization serve the common good? Questions regarding character transformation and the cultivation of the virtues are scarcely mentioned by most management gurus; questions of narrative transformation, character, and the virtues each merit fuller examination.

My central purpose in this chapter is to puzzle through these issues, beginning with an intense consideration of the relationship of friendship that can develop between reader and author. How might narratives shared in a reader–author friendship help bring about a transformation in the character of the reader? Pursuing this may take us at times seemingly far afield from the concerns about the manager, but this journey is meant not as a diversion along a side path, but as an effort to gain deeper insight into the way that moral philosophers can contribute to the task of transforming the character of the manager.

As mentioned in previous chapters, Alasdair MacIntyre has played a key role in reviving interest in dramatic narrative. Despite this, he has written relatively little about the important place of the *narrator* in a narrative. One exception, ripe with implications, is an offhanded remark in which MacIntyre states that the "collaboration between author and reader that takes place in the reading of a philosophical text is important."[10] What does this mean? How do author and reader collaborate? What can be learned about the narrative of transformation from focusing on the relationship between author and reader?

As Scholes and Kellogg put it in their seminal work on the nature of narrative, "for writing to be a narrative no more and no less than a teller and a tale are required."[11] Every narrative includes a story, a storyteller, and an audience. In oral narratives, the storyteller engages in a face-to-face encounter with the audience.[12] Such storytellers are able to respond to cues from the audience to determine how much background is needed, when to move the story along, how much repetition is needed, and so forth. In such a context, the relationship between narrator and audience involves a significant degree of non-verbal communication. The situation is quite different in written narratives. The narrator of a text is faced with the challenge of telling a story to an audience who is not actually present. As Walter Ong put it, "The writer's audience is always a fiction. The historian, the scholar or scientist, and the simple letter writer all fictionalize their audiences, casting them in a made-up role and calling on them to play the role assigned."[13] Writers must learn to fictionalize their audience, constructing a role for the reader to play.[14]

This insight, explored by literary critics in the context of literature, fiction, and novels, can be extended to every genre of writing, including moral philosophy. Writers must construct fictional, implied versions of themselves and imagine themselves as part of their own audience. Henry James described this character as the "mock reader," and Wayne C. Booth calls this the "implied reader." As Booth puts it, the writer "must make his reader, very much as he makes his characters."[15]

Corresponding to the implied reader (constructed by the author), Booth also writes of the implied author (constructed by the reader in the activity of reading). Understood this way, reading and writing narratives always involves more than simply a reader, a writer, and a story. Reading and writing a written narrative always involves a collaborative effort between author and audience. There is a complexity of roles that is a pervasive feature of writing and reading narratives. A polyphony of voices is present and hidden in all written narrative:

1) the flesh-and-blood author,
2) the implied author,
3) the immediate narrator,
4) the various characters in the story,
5) the immediate reader,
6) the implied reader, and
7) the flesh-and-blood reader.

Consider these seven roles in the example of Aesop's well-known fable of the goose who laid the golden egg. The story is familiar and brief:

A man and his wife had the good fortune to possess a goose that laid a golden egg every day.

"Just think," said the man's wife, "If we could have all the golden eggs that are inside the goose, we could be richer much faster."

"You're right," said her husband, "We wouldn't have to wait for the goose to lay her egg every day."

But when they cut it open they found it was just like any other goose. Thus, they neither got rich all at once, as they had hoped, nor enjoyed any longer the daily addition to their wealth.

Despite the apparent simplicity of the tale, the cast of characters involved in the activity of reading this narrative goes well beyond the man, his wife, and the goose. The seven voices identified earlier are all present, actually or implicitly, in the telling of the tale. Each is, to varying degrees, operative in the narrative.

We know very little about 1) flesh-and-blood Aesop; he is thought to be a Greek slave who lived a century before Socrates. Regarding his birthplace, he has been claimed by Athens, Thrace, Phrygia, Egypt, Ethiopia, and elsewhere. Apart from flesh-and-blood Aesop, 2) Aesop as implied author is the narrating voice of ancient practical wisdom discovered in this and many other fables. Aesop's voice is one that we, as receivers of the story, implicitly encounter in the activity of listening or reading. More directly and immediately, we encounter 3) the immediate narrator. Because the tale is told in the third person, the immediate narrator is hidden, present primarily as a narrating voice. Within the tale and its plot and setting, we encounter 4) the various characters, in this case, the man, his wife, and the goose. To receive the story, it is necessary for us as listeners or readers to take in the words. In giving our attention as 5) the immediate listener or reader, we must attend not only to the words, but to the unfolding of the story's plot. Beyond this immediate role, Aesop has presumed a set of beliefs in his audience. Aesop invites us, as 6) his implied readers, to pretend that, for the sake of the story, there could exist a golden-egg-laying goose. We know that no such geese exist, and we know that Aesop knows that there are no such geese, but we also know that, for the sake of the story, suspending our disbelief will help the fable. Aesop imagines that of us, and we hold a corresponding belief about Aesop. Further, Aesop takes it for granted that his implied audience thinks that gold is good, and he presumes that we are tempted both to overvalue gold and to be impatient.[16] As Aesop's implied readers, we can discern his goal for us; he wants to move his implied reader away from an attraction to greed and impatience toward a character state of patient satisfaction with the material goods of one's life. While Aesop's tale tries to move the dispositions of 7) the flesh-and-blood reader, the story leaves a space between implied reader and the flesh-and-blood reader; Aesop leaves it to the flesh-and-blood reader to affirm the truth and importance of becoming a person who patiently stands firm in the face of temptations.

Or consider the way these voices are present in Twain's novel, *The Adventures of Huckleberry Finn*. 1) Samuel Langhorne Clemens (the man behind the pseudonym Mark Twain) is the flesh-and-blood author of the text. In the case of living authors, we can learn about the author's flesh-and-blood life from those who know the author in other social contexts. For those of us who are separated historically from the life of Samuel Clemens, we can learn about his flesh-and-blood existence from biographers, curators, and critics who have studied and attended to features of the author's life. These details may be attractive for historical value, but frequently they also lend insight into an author's published works.[17] 2) The implied author of *Huckleberry Finn* is Mark Twain. This is evident not only from the pen name that appears on the novel, but also from the opening line. "You don't know about me without you have read a book by the name of *The Adventures of Tom Sawyer;* but that ain't no matter. That book was made by Mr. Mark Twain, and he told the truth, mainly." As an authorial presence distinct from both Samuel Clemens and Huck, the reader discovers Twain's character in the activity of reading the text. From the writing, we can discern Twain's attitudes, feelings, and desires. Twain invites us imaginatively to enter into life in Hannibal and enjoy a leisurely float down the Mississippi. Along the way, we discern that Twain wants us to engage in moral reflection, to question Huck, and to take up questions about Huck's relation with Jim and Huck's malformed conscience. Twain offers us a world that is at once both lighthearted and serious, a space capable of awakening us to the possibility of our own participation in social structures that distort the way we relate to others. While Twain is the implied author, 3) the immediate narrator of the story is Huckleberry Finn. Unlike the fable of the goose who laid golden eggs, which is told in the third person, this is a story told in the first person. Huck Finn both narrates the story and acts as the central character. 4) In addition to Huck, the story includes other familiar characters: Jim, Tom Sawyer, Becky Thatcher, Widow Douglas, Huck's father "Pap," the Duke and Dauphin, Aunt Polly, and others. As one is immersed in the activity of reading and attending to the words of the text and the unfolding of the plot, one plays the role of 5) the immediate reader. *The Adventures of Huckleberry Finn*, like all well-written works, is addressed to 6) an implied reader. The novel addresses this imagined character in the very first word: "You." The opening line helps us, as Twain's readers, know the role that we are supposed to play. "You don't know about me without you have read a book by the name of *The Adventures of Tom Sawyer*, but that ain't no matter." As readers, Twain invites us, through his casual familiarity, to play the role of Huck's contemporaries. By reading the novel this way, we cooperate with Huck, with Mark Twain, and even in a way with Samuel Clemens. While reading the novel this way, the reader may feel the exuberance of youthful adolescence even though as 7) flesh-and-blood reader one may inhabit a very different social setting or stage in life.

Twain's novel is an invitation to the flesh-and-blood reader to undergo at the level of one's imagination the transformation that the novel proposes. As with all great storytellers, Twain leaves a space for his reader between the imagined transformation of the narrative and the possibility of undergoing an existential conversion, a change of heart with regard to one's flesh-and-blood dispositions. The flesh-and-blood reader plays an important role in affirming or denying, at the level of one's personal existence, the transformation proposed by the narrative.

In addition to the complicated set of relations between the various voices at play in a written narrative, especially the relationship between implied author and implied reader, there is an "*implied narrative*" beyond the basic plot of the story. Narratives involve both the explicit tale that is told and an implied narrative, a story of hoped-for transformation in the character of the audience. The implied narrative is a story of moral transformation that is intended to occur in the character of the flesh-and-blood reader. The setting of the implied narrative is the state of character of the implied audience. The central plot of the implied narrative involves the audience properly attending to the tale, and then, the implied reader is invited to undergo a transformation to a new set of beliefs, feelings, desires, and social relations or to become more deeply confirmed in those traits being affirmed by the narrative.

How can the implied narrative become recognizable? In Aesop's fable of "The Goose Who Laid the Golden Eggs," the implied narrative becomes explicit when the fable's moral is added: "much wants more and loses all." Aesop, as implied author, wants his implied audience to undergo a transformative journey, moving away from greed and impatience toward patient satisfaction with the small fortune's in one's life. In *Huckleberry Finn*, the implied narrative is a coming-of-age story; Twain wants to provoke in his reader a moral transformation, a more mature conscience beyond the naïve innocence and unexamined loyalties of Huck's Hannibal days.[18]

So, narratives involve not only the features of the tale (such as setting, plot, and characters) but also the complex set of relations that develop among teller, audience, and tale.[19] Booth helpfully uses this framework to evaluate moral features of the relationship between reader and author in terms of friendship. After all, the author is inviting the reader into a relationship. How might one characterize one's relationship with a particular author in terms of the three kinds of friendship famously described by Aristotle?[20] Is it a friendship of utility, where each is attracted to the other simply because of the benefits provided by the other? Is it a friendship of pleasure, where author and reader are attracted for the sake of a shared pleasure? Can an author and reader develop a relationship that has the qualities of a complete friendship, where each wishes well alike to each other *qua* good?[21] Readers sometimes refer to texts and authors as "good friends." What goes into such a relationship? After all, reader–author relationships can vary as much as flesh-and-blood relationships. One's relationship to the author of *The Complete Idiot's Guide to Simple Home Repair* is likely to be different from one's relationship to Mark Twain. Using Aristotle's taxonomy of the kinds of friendship brings order to understanding reader–author relationships.

Initially, a reader must discern both the qualities of character in the implied author and the nature of the author's invitation. Readers have a range of resources to draw upon to take up these sorts of evaluations. The most obvious of these is the text itself. Careful readers can find in the text a wealth of clues about the implied author. Because the implied author is an authorial voice behind the text, that is, an intervening persona distinct from both the immediate narrator and the historical flesh-and-blood author, this is a character discovered in the activity of reading. The style, tone, and technique of the writer's artistry allow the reader's imagination to assimilate information about the implied author. From the writing, we can discern aspects of the character of the implied author's attitudes, feelings, and desires. Is this author a friend or a foe? If the author is a friend, what sort of friendship is on offer? To what extent is the implied author willing to reveal vulnerabilities or grant responsibility to us as readers? Is it prudent for us, as readers, to respond to this invitation and to deepen this author–reader relationship?

For the flesh-and-blood reader, reading may seem like a solitary activity. The reader is alone with the text. However, this solitariness is always at most apparent. While alone with the text, the reader is together with the author. Reader and author are alone together. Just as friends or lovers find joy when they withdraw together from the wider social world in order to develop a deeper sense of intimacy, a reader withdraws, in a sense, from the social context of the wider world to immerse oneself in a different (implied) social context.

In order to read well, the reader must become vulnerable in certain ways to the author. Sartre claimed that the writer requires of the reader, "the gift of his whole person, with his passions, his prepossessions, his sympathies."[22] As with any relationship of intimacy, the author–reader relationship is an invitation to trust. But as a reader, I might ask myself,

"Who is this person that I am entrusting myself to? Is this a trustworthy character?" Readers are continually required to assess whether the implied author is a companion or a rival. In order to avoid manipulation, one must learn, as MacIntyre puts it, "how to read antagonistically without defeating oneself."[23]

As a reader, I might ask myself three questions. 1) Who is this person that I am entrusting myself to? In other words, is this a trustworthy character? In addition, I might ask 2) What is the author's conception of his or her audience? In asking this question, I can determine how much is required of me to take up the role demanded by the author. Finally, I might wonder, 3) What is the nature of this author's invitation? Is the author inviting me, as reader, to enter into a kind of friendship? What is the nature of this friendship?

These sorts of questions are crucial for inquiry into the purpose of the manager and the possibility of reconceiving the character of the manager as wise steward. Joseph Pieper has suggested that the ability to reason well about questions of purpose is cultivated and developed in the context of friendship. "It is possible for a friend – only for a friend and only for a prudent friend – to help with counsel and direction to shape a friend's decision."[24] A good friend, not simply a friend based on shared benefits or pleasures, but a friend who wants the good for the other, can, by virtue of the oneness established in the friendship, help one to visualize the concrete situation calling for a decision by seeing it almost from the inside. Then, with the fresh eyes of the friend, one is able to seek counsel to reshape one's understanding of the situation. As Pieper puts it, "only this empowers another to offer the kind of direction which – almost! – conforms to the concrete situation in which the decision must be made."[25] For the virtue of practical wisdom (in the Aristotelian–Thomistic sense) to be cultivated, part of what is needed is a relationship of friendship.[26]

Is it possible for an author to cultivate in one's reader the traits that make for a good human life? Can an author help cultivate in a reader a disposition toward practical wisdom? If so, how? How might one acquire the habit of reasoning well about purposes? After all, protesting demonstrators might be successful at calling attention to income disparities, but a program of confrontation seems like it will do little to encourage a forum for shared deliberation about organizational goals and the common good. Even Gary Hamel's very suggestive call for a new leader who acts as a "wise steward" seems undermined by both his emphasis on "winning" and the medium of his message. In the genre of the management guru who sells a message for a profit, the relationship between author and reader might seem to be a friendship of utility where the reader wins by gaining new tools for winning in a world of ferocious competition while the author wins by merchandising a message about the need for managers to act with prudent wisdom. Besides, Hamel and the other contemporary management writers have done comparatively little to explore and explain the traditional understanding of these virtues in the great thinkers of the Western canon.

Aristotle and St Thomas Aquinas both prized highly the virtue of reasoning well about how to make practical decisions. Aristotle termed this trait *phronesis*. St Thomas and his contemporaries named this trait *prudentia*. The person who has this quality, that is, the person of practical wisdom, is excellent at taking in the complexities of a situation, deliberating, making a judgment about the best course of action in one's concrete situation, and then properly executing that judgment in action. Is it possible for an author to cultivate this sort of excellence in practical reasoning in one's readers?

In a sense, it seems impossible to form the sort of friendship that Aristotle describes as "complete" in an author–reader relationship. After all, as Aristotle states, living together seems to be a crucial component for a complete friendship, but the sort of relationship where a reader refers to an author as a "good friend" almost always involves parties who are separated by space, time, or both. Further, one might question whether author–reader relationships that are cultivated in reading and writing destroy the more basic sorts of face-to-face relationships that occur when a strong emphasis is placed on the spoken word. For example, objections might be raised such as those mentioned by Plato in the *Phaedrus* (through the voice of Socrates) and in the *Seventh Letter*. [27] In those texts, Plato raises four concerns about writing. 1) Writing is a manufactured product that pretends to capture outside the mind a reality that is properly an intellectual activity. 2) Writing weakens the mind by undermining memory. 3) Written texts are unresponsive. It seems to be a sort of foolishness to form a friendship with a book. 4) Written words are essentially passive and incapable of participating in the give-and-take that is an integral part of genuine human friendship.

In response to these and similar objections, I concede that the author–reader relationship is certainly not primary in human experience, and it can be a vice to allow one's relationship with texts to shape one's existence to such a degree that one becomes unresponsive to flesh-and-blood persons. Obviously, it is foolish to think that the sort of friendship formed between readers and authors, especially in the activity of reading, is no different from the "complete friendship" that Aristotle describes. With that said, it seems too strong to complain that texts are entirely unresponsive, passive, and incapable of generating a certain sort of give-and-take. In particular, this occurs when a community of readers develops a conversation in response to a text. Certain texts have a way of inviting an extended conversation. Indeed, part of the fecundity of great writers (such as Plato and Aristotle) stems from the multiple ways in which their writings have spawned fruitful responses. Classic texts such as these make it possible for members of a community in one time and place to engage insights from others situated in different times and places. It is this sort of friendship – an author–reader friendship – that I am suggesting we might extend more deeply in order to cultivate the virtue of practical wisdom. Before taking this up in greater detail, let's spend more time examining character transforming arguments.

11
Transforming the Character of the Moral Philosopher

MacIntyre suggests that we are confronted with competing understandings of what it means to be a "philosopher." The philosopher as technical specialist is akin to the character of the manager. MacIntyre describes this character not only to diagnose, but also to arouse. His purpose is to awaken his readers to the hollowness of this sort of philosopher, pointing to the gap between this character's activities in the professional context as compared with the everyday life of this kind of philosopher. He thereby hopes to dispose his reader to turn away from the conception of the philosopher as technical specialist. MacIntyre draws upon the character of the "plain person" to encourage a transformed conception of the philosopher, from professional specialist to seeker of understanding.

As MacIntyre once put it, "Ours is a culture dominated by experts, experts who profess to assist the rest of us, but who often instead make us their victims."[1] This tendency toward narrow expertise applies not only to managers, but also to professional philosophers, especially with regard to the tendency to turn questions about the good and the nature of things into intellectual puzzles formulated in a specialized technical jargon and disconnected from concrete human existence. In the preceding chapters, I showed how MacIntyre's work problematizes the manager as a character. I pointed to the need for a business humanities approach and a transformed conception of the manager. In this chapter and the next two, I bring into focus the notion of a *character-transforming argument*. In order for moral philosophy to contribute to the many calls for a new sort of manager, part of what is needed is a transformed conception of moral philosophy. My goal in this chapter is to focus on the character of the philosopher to show that MacIntyre has advanced a character-transforming argument with regard to the moral philosopher, if not with regard to the character of the manager.

MacIntyre's character-transforming argument concerning the philosopher has the following shape. First, he focuses on the professional philosopher, aiming to sting his contemporaries in order to awaken them to a sort of hollowness in their activities. Then, he contrasts the concerns of the professional philosopher with those of the everyday plain person. Finally, he argues that, in order for philosophers to become masterful in the activities of their practice, they need to retrieve an older and more substantive understanding of philosophy as the pursuit of wisdom in service to the common good. In order to work through the details of MacIntyre's character-transforming argument with regard to the philosopher, it is necessary to focus on three steps in his argument: 1) his stinging criticism of the contemporary professional philosopher; 2) his description of the character of the "plain person," and 3) his account of the transformed philosopher.

Already in MacIntyre's early writings, his criticisms of professional philosophy are evident. In his 1958 article, "On not Misrepresenting Philosophy," MacIntyre expressed disapproval of "the kind of objectivity that dwells in the ivory tower."[2] By the end of the 1970s, the tone of MacIntyre's criticisms of professional philosophy had become stinging and sarcastic: "The increase in the number of philosophical journals – and the pressure to write that produces that increase – are almost unmitigated evils. The case for making nonpublication a prerequisite for tenure or promotion is becoming very strong."[3]

MacIntyre traces the well-known development of specialization (and hyper-specialization) in the academic disciplines of modern research universities. At such institutions, where aspiring college and university professors pursue their doctoral studies, each academic discipline frequently is treated as autonomous and self-defining. Prestige and influence at such universities is often associated with intensely and narrowly specialized research and scholarship. In such a context, it might seem imprudent to spend time learning or focusing on any discipline other than one's own. The same is true of the discipline of philosophy, at least according to a widely held contemporary attitude. For example, Scott Soames has written that contemporary philosophy "has become an aggregate of related, but semi-independent investigations, very much like other academic disciplines."[4] Considered this way, philosophy is done by and for specialists.

In appropriate contexts, specialization obviously is good. In contexts where specialized knowledge is needed to solve a particular problem, expertise is certainly helpful. Whether one's arena is research (as with the scientist), corporate effectiveness (as with the manager), or philosophical problem solving (as with the professional philosopher) each specialist claims expertise based on effective problem-solving ability drawn from skilled analysis. The expert's analytic method, relative to each field, involves breaking things down to fix manageable problems. Higher education and professional schools have become outstanding at producing countless experts.

Despite the benefits that come from expertise, the culture of specialization has several shortcomings, including hyper-specialization and fragmentation. The result seems to be that there is an expert for every perceived problem. In that context, several problems have remained largely hidden and unaddressed. In some instances, experts who profess to assist us actually end up doing damage. Frequently, what is needed is not another expert with specialized knowledge; rather, what is needed is the practical wisdom to determine whether or not the one offering expertise is promoting human flourishing or harm.

The culture of specialization leaves us with another problem. There seems to be no expert or specialist who can address the question as to whether human life has any integrated meaning or deeper purpose. Contemporary culture, that is, the culture of endless specialists, leaves us without any rational way to evaluate the various attempts to provide such a synthesis. Every effort to discern an integrated understanding about what makes for a good human life seems to get reduced to individual preferences.

MacIntyre contrasts the "professional philosopher with specialized expertise" with the character of the "everyday plain person." The "plain person" appears in *Three Rival Versions of Moral Inquiry* and then repeatedly in MacIntyre's later work.[5] This character is "plain" in the sense that he or she is not a professional philosopher and not someone who has studied academic philosophy. This character is an "everyday person" in the sense that he or she is an individual with an everyday life who is engaged in concrete social practices with internal excellences, the pursuit of which promotes the cultivation of the virtues, allowing the possessor to take up the quest for life's deeper questions.[6]

Everyday plain persons may live without sensing a desire to reflect on questions of purpose and meaning. In this mode, which may extend for long periods, plain persons may seem unreflective and not philosophical. While existing in this unreflective state, the plain person unwittingly presumes the philosophical views embedded in the customs and culture in which one has been raised, perhaps in a fragmentary manner filled with unnoticed inconsistencies. In that context, the plain person may be confronted by a crisis that provokes deep questions. As MacIntyre writes,

> Someone who has believed that he was highly valued by his employers and colleagues is suddenly fired; someone proposed for membership of a club whose members were all, so he believed, close friends is blackballed. Or someone falls in love and needs to know what the loved one *really* feels; someone falls out of love and needs to know how he or she can possibly have been so mistaken in the other.[7]

Confronted by such a crisis of meaning, the plain person finds himself or herself asking philosophical questions. Is it possible to distinguish appearance from reality? Can we know the thoughts and inner life of another? Can we reliably predict the future based on generalizations from the past? Who am I? Where have I come from and where am I going? Why is there evil? What is there after this life? How shall we live? What makes for a good life? How can we shape the communities of which we are members to help make them just, humane, and civil? These are not the questions of specialists. Such questions arise in the lives of ordinary persons.

Faced with these sorts of questions, the plain person finds himself or herself on a quest. To take up that quest with seriousness, MacIntyre proposes that the plain person will need to withstand the temptation to dismiss that search as nonrational, thereby learning to use practical reason with others to uncover the order implicit yet actually present in the world while calling into question the norms espoused by one's contemporaries.

MacIntyre further suggests that taking up this quest will be particularly difficult for plain persons situated in the contemporary culture of advanced capitalism influenced by the enlightenment liberalism of modern Western society, and this for two reasons. First, we lack an institutional arena in which plain persons "are able to engage together in systematic reasoned debate designed to arrive at a rationally well-founded common mind."[8] Additionally, if the plain person turns to philosophy – which might appear to be the discipline best suited to take up questions of deep purpose – one regrettably finds too often a deep split between what philosophers say (in their professional articles or in the seminar room) compared to what those same philosophers do as flesh-and-blood persons. Indeed, MacIntyre advances this not only as an indictment, but as a confession of his own past shortcomings.[9]

Let's focus explicitly now on MacIntyre's treatment of the "philosopher" and the distinction he draws between two different "kinds of philosophers."[10] As we have seen, one kind conceives of philosophy as a specialized "set of argumentative and analytic skills."[11] This sort of philosopher does his or her work typically "in the professionalized and specialized enquiries"[12] of seminars and conferences. The main genre of writing for such philosophers is the journal article. This character can be called the professional philosopher as "technical specialist." When the philosopher is conceived in this manner, the philosopher's activity is characterized by three qualities.

1) The philosopher (as technical specialist) is one who has training in a set of specific analytic skills. "Entering into philosophy is a matter of training in the requisite skills and question about the ends of life are taken to be of interest to philosophers just insofar as they provide subject matter for the exercise of those skills."[13]

2) The philosopher (as technical specialist) engages in the activity of exercising those special analytic skills as a sort of diversion. While exercising such skills, one is also concealing from oneself "how desperate our human condition is and how urgently we need answers to our questions."[14] Those who are not professional philosophers use other diversions: hunting, backgammon, dining, drinking, etc., to evade painful reflection about matters of deep purpose. The philosopher as technical specialist engages in the exercise of argumentative skills as a similar form of diversion.

3) The philosopher (as technical specialist) is unavoidably a human person faced with concrete questions about the purpose of life. "Just because this kind of philosophy distances and defends those individuals who practise it from personal engagement with questions about the ends of life, it does not follow that they do not in their lives even if not in their philosophy, presuppose answers to those questions, answers all the more influential for being taken for granted and remaining philosophically unexamined."[15] While second-order reflection serves as a shield to protect oneself from having to engage questions of purpose in a personal, first-order manner, those questions will be answered in the person's everyday life, typically by adopting the cultural ethos that one inhabits.

MacIntyre describes the philosopher as technical specialist for the purpose of awakening. His aim (akin to his purpose in describing the character of the manager) is to awaken his reader to the hollowness and internal contradictions of this form of life. His goal is to hold up a mirror in order to show that the philosopher as technical specialist frequently lives a life that is unphilosophical.

MacIntyre contrasts the philosopher as technical specialist with "the kind who by their writing send us beyond philosophy into an immediate encounter with the ends of life."[16] In the contemporary culture of specialists, this sort of philosopher does his or her work frequently from the margins. Let's call this character the philosopher as "seeker of understanding." The philosopher as seeker of understanding engages in "serious and systematic questioning of oneself and others about the nature of the human good and the order of things" including especially a willingness to question dominant cultural norms.[17] Three qualities characterize the activities of the philosopher as seeker of understanding.

1) Philosophers (as seekers of understanding) are "engaged by questions about the ends of life as questioning human beings and not just as philosophers."[18] The questions that such philosophers investigate are the very same questions that confront the everyday plain person who is confronted by an epistemological crisis. All human beings are, in some sense, philosophers of this sort.

2) Philosophers (as seekers of understanding) conceive of their enquiries "as contributing to an ongoing philosophical conversation, a conversation that has had a long history before they became a part of it and that would continue after they had fallen silent."[19] Accordingly, this sort of philosopher is thereby enabled to treat his or her reader (or listener) as a fellow contributor to a common dialogue.

3) Philosophers (as seekers of understanding) recognize that "the end of the conversation and the good of those who participate in it is truth and the nature of truth, of good, of rational justification, and of meaning."[20] Therefore, these issues will have to become central conversation topics, not as "a set of independent and heterogeneous enquiries into distinct and unconnected problems,"[21] but as integrated aspects of a comprehensive vision toward which we aspire. The effort to pursue in an orderly and systematic way an understanding of the human good and of the nature of things may involve technical treatment. While those technical issues may require various specialized skills, each with their own intrinsic intellectual attractions, those are conceived as ultimately subordinated to the substantive purposes of the conversation.

MacIntyre describes the philosopher as seeker of understanding for the purpose of building up in his reader the dispositions needed to become this sort of philosopher. He wants his reader to shed the vices associated with the philosopher as technical specialist and then, by inviting his reader to take up the role of the everyday plain person, he seeks to encourage his reader to envision human life as a quest for understanding and to build up in his reader those dispositions needed to pursue a life that is philosophical in the sense of seeking understanding. MacIntyre reminds his reader, "philosophy is a matter of concern for plain persons before it is a matter of concern for professional philosophers."[22] Accordingly, he invites his readers who have become technical experts to retrieve those questions and concerns of plain persons that served as the original motivation to pursue expertise in philosophy. By inviting his reader to take up the role of the everyday plain person, he hopes to bring about a transformation and then to build up the qualities of character needed to undertake such a journey.

One way to understand MacIntyre's distinction between these two kinds of philosophers is to set it against the backdrop of the argument he makes in two books: *Three Rival Versions* and *Whose Justice?* In those books, MacIntyre gave a detailed history of moral philosophy in order to show why contemporary moral debates appear interminable. He offered both a diagnosis and a proposed cure for the disorder of contemporary moral life. Our moral discourse is drawn from fragments that now lack the contexts from which their significance originally derived. MacIntyre draws a comparison with the natural sciences where there was a series of paradigm shifts. Aristotle, Galileo, and Einstein were each concerned with matter, energy, and nature. However, those concepts came to mean different things in each paradigm. In an analogous manner, moral discourse involves multiple paradigms, each apparently using the same terms to debate justice while unwittingly drawing from diverse moral grammars. The cure, proposes MacIntyre, is to recast our understanding of our contemporary situation through a history that accounts for the current disorder. We are confronted by (and participants in) rival traditions of moral enquiry. Each is concerned with justice and rationality, but those terms are understood in different, even incompatible ways. The standoff between modern culture (which prizes objective neutrality) and postmodern genealogy (which prizes unmasking the pretensions of those who claim to be objective and neutral) is interminable – unless the resources of an earlier culture are retrieved.

In a parallel manner, MacIntyre suggests that we are confronted with competing understandings of what it means to be a "philosopher."

The philosopher as technical specialist is akin to the character of the manager. MacIntyre describes this character not only to diagnose, but also to arouse. His purpose is to awaken his readers to the hollowness of this sort of philosopher. He does so by pointing to the gap between the activities of such a character in the professional context as compared with the everyday life of this kind of philosopher. He thereby hopes to dispose his reader to turn away from the conception of the philosopher as technical specialist.

Another way to understand MacIntyre's distinction between the two kinds of philosophers is to set the distinction against the backdrop of his book, *Edith Stein*. In that book, MacIntyre addresses an audience of professional philosophers who are, he presumes, mostly unfamiliar with Stein's writing. MacIntyre notes that "there is no entry for Edith Stein in the *Oxford Dictionary of Philosophy*, the *Cambridge Dictionary of Philosophy*, the *Oxford Companion to Philosophy*, or the *Routledge Encyclopedia of Philosophy*."[23] So, part of his purpose is to show that Stein's work merits philosophical attention. However, MacIntyre's greater accomplishment in his book on Stein is that he forges a new genre of philosophical writing.

In his essay, "The Ends of Life, the Ends of Philosophical Writing," MacIntyre proposed a need to invent a new mode of philosophical writing that would move beyond both biography and the history of philosophy. He names this proposed new genre "the history of philosophers."[24] Authors who write in this mode would explore the relationship between attitudes expressed in a philosopher's writing compared to the philosopher's life. MacIntyre's book on Edith Stein is an instance of this genre. His subject matter is the relationship between writing and life in Stein. Stein was raised in a secular Jewish context and studied under Edmund Husserl. She later parted philosophically from Husserl on certain basic points, but she remained personally on good terms with him, even as she became a Roman Catholic and entered a Carmelite monastery. During World War II, she was killed in a Nazi prison camp. What emerges from MacIntyre's text is an investigation of what it means to live a philosophical life. Many of the early chapters aim to explain Husserlian phenomenology (and Stein's philosophical formation in that approach) to an audience of philosophers trained in the analytic, rather than the continental, mode. However, MacIntyre's central purpose in his book on Stein is neither to explain her doctrines nor to compose a "lives-of-the-saints" biography. Instead, MacIntyre wants to dispose his reader to see that Stein's life, her flesh-and-blood existence, is far more philosophical than that of her better-known contemporaries such as Martin Heidegger.[25] MacIntyre wants to dispose his reader to embrace a conception of the philosopher as "seeker of understanding." To do so, he encourages his reader to take up the role of the plain person and to retrieve the deep questions that he presumes drew his readers to the discipline of philosophy in the first place. "Philosophy is a matter of concern for plain persons before it is a matter of concern for professional philosophers."[26]

In *God, Philosophy, Universities*, MacIntyre extends this distinction between two different kinds of philosophers. His aim is to retrieve and build up a conception of the character of the philosopher as one whose task is to cultivate a set of dispositions that make it fruitful to address the philosophical questions faced by everyday plain persons. To excel in this practice, one must learn not only how to analyze arguments, but also how to understand, describe, and evaluate the history of the debates that are integral to philosophy and which have been sustained through multiple generations. Further, philosophers need to recall that, although it is altogether appropriate for their work to become rigorous and for their discipline to develop a technical vocabulary, their enquiries "begin from and extend the enquiries of plain persons."[27] Philosophers should, according to MacIntyre's reconceived notion of what it means to be a philosopher, engage in their activities "for the common good" and while taking "the trouble to engage in sustained conversation with plain persons, so as not to lose sight of the relationship between their enquiries, no matter how sophisticated, and the questions initially posed by plain persons."[28]

In suggesting that there is a parallel between the role played by the manager and the philosopher-as-technical-specialist in MacIntyre's authorship, I want to note one important difference. With regard to the character of the manager, MacIntyre aims to sound an alarm. He is warning that the manager is a dangerous character, and that beneath the veneer of neutral rationality lies barbarism, destructive tendencies, and a will-to-power unchecked by rational deliberation. In contrast, MacIntyre describes the philosopher-as-technical-specialist not as dangerous, but as pathetic. The professional philosopher is a marginal figure in contemporary culture. Professional philosophers debate insular problems of interest primarily only to other professional philosophers. So, there is a similarity with regard to the manager and the professional philosopher: in both cases, MacIntyre aims to arouse. However, there is an important difference: the manager is, according to MacIntyre, more central and more dangerous.

While I have come to appreciate deeply MacIntyre's approach, I want to point to a shortcoming that has important implications with regard to the character of the manager. Let me first summarize my reasoning in this chapter.

I have argued that MacIntyre's authorship has a twofold purpose.

First, MacIntyre aims to awaken his reader to the deep disorder in contemporary moral life and to our inability to move forward in any nonarbitrary manner (unless we retrieve insights from a culture alien to secular modernity). In order to awaken his reader, one of MacIntyre's central strategies involves describing *characters*, especially the character of the manager. In doing so, he hopes to provoke reflection and recognition of this character's moral emptiness and internal contradictions. For the same purpose, he describes the therapist, the aesthete, and the philosopher-as-technical-specialist.

Next, MacIntyre aims to build up in his reader those dispositions needed to pursue a quest for life's deeper questions. In order to build up understanding and practical wisdom, he invites his reader to take up the role of the everyday plain person and then, through a sort of friendship between author and reader, to reshape one's understanding by learning to see one's concrete situation anew through the fresh eyes of a friend. Practical wisdom, that is, the intellectual excellence of habitually opening oneself to the complexities of a situation, evaluating the worth of the given ends in light of higher goods, deliberating well, making sound judgments, and then properly executing those judgments in one's concrete situation, can be acquired by learning to see things through the eyes of a friend who has these dispositions.

MacIntyre wants to hold up a mirror to his reader. He describes these characters for the purpose of arousing his reader. He uses the character of the everyday plain person in a different manner and for a different purpose. Rather than holding up a mirror to this role (so that his reader might reflect on deficiencies), he invites his reader to inhabit this role (so that his reader might begin to see his or her situation through fresh eyes).

With this interpretation in hand, allow me to suggest a possible deficiency with this approach, especially as it applies to the character of the manager. MacIntyre has warned repeatedly: Do not take up the role of the Weberian bureaucratic manager. However, he has done comparatively little to propose an alternative conception of this role. After all, so long as human beings form communities and engage in common projects, we will need individual persons to take up the role of organizing, leading, planning, and monitoring such groups. MacIntyre has done very little to build up an alternative conception of this role.

Notice a contrast with MacIntyre's treatment of the philosopher. He describes two kinds of philosophers: the technical specialist and the seeker of understanding. In order to arouse his reader to the deficiencies of the philosopher as technical specialist, he describes this character and points to deficiencies and internal contradictions. Then, he proposes a solution: he invites his reader to take up the role of the everyday plain person and to retrieve the sort of questions that such persons ask. He aims to show that philosophers need to change their conception of what it is to engage in philosophy. Indeed, much of MacIntyre's career has been devoted precisely to this sort of project, to show how philosophers can take up the concerns of plain persons by employing narrative, drawing from the history of philosophy, writing in a manner that is accessible to an audience beyond specialists, and seeking to build up (rather than simply seeking to analyze arguments).

So, I am suggesting that MacIntyre's project is incomplete with regard to the character of the manager. He has left undone for the character of the manager (to a very great extent[29]) what he has done in much more detail for the character of the philosopher.

12
Transforming Character: The Manager and the Aesthete

MacIntyre describes the manager as one of three central contemporary characters; the others are the therapist and the aesthete. The aesthete is a character we meet in reading the works of Søren Kierkegaard. MacIntyre's interpretation of Kierkegaard emphasizes a criterionless choice. Widely criticized by Kierkegaardians, MacIntyre acknowledged the flaw in his earlier interpretation and called for more conversation. The encounter between MacIntyreans and Kierkegaardians has been fruitful. As Anthony Rudd has shown, Kierkegaard's writing provides helpful resources for advancing the project of MacIntyre's virtue ethics. Kierkegaard writes of the aesthete to bring about a transformation in the reader's character and understanding of the aesthetic life. From the art of Kierkegaard's writing we can gain insights about the art of character.

The heart of the argumentative strategy that I employ in the remainder of the book, indeed throughout this book as a whole, is borrowed from the Danish philosopher, social critic, literary prose artist, and religious writer, Søren Kierkegaard (1813–1855). To explain Kierkegaard's character-transforming argumentative strategy, a long tangent is required.

I focus in this chapter on the *aesthete*, a character that figures prominently in Kierkegaard's authorship. I do so in order to advance my argument about the character of the manager. In particular, my goal is to show how those of us concerned with transforming the character of the manager might learn from the character-transforming argument used by Kierkegaard with regard to the aesthete.

As I discussed earlier, MacIntyre describes the manager as one of three central contemporary characters; the others are the therapist and the aesthete.[1] Regarding the aesthete, MacIntyre refers explicitly to that character we meet in reading Kierkegaard's *Either/Or*. The aesthete is an urbane, wealthy, cosmopolitan young man who restlessly aims to fend off boredom and to pursue his own enjoyment and interests. Although the name for this character, the "aesthete," may not be familiar today, the aesthete's attitudes and dispositions permeate contemporary culture. As the philosopher Charles Taylor observes, an outlook invented by 19th-century romantics has now become a mass phenomenon.[2] The aesthete desires enjoyment, but not vulgar selfishness. This sort of person is interested in a "higher selfishness." Today, such a person might advise that it is important to "get the most out of yourself." In the 19th century, the aesthete typically was the inheritor of significant wealth. Aesthetes in the early 21st century typically have to work in order to support oneself, but this involves aspiring to a job and a life that is interesting, "spiritually fulfilling, socially constructive, experientially diverse, emotionally enriching, self-esteem boosting, perpetually challenging, and eternally edifying."[3]

In order to describe the aesthete, MacIntyre points not only to Kierkegaard's writing, but also to Diderot and Henry James.[4] The aesthete MacIntyre describes is a flat, stock character. In contrast, the literary style of Kierkegaard's writing presents us with a rather more complex character.[5] We meet Kierkegaard's aesthete as the anonymous narrating voice of the first volume of Kierkegaard's *Either/Or* and the intended audience of the three letters from the fictitious Judge Wilhelm that make up the second volume. This character is sophisticated, post-religious, and highly educated. He is at once both cynical and impassioned, detached, and at times brooding. He has a passion for authentically pursuing his interests so long as he finds them engaging, for drinking deeply from his individual experiences, and then expressing his ecstasies and inner loneliness, perhaps secretly, but always in an unconventional manner without the constraints of traditional social norms.

MacIntyre's interpretation of Kierkegaard and the character of the aesthete sparked significant debate among the specialized literature of Kierkegaardians.[6] Reviewing these debates brings into focus Kierkegaard's distinctive "character-transforming argumentative strategy."

MacIntyre wrote about Kierkegaard at a number of points in his career, and his views have shifted about how Kierkegaard should be interpreted. In the 1960s, MacIntyre published three pieces on Kierkegaard; each covers the same ground, gives the same interpretation, and criticizes Kierkegaard in the same way in light of that interpretation. Those essays form the basis for the interpretation that MacIntyre presents in *After Virtue*. As Anthony Rudd summarizes, "On MacIntyre's reading, Kierkegaard claims that one's fundamental commitments – in particular to an aesthetic, ethical, or religious way of life – have to be chosen, and that this choice cannot be a rational one."[7] In short, MacIntyre presents Kierkegaard as an advocate of criterionless, arbitrary, existential choice. The aesthete and the judge represent a choice: A or B? "A" commends the aesthetic manner of living; "B" extols the ethical life. "Each of the two ways of life is informed by different concepts, incompatible attitudes, rival premises."[8] Interpreted this way, Kierkegaard's *Either/Or* presents the reader not only with two very different characters, but also with a radical, existential choice. "The principles which depict the ethical way of life are to be adopted for no reason, but for a choice that lies beyond reasons, just because it is the choice of what is to count for us as a reason."[9]

In fairness, it should be noted that MacIntyre acknowledged in *After Virtue* that his interpretation of Kierkegaard is crucially different from both that of the best Kierkegaard scholars and "that given by Kierkegaard himself."[10] In response to the interpretation of Kierkegaard by MacIntyre in *After Virtue*, a generation of Kierkegaardians, myself included, raised a series of objections to the "arbitrary choice" interpretation.[11] As it turned out, MacIntyre's reading of Kierkegaard did not stand up to critical scrutiny, and he conceded as much in his 2001 essay at the end of the volume by Davenport and Rudd, *Kierkegaard After MacIntyre*.[12] However, the disagreement provoked by MacIntyre has been fruitful. Edward Mooney has written that Kierkegaardians owe a simple debt to MacIntyre. "Whatever hesitation we may have about the details of MacIntyre's account of Kierkegaard, we should be grateful that he brought Kierkegaard to center stage in a narrative of moral theory written well within the mainstream of English speaking philosophy – a place where Kierkegaard till then was conspicuously absent."[13] Mooney, along with Anthony Rudd and others, have shown that there is a great deal shared by the projects of both MacIntyre and Kierkegaard.

Consider these parallels, some of which are obvious, others of which are subtler. Both MacIntyre and Kierkegaard are writers with large projects; both are concerned with retrieving a form of life that emphasizes practicing the virtues while criticizing modern social practices. Both could be described as moral and religious "grammarians," as both dedicate parts of their writing to the task of drawing out competing moral vocabularies, and both are attentive to the ways a single name for a virtue is used differently in competing social contexts. Both aim to awaken and build up. Both have a similar strategy for defeating cultural relativism. Both propose a teleological moral and religious philosophy that is deeply influenced by ancient Greek philosophy and its interaction with Christianity. Both have a post-Hegelian emphasis on social life and practice. Both emphasize the unity of one's life and the understanding of one's life in narrative terms. Both emphasize the importance of the first person in moral philosophy and in the acquisition and evaluation of a moral grammar. Both see in the human person capacities, gifts, and abilities waiting to be realized (rather than problems needing to be solved). Both come to an understanding of the human person that is metaphysical in character involving a synthesis of two poles – the physical and the psychical. Both do philosophy, in certain ways, "from the margins." Finally, both Kierkegaard and MacIntyre have deep criticisms of a pernicious "character" that is superficially attractive but actually morally hollow; for Kierkegaard, this character is the aesthete, and for MacIntyre, it is the manager. In recent years, the two approaches have become rich conversation partners.

In order to motivate a non-MacIntyrean interpretation of the role of the aesthete in Kierkegaard's authorship, let me trace briefly the arc of Kierkegaard's concerns with the character of the aesthete throughout his career as an author. As a student, Kierkegaard immersed himself in a study of romanticism and the form of life proposed by the romantics. The journals that Kierkegaard kept while a student are filled with notes about his study of romanticism.[14]

Criticizing dehumanizing features of early industrialization, impersonal aspects of modern science, and the detachment of the enlightenment and its claims to objective neutrality, the romantics extolled passion while developing an appreciation of medieval romance narratives. Romantic tales involve flights into the imagination with knights traveling to exotic lands inspired by the unrequited love of a pure young maiden but separated by an intervening element that makes the quest both noble and futile. The romantics delighted in the tension that comes from escaping the constraints of the here-and-now while finding solace in the despairing self-contradiction of knowing one's fanciful wishes can never be realized.

The 22-year-old Kierkegaard, writing in 1835 to a family friend who traveled to Brazil to work as a paleontologist, expressed a desire to travel the earth to survey the natural world; later in the letter, he gropes for a deeper sense of his calling in life.[15] The young Kierkegaard shared with the romantics a fascination with the natural world outside the city. The romantics viewed nature as a companion and teacher who speaks in a mysterious language of symbols. They developed the cult of the individual, holding up the poet and artist as prophets who reject traditional social norms and provide a novel access into deeper truths by articulating personal experiences. The romantic poet takes up a journey, wandering in search of new lands, new places in the imagination, and new vistas for the soul. Consciously and energetically setting out to abandon traditional life, the romantics elevated the imagination, viewing it as the supreme faculty that allows each person to propose a radically alternative way to perceive the world, reconcile opposites, and read nature as a system of symbols. With passion, the poet aims at the beauty of creating one's own way of life, defining oneself in a manner where one is constantly free to reinvent oneself.

Although drawn to certain qualities extolled by the romantics, Kierkegaard became an intense critic of their form of life and the dispositions they encouraged. These criticisms are present in his earliest published writings, including his 1838 polemic against Hans Christian Andersen. The young Kierkegaard launched into a densely argued attack charging that Andersen's work lacks artistry because his life lacks a deep and earnest embracing of his given actuality.[16] On Kierkegaard's view, an artist must form "a positive relation to actuality through striving toward a single goal in life."[17] Kierkegaard reasons that if an artist does not have a focused life goal, the artist's work becomes "nothing more than an egotistical projection of the writer's own moods and life experiences."[18] Kierkegaard further criticized Andersen as a novelist, claiming that Andersen lacked a developed life view or a comprehensive way of engaging the world and others.

Kierkegaard's favorite professor at the University of Cophenhagen was the poet and Aristotle scholar, Poul Martin Møller.[19] Møller taught Kierkegaard to have a great enthusiasm for the ancient Greek and Roman writers, and in particular for the themes of moral development, the cultivation of an integrated life, and the desire for a philosophy that one might embody concretely in one's existence.[20] Tragically, Møller died in 1838, just as Kierkegaard began the dissertation phase of his studies. Faced with the need to choose a different mentor, Kierkegaard wrote instead under the direction of the university's Plato scholar.

Despite the young Kierkegaard's criticisms of Andersen and romanticism, he was drawn to the romantic ideal of "living poetically." The romantic concern for producing beauty went beyond a desire to create art; the romantics believed that the ultimate work of art is a human life.[21] Kierkegaard adopts this notion from the romantics, that one's life is a work of art to be lived in a way that is beautiful, true, and good.

Kierkegaard's argument against romanticism is extended and made more explicit in his dissertation, *The Concept of Irony*. In his dissertation, Kierkegaard praised the artistic mastery required to understand one's life as a work of art while rejecting as not serious the cult of the *avante garde* akin to the hipster ethic with its pretense that continually and playfully inventing a new self *ex nihilo* makes for a beautiful life.[22] Kierkegaard criticizes several romantic thinkers (Schlegel, Tieck, and Solger), advancing three arguments against them. Kierkegaard reasons that romanticism 1) is not true, 2) is not good, and 3) is not beautiful. First, he thinks that romantic poets and artists flee from actuality, taking flight into ideality and turning away from the truth of concrete historical actuality. The romantic, in an effort to preserve unlimited freedom for the self, is misrelated to actuality.[23] Related to this flight from actuality, Kierkegaard criticizes the romantics for their lack of seriousness.[24] The romantics extol the beautiful freedom of poetically claiming victory over the world, but they are left with the sense that life is like an electronic game where you can always press restart if you don't like where you are. "It knows it has the power to start all over again if it so pleases; anything that happened before is not binding."[25] Second, Kierkegaard thinks that the romantics are left with a view of life that is not good. They extol the "I" as absolute and freedom's unlimited ability to choose, but because this freedom is detached from actuality, it ends up collapsing into sensuousness that is no different from the bourgeois philistinism that it began criticizing. Kierkegaard argues that Schlegel's *Lucinde* demonstrates this collapse. "Because the *I* wants a higher freedom, it negates the ethical spirit and thereby falls under the laws of the flesh and of drives."[26] The romantic self is left with an unhealthy, unbalanced vacillation between flights of disengaged detachment and periods of uncontrolled immersion into sensuality. Finally, Kierkegaard thinks that the romantic quest for absolute freedom detached from the concrete facticity of the here-and-now is not just false and destructive, but that the romantic self is, ultimately, not beautiful. The romantics extol love, but "it is a love without any real content, and the eternity so frequently talked about is nothing but what could be called the eternal moment of enjoyment, an infinity that is no infinity and as such is unpoetic."[27] Kierkegaard argues that what is needed is the ability to see one's life and the cultivation of one's character as a beautiful work of art; the task of the poet is identical to the task of every human, that is, to become composed poetically. Near the end of his dissertation, Kierkegaard speaks with a theological tone: "the Christian comes to the aid of God, becomes, so to speak, his co-worker in completing the good work God himself has begun."[28]

A version of this same argument is embodied in Kierkegaard's *Either/Or*, an ingenious literary production that was the first book he published after completing his dissertation. Kierkegaard's concern with character and narrative shows itself in the plot and characters of this masterful work. The pseudonymous "editor" of *Either/Or* describes in the preface how he came upon the two volumes hidden in a secret compartment of a desk he had purchased from a second-hand furniture shop. The aesthete is the narrating voice of the first volume of *Either/Or*, an amalgam of three characters revived from medieval lore: Don Giovanni, the sensualist; Faust, the doubter; and Ahasuerus, the despairing Wandering Jew. The aesthete is cosmopolitan, well-educated, and well-to-do; he wants an interesting, beautiful life without the undesirable constraints of social commitment. To a restless young man, one of the most interesting and desirable pursuits is, quite obviously, the attraction of a lovely young woman. The aesthete's writings consist in random thoughts and moody desires, a discourse on Mozart's *Don Giovanni*, reflections on ancient and modern theater, a review of a novella on first love, essays on life and death, and a diary recounting the seduction of the alluring Cordelia with the interesting possibility that she might freely and completely give herself to her suitor.

The second volume of *Either/Or* consists in long letters from Judge Wilhelm, written in a spirit of friendship, to the aesthete who is the author of volume one. The heart of the Judge's efforts to persuade the young man to take up a different form of life consists in an analysis of love and in his claim that the longed-for beauty of the aesthete can only be found within the stability of the ethical life. The aesthetic young man is aware of the erotic, sensual urgings of romantic love as well as love's yearning to taste an eternal ideal. The young man, although interested in the sensual, wants more than lust. His interest takes him to desire the sort of love where his beloved is willing to give herself to him and him alone, to give herself completely, not just sensually, but in her emotions and thoughts, in her entire being. He knows that more interesting than lust is the love that has the stamp of the eternal.

Of course, the young man doesn't want the duties of marriage. He finds those boring. So the task of the judge is to convince the young man that the kind of love he desires (romantic love, first love, a love in which the sensual is taken up into the eternal) is found in married love. In other words, the judge's argument is that romantic love (which is attractive to the young man) finds its fulfillment in married love, and it does so in such a way that the aesthetic element in romantic love is not annihilated, but rather is sustained and deepened. Romantic first love entails an openness, a receptivity to the gift of the other. But in order to open oneself to the gift of the other, one must surrender oneself, and in order to surrender oneself, one must be self-possessed. Only one who is self-possessed can give of oneself to one's beloved.[29] This complete reciprocated self-giving and self-receiving, which is the teleological drive toward which romantic love is ordered, is more than romantic love, and it is more beautiful than romantic love.

The judge's argument flows from his effort to convince the aesthete to reframe a possible answer to the question, "Why get married?" To answer this question, the judge draws a distinction between goods internal to marriage and benefits that are external to marriage. The young man is drawn to the activity of love, especially to the sense of ecstatic rapture associated with first love, while the young man is disposed to conceive of marriage as boring, constricting, and bound to annihilate romantic love. The standard reasons given for marrying strike the young man as ludicrous and alien: to cultivate one's character or a stable life at home, or to have children, or to develop responsibility. However, the judge turns the focus away from these purposes and insists that for marriage, there is only marriage's own why.[30] The only real reason to marry is internal to the activity of self-giving love. As the judge puts it, "The less 'why' the more love."[31]

What are the features of this sort of love as complete self-gift? The judge answers by quoting the virtuous dispositions extolled by St Paul: "Love is patient and kind, love is not jealous or boastful; it is not arrogant or rude. Love does not insist on its own way, it is not irritable or resentful, it does not rejoice at wrong but rejoices in the right. Love bears all things, believes all things, hopes all things, endures all things."[32] The judge urges the young man to focus on those dispositions and to see them as the aesthetic fulfillment of his desire for romantic love. "Think of these beautiful words by one of the Lord's apostles; think of them applied to a whole life.... Think of a married couple, that they dare to say these words to each other in such a way that the main impression still remains joyous, what a blessing there is in this."[33]

The judge concludes that the young man's strategy for living, his quest for the interesting coupled with his unwillingness to enter into a relationship of reciprocated self-giving, is a boring recipe for despair. In contrast, the judge, writing in a spirit of friendship, invites his young friend to develop a different grammar of love and marriage by seeing it from the inside. The aesthetic is incommensurable for artistic portrayal, except "by living it, by realizing it in the life of actuality."[34] He who practices the virtues in human existence with "courage and humility enough to let himself be esthetically transformed, he who feels himself present as a character in a drama" is able to bring "into actual existence the highest aesthetics."[35] In this way, the judge hopes that the young man might glimpse in his imagination those goods internal to married love.

The judge writes to the young man as a friend, and he tries to get him to see that the young man's cynical view of friendship is unattractive.

In other words, Kierkegaard is not proposing a nonrational, arbitrary choice. Instead, his strategy is to invite his reader to conceive of a different form of life, to learn a different grammar, and to reconceive what it is to be an aesthete. As many Kierkegaard interpreters have noted, Plato's *Symposium*, with its multiple speeches in praise of *eros* progressively ascending from the sensual to divine love, structurally and thematically influenced the argument of *Either/Or*.[36] Writing in the terms of his contemporaries, Kierkegaard presents Plato's dialectic of eros as a path to the divine, but he does so in order to show the limits of Platonic *eros* while inviting his reader to consider afresh the grammar of Christian *agape*. Kierkegaard's strategy is to get his reader to reconceive what it is to be one who loves beauty. His goal is to shape the moods, desires, and dispositions of his reader such that the gift of self-giving love proposed in New Testament Christianity comes to be seen as an alternative that is better and more attractive than the endless questing of the aesthete as romantic ironist. Kierkegaard recognizes that his reader is not disposed to see love in the activity of traditional marriage or in the life of Christian discipleship; his goal as an author is to bring about a changed disposition, a transformation in the character of his reader. Presuming that his reader is a cultured despiser of bourgeois Christendom, his task is to extend an invitation to consider an overlooked form of life, suggesting as a friend that existential fulfillment consists in appropriating the goods internal to a way of life that, from the outside, seems unattractive, constricting, boring, and certainly not in one's interests.

As a religious author, Kierkegaard's argument stretches beyond the suggestion that a life shaped by commitments to marriage, family, and social responsibility is beautiful and good. He seeks to invite his reader to become open to the possibility that the dispositions developed and practiced in the life of Christian discipleship are integral to living truly a beautiful and good human life. In *Either/Or*, this is intimated near the end of the book when the reader is introduced to another character, a Lutheran pastor that the judge describes as "a stocky little fellow, lively, cheerful, and unusually jovial ... stuck out in a little parish on the heath of Jylland."[37] *Either/Or* concludes with a sermon, written but never delivered, by this pastor. The pastor's sermon presents a conception of the life of love quite distinct from both the aesthete and the judge.

For the aesthete, the beautiful life involves the pursuit of a sort of higher selfishness, making sure "you get the most out of yourself." For the judge, the beautiful life involves becoming self-possessed in order that one can give of oneself, to one's spouse, one's children, and one's fellow citizens. For the pastor, the beautiful life involves receptivity to divine grace: "only in an infinitely free relationship with God could his cares be turned to joy."[38] The pastor's sermon, in a haunting and rather penetrating manner, points to the life of faith as the most beautiful form of life for a human being. It is not a call to abandon the life of the aesthete, but to reconceive what it is to live a beautiful life.

Regardless of whether one is persuaded by Kierkegaard's form of ethical and religious argumentation, my aim is to call attention to the character-transforming argument that he employed. In a letter to his fiancé, Kierkegaard once wrote, "I have now read so much by Plato on love."[39] In his authorship, Kierkegaard borrowed from the speeches and arguments of the characters in Plato's *Symposium* and the *Phaedrus* to move the reader up toward higher concerns while allowing one to become open to the otherness made possible through intensely particularized passion.

On the interpretation that I am suggesting, Kierkegaard is not positioning his reader to make a criterionless choice for or against the aesthete. Neither is Kierkegaard, as the implied author behind the immediate narrator of the text, aiming to convince his reader to turn away from the quest for a life that is beautiful. To the contrary, he wants his reader to reconceive what it means to live a beautiful life. Judge Wilhelm wants the young man to see that his constant uncommitted questing is hollow, not serious, and not beautiful. The pastor's sermon awakens the reader to the possibility that a life immersed in social roles, such as Judge Wilhelm's roles as husband, father, and civil servant, is subject to a different kind of despair; in that way, the pastor's words are an invitation for the judge to consider his life and his work under the prism of a higher, more "beautiful law."[40]

Kierkegaard wrote entirely in Danish – very much a minor language. His fate, he feared, was to be a forgotten writer from a provincial market town: "I write books which presumably will not be read." Even in Denmark, none of his dozens of volumes sold more than a thousand copies during his life. *Either/Or* is the only book that called for a second edition during Kierkegaard's life. Accompanying the second printing of *Either/Or* was a set of short devotional discourses. These have been called "the most beautiful, indeed sublime set of discourses ever written by Søren Kierkegaard."[41] The first of these is a discourse on silence; it is a meditation on the lilies of the field and the birds of the air. In the discourse, Kierkegaard addresses himself to "the poet." The sort of "poet" he has in mind is a character with the same dispositions and tendencies as the aesthete.[42] Kierkegaard's purpose in the discourse is to move the reader from the dispositional attitude of romanticism to adopt a personal trait advanced by the Christian gospels of attentively opening oneself to God.[43] Kierkegaard tries to show that the attitude toward the birds and the flowers typical among romantic poets, while appearing beautiful, is actually a frustrated self-contradiction. Kierkegaard aims to move the reader beyond the life-view of the romantic poet to seek something more than the poet's empty despair. By encouraging his reader to cultivate the practice of silence, Kierkegaard hopes to bring about a transformation to a religious form of life that sees the divine as present throughout the connected narrative of the everyday strivings of human life.

Let's return for a moment to the character of the manager. If we were to apply Kierkegaard's strategy as a writer to this character, we would see that what is needed is both awakening and upbuilding. Further, we could see that MacIntyre has been successful in the first task, but with regard to the character of the manager, he has fallen short in the second task. While MacIntyre's writing is successful with regard to the task of awakening – he does plenty to alert his reader to shortcomings in the Weberian manager – he has done relatively little to build up an alternative conception of the manager. His diagnosis is insightful, but his cure – that we await a new Benedict while retreating into small-scale communities where the tradition of the virtues might be sustained – seems lacking in realism, truth, and beauty.

Those of us who use telephones and computers engage, perhaps unwittingly, in large-scale projects. Even if we try to simplify our lives and avoid getting caught up in cutting-edge global capitalism, it seems unrealistic to think that we can purge ourselves of participation in large-scale institutions. Those projects need managers, so a social world without managers seems unrealistic. Further, the retreat into a balkanized world of distinct communities stands in denial of the solidarity that is a deep feature of our humanity. Finally, even if we retreated into small-scale communities, we would still need leaders charged with the tasks of organizing, leading, planning, monitoring, correcting, and celebrating the activities of social groups. MacIntyre has offered very little with regard to a proposal about how to engage in these activities in a manner that is beautiful and excellent.

According to MacIntyre, "insofar as any philosophical project enlarges the possibilities for conversation between different and rival philosophical standpoints, it serves that ongoing conversation."[44] It is appropriate that MacIntyre calls for the conversation to continue between virtue ethicists and Kierkegaardians.[45] One way to press beyond MacIntyre's sounding of the alarm in his criticisms of the manager is to learn from the art of character that we find in the art of Kierkegaard's writing as a career author. However, Kierkegaard is not the inventor of this way of engaging in the practice of philosophy; he learned it from the ancients, especially the writings of Plato and Aristotle. It is to them I now turn.

13
Transforming the Character of the Rhetorician

The writings of Plato and Aristotle provide character-transforming arguments. Both Plato and Aristotle treat the rhetorician Gorgias as an untrustworthy character and as an archetype of those willing to use sophistical deception. When rhetoric is defined in terms of outcomes, the rhetorician will do anything to persuade. Plato and Aristotle rejected Gorgias' outcome orientation while advancing arguments for a true art of rhetoric with internal standards of excellence. They transformed the character of the rhetorician, from sophist to statesman. Mastering the art of rhetoric involves becoming a person of practical wisdom. This sort of transformed rhetorician is embodied in Cicero's eloquent and ethical concern for the common good and St Augustine's eloquent oration on the deepest longings of the restless heart.

In this chapter, I trace the character-transforming arguments of Plato and Aristotle with regard to the rhetorician. Both Plato and Aristotle wrote dialogues focusing on rhetoric. Of course, Aristotle's dialogues have been lost to history, though his great work on rhetoric remains and continues to yield fruitful insights for those who engage its arguments. Cicero, the great Roman rhetorician, famously compared the prose in Plato's dialogues to silver, and then added that Aristotle's writing was a "flowing river of gold."[1] Cicero must have been referring to manuscripts that were later lost, because the writing in the texts from Aristotle that we have employ a style that is more like lead than gold. The texts from Aristotle we possess are in the style of compressed lecture notes rather than dialogues akin to the writings of Plato. Diogenes Laertius, writing in the 3rd century AD in his biography of eminent philosophers, listed dialogues by Aristotle of which we now have only a few fragments. The dialogue generally considered to be Aristotle's first, the Grullos, focused on rhetoric. We know too little about the text to speculate about the contents, except the obvious point that Aristotle, like Plato, was concerned with the practice of rhetoric and the characters of those who engaged in the activity of persuasive public speaking. Diogenes Laertius recorded that Aristotle wrote dialogues on the "Sophist" and the "Statesman," but these too have been lost. Who are the sophist and the statesman? Why were the ancients concerned with character generally, and especially with rhetoricians, sophists, and statesmen? What can we learn about the manager as wise steward from the character-transforming arguments of Plato and Aristotle with regard to the rhetorician? I take up these questions in this chapter to show the way that Plato and Aristotle transformed the conception of what it means to be a rhetorician, from sophist to statesman.

In Chapter 2, I pointed to the new class of specialists that developed in the social context of the early form of democracy practiced in the golden age of ancient Greece. They claimed expert knowledge about how to achieve success in persuasive public speaking, especially in courts, elections, and legislative assemblies. To secure one's interests, they suggested, one needs persuasive power. The birthplace of democracy was also the cradle of elocution, or at least of those who made their living by merchandising their claims of expertise in persuasive power.

One such character repeatedly criticized by both Plato and Aristotle was the rhetorician Gorgias. A contemporary of Socrates, Gorgias was a historical figure, a native of Sicily who spent time in Athens. His speeches continue to be studied, including his address in praise of Helen, his defense of Palamedes, his funeral eulogies, and his Olympic oration. Gorgias wrote manuals for rhetorical instruction of which extensive fragments still exist. His style of speaking was highly ornamental, full of rhythms and rhymes, and quite dignified; he attracted students by displaying his ability to give bold and grand answers on any topic in impromptu speeches. Both Plato and Aristotle treat Gorgias as an untrustworthy character and as an archetype of those who will do almost anything to persuade: employing deceptive tricks, pandering to the emotions of the audience, and deliberately using flawed arguments. The character Gorgias that appears in the dialogues of Plato is as much a type as he is a historical figure. In addition to being a central character in the dialogue that bears his name, Gorgias is mentioned in seven of Plato's other dialogues.[2] Aristotle's work, *In Reply to the Opinions of Gorgias*, has been lost, but the title suggests that Aristotle, like Plato, thought Gorgias held views that merited a reply. Indeed, I want to suggest that Aristotle's *Rhetoric* is like Plato's *Gorgias* in that both works are a reply to the Gorgias-type rhetorician. The works of Plato and

Aristotle present a character-transforming argument that aims to move the reader from the Gorgias-type rhetorician to the artful and virtuous rhetoric of the statesman.

The conversation between Socrates and Gorgias, as recorded by Plato, begins with Socrates expressing his desire to find out from Gorgias "who he is."[3] In a sense, the entire dialogue is a character study.[4] Set at the house of Callicles, the plot of the dialogue is divided into two main phases. In the first half, Socrates prosecutes his case against the rhetoricians; in the second part, Socrates defends philosophy against the charges of the Gorgias-type rhetoricians. At the heart of both the prosecution and the defense is a question of character. Plato wants to unmask for his reader the pretensions of Gorgias, who appears at first as a smooth-talking, eloquent speaker who has mastered a value-neutral skill. His expertise has brought him fame and fortune; crowds applaud his eloquence, and pupils with money show a willingness to pay him in order to acquire what he knows about the art of persuasive speaking.

As the plot unfolds, the character of Gorgias is revealed. "Who he is" is disclosed in "what he does" and the way he does it. His practice, of course, is the "art of rhetoric," which Gorgias defines in terms of results: the rhetorician is a producer of persuasion.[5] I want to call attention here to the similarity between this sort of rhetorician and MacIntyre's chess-playing child in the initial phase of the story: both understand their role in terms of results. So long as the child is motivated by money-for-candy, the child agrees to play chess, and will do anything to win. The child plays chess in order to win so he can acquire money and candy. So motivated, the child becomes quite crafty, and uses his cleverness to rearrange the chess pieces when the opponent is distracted. The analogue with a Gorgias-like rhetorician is obvious: so long as rhetoric is defined in terms of outcomes, then the rhetorician will do whatever it takes to persuade one's audience: playing on the emotions of the audience, manipulating the jury, influencing the judge, tampering with election results, or doing whatever it takes to win. It is this sort of rhetorician as the smooth-talking deceiver that motivates ongoing distrust of slick lawyers and dishonest politicians; their speeches are dismissed as "mere rhetoric." Indeed, Socrates exposes the contradiction in this understanding of the rhetorician's task early in his dialogue with Gorgias.

The central action in the *Gorgias* begins as Socrates comes in late to the house of Callicles after Gorgias just completed a display of his rhetorical expertise. The plot centers on the conversation between Socrates and Gorgias – and the collision between two very different characters – and two competing ways of life.[6] Socrates focuses his questions on the character of Gorgias and the nature of rhetoric: Who is Gorgias? What is rhetoric? As the conversation unfolds, it becomes apparent that Gorgias conceives of his expertise in terms of outcomes; he claims expertise in the art of persuasion, boldly proclaiming his ability to deliver persuasive speeches in courts and in assemblies while affirming that he can teach others to become rhetoricians.[7] Early in the conversation, Socrates brings to light a contradiction in the character of Gorgias – and in his conception of the art of rhetoric. Initially, Gorgias claims that the persuasive skill he teaches is a value-free technique no different from boxing or skill in martial arts; such skills can be used for good or bad ends, while the skill itself, so it is claimed, is morally neutral.[8] However, rhetoric is closely connected with moral and intellectual virtue, and this for several reasons. Rhetoric is practiced quite prominently in courts of justice and in legislative assemblies where the issues under debate certainly are not morally neutral. Further, one of the most important resources of the rhetorician is trust; speakers must present themselves as trustworthy. If an audience concludes that a speaker cannot be trusted, then the power of persuasion dissipates. How does a speaker establish trust? Three things are crucial: 1) the speaker has to be perceived as a person of good moral character, 2) the speaker has to be perceived as a person with good judgment, and 3) the speaker has to be perceived as having good will toward the audience.[9] For this reason, the power to persuade is never a merely "morally neutral" power, for exercising the power involves establishing trust with one's audience through showing that one has a command of one's desires and moods, good judgment, and a concern for the well-being of others. In the dialogue, Gorgias and Polus each are shamed by Socrates as he trips them up and catches them in a contradiction that arises from failing to acknowledge that the practice of rhetoric is inextricably tied up with the art of character.

Gorgias wants to look good before the crowd. Not only does he brag of the power of his persuasive skills and the effectiveness of his abilities as a teacher; when pressed, he affirms that he teaches his students how to use rhetorical skill in a just manner. After all, if he denied this in front of the crowd, he would appear to be amoral and ruthless. At the same time, Gorgias insists that, were any of his pupils to use their persuasive skill without concern for justice, the fault would be their own, and that he should not be held accountable for the shortcomings of his students. Socrates catches him in a plain contradiction: either Gorgias is a poor teacher (unable to teach justice, as he claims he can) or he dangerously teaches the art of winning cases without teaching a concern for truth and justice. Trapped, Gorgias becomes ashamed and recedes into silence for much of the rest of the dialogue.[10]

The character of the one who engages in the activities of the Gorgias-like rhetorician is further disclosed as Socrates continues the conversation with Polus, a pupil of Gorgias, and later with Callicles, the host who admires Gorgias's rhetorical power. Polus tries to extend the defense of the rhetoric of Gorgias. A significant part of the debate centers on the question of whether "the rhetoric Gorgias pursues"[11] is a τέχνη (*techne*, art, reasoned productive activity) or a mere knack for persuading uninformed audiences using the lure of enjoyment to gain the trust of foolish crowds. The dialogue contains a strong distinction between two different ways of being a rhetorician. The rhetoric of Gorgias is outcome based; its claims to respectability are based on its success ratio. In contrast, Socrates engages in a different sort of "rhetoric." Indeed, Socrates delivers several speeches in the dialogue, but these differ from the speeches of Gorgias, Polus, and Callicles in important ways. Socrates prefers a conversation with an informed dialogue partner where each is given the opportunity to question and cross-examine. Socrates does not appeal to external success as an indicator of the worth of his speeches. Indeed, the most famous speech of Socrates, the defense he offered at his own trial, was a failure when measured in such terms; the jury found him guilty and sentenced him to death. The excellence of a true art of rhetoric is internal to the very activity of advancing arguments in speech to an audience. Socrates concludes his conversation with Gorgias by delivering a speech in defense of the philosophical life, but it is also a speech in defense of "the way one ought to make use of rhetoric."[12]

The largest part of the dialogue occurs after Gorgias and his pupil, Polus feel shamed and unable to respond to Socrates' unmasking of their inconsistencies. Callicles, the host, takes over the conversation. He offers a candid attack of both Socrates and philosophy. Callicles ridicules adults who devote themselves to philosophical pursuits; it is like "a grown man talking baby talk... ridiculous, unmanly, and something deserving a beating."[13] Callicles thinks it is an ugly waste of one's natural gifts and intellectual talents to spend one's time pursuing philosophy rather than the pursuits of business or politics that are more fitting for a man. Callicles sarcastically notes that if a philosopher such as Socrates were brought to court on false charges, experience in the practice of philosophy would leave such a person defenseless. Callicles warns Socrates that he is throwing away his life. "If anyone were to grab you now, or anyone else at all of your sort, and drag you off to prison, claiming you'd committed an injustice when you'd committed none, you know that you'd have no clue how to handle yourself."[14] Callicles mockingly asks Socrates, "How wise can that be?" Because Callicles is more candid than Gorgias or Polus, and thus less concerned about the way he appears to the crowd, he is seemingly able to cut through Socrates' arguments as a formidable opponent. However, Socrates is able to withstand the attacks of Callicles while showing the contradictions that underlie Callicles' desires for power and pleasure. In response to Callicles, Socrates presents a defense of the virtuous life. Callicles, in contrast, appears unable to control his moods and desires, unconcerned with anyone but himself, and finally unwise.

The dialogue ends with a long speech by Socrates in which he summarizes his defense of the virtuous life, proposes that practicing the virtues is the best policy for a good human life, and praises the speech that points to the power of deliberation that emerges in those who have cultivated the virtues. Is it possible to engage in the practice of rhetoric in a manner that is artful? Socrates investigates *techne* – artful reasoned productive activity – by pointing especially to the practice of medicine. The physician who practices the art of medicine has knowledge of the subject matter (not simply in terms of familiarity with particular cases, but in terms of underlying principles), an awareness of the limits of one's understanding, and a commitment to using this productive knowledge for the purpose of health to promote the well-being of one's patients. Socrates contrasts the practice of medicine with those who cater to the desires of the ill by offering tasty pastries, perhaps soaked in rum or some other delight, providing short-term comfort, treating one's customers as occasions for profit without genuine concern for their health or well-being. Rhetoric, as an analogue to this sort of pastry baking, is sharply criticized by Socrates as not artful, but trickery; not rational, but harmful; not honest, but a deceitful "low class thing unfit for free people."[15]

Plato's task, as the author of dialogues that bring into focus this sort of rhetorician, is complicated. Socrates and Gorgias are presented as exemplars of a competing set of dispositions. Through the story narrated in the dialogue, Plato, as the implied author and narrating voice behind the text, creates the conditions whereby author and reader together can examine the character traits exemplified by Gorgias and Socrates. The reader at first may be drawn to certain qualities in Gorgias, especially his eloquence, his boldness, and his success. In contrast, Socrates may seem at first less attractive in certain ways; Socrates appears less successful than Gorgias. Through the dialogue, Plato invites his reader to call into question whether the character traits exemplified by Gorgias satisfy or frustrate human flourishing. As Gorgias gives way to Polus and then to Callicles, the reader is invited to see that the bold confidence and grand eloquence of this sort of rhetorician actually frustrates human flourishing. Socrates is proposed as a model of a different sort of rhetorician, as one who gives speeches "the way one ought to make use of rhetoric."[16] Plato's goal is to help cultivate in his reader a different set of dispositions; rather than questing for success as measurable in quantifiable terms of victories, money, power, and pleasure, his writing aims to nurture a different set of thoughts, emotions, and perceptions with regard to the activities of the rhetorician. The notion that Socrates is a model of one who truly practices the art of rhetoric may perhaps appear strange or unusual. After all, his record in court was no victories and one loss, and he had virtually no record at all in legislative assemblies. Despite this lack of success, Plato aims to encourage his reader to appropriate the character traits exemplified by Socrates to become the sort of rhetorician who practices the art of rhetoric with knowledge of the subject matter at hand, an awareness of the limits of one's understanding, and a commitment to use the art of rhetoric for the well-being of others.

Interpreted this way, Plato's task in the *Gorgias* may be described as an effort to reconceive the rhetorician, to transform the social understanding of what it means to engage in the art of rhetoric, and to bring about a change in character of the rhetorician, from sophist to statesman. Socrates is a rhetorician of a sort, but not in the same sense as Gorgias. It is not that rhetoric, the practice of making persuasive speeches, is shameful. Indeed, Socrates engages in the practice of delivering speeches; he delivers several speeches in the *Gorgias* – and in many of Plato's other dialogues. In the *Phaedrus*, Socrates is critical of the speeches of Lysias in a way that is analogous to his famous criticism of poetry in the *Republic* and the "old quarrel between philosophy and poetry."[17] The quarrel between philosophy and rhetoric is directed at a specific conception of the practice of rhetoric, that is, the Gorgias-like view that rhetoric is a strictly outcome-based activity that produces persuasion. In his dialogue with Phaedrus, Socrates argues that this way of thinking of rhetoric leaves one tone deaf to the standards of excellence internal to the activity of persuasive speaking. Socrates emphasizes the importance of a speech having a well-organized body with a clear thesis and a strong middle, well-structured in manner that is appropriate to its kind. Further, Socrates demonstrates that he can advance a strong argument on either side of a case, as was the practice of Gorgias and the other teachers of rhetoric; however, the purpose of learning how to present the best argument on either side of a case is to achieve a more refined understanding of the truth in a manner that anticipates likely objections, not to merchandise one's skills to the highest bidder. Socrates argues that the lover of wisdom is the one who practices a true rhetoric. "It's not speaking or writing well that's shameful; what's really shameful is to engage in either of them shamefully or badly."[18] Considered this way, it is Gorgias-like rhetoric that lacks art. What is needed, claims Socrates, is to turn away from the outcome-oriented motivations of speakers like Gorgias while seeking to develop a true art of rhetoric.[19]

Plato's dialogues, the *Sophist* and the *Statesman*, focus on three characters: the sophist, the statesman, and the philosopher. In the *Sophist*, the dialogue partners go on a playful search to identify the essence of the character of the sophist. To do so, they gather together disparate parts into organized wholes while also drawing subtle distinctions in order to get at the essence of each character. The conversation playfully speaks of a hunt. Distinction after distinction is drawn with regard to the various productive and acquisitive practices: productive arts are distinct from acquisitive arts; acquiring in battle is distinct from acquiring by hunting; hunting on land is distinct from hunting on water; hunting water fowl is distinct from fishing; fishing with a net is distinct from fishing with a baited hook. The sophist, it is suggested, is a sort of angler, fishing for "young men of wealth and rank" using the lure of "the semblance of education" and the promise that wisdom and sophistication can be taught.[20]

The term "sophist" is drawn, of course, from the Greek term *sophos*, a wise person. Socrates never quite refers to Gorgias as a *sophist*, but he comes close: "Sophists and rhetoricians get mixed together in the same place dealing with the same subjects."[21] Plato and Aristotle used the name "sophist" as a term of derision, referring to those who pretended to have more wisdom than they actually possess. Plato and Aristotle criticized the sophists especially for claiming that wisdom could be taught, retailed, and wholesaled as if wisdom about how to make good decisions were a kind of technical expertise.[22]

The search for the sophist and the statesman continues in this playful dialectic. In taking up a quest to better understand the essence of these characters, Plato demonstrates a concern with mundane forms of life and the practical sort of knowledge required for human beings who take up those roles in order to make a living and for the members of the community to flourish together in their lives. As such, the philosopher is not simply a head-in-the-clouds thinker concerned with abstract ideals. The method of dialectic, of gathering and dividing, offers a research program to discover the essence of various kinds of social practices.

In the *Statesman*, the weaver is presented as an analogue for the statesman (*politikos*), the character who is charged with planning, leading, and organizing the community (*polis*). The statesman weaves together disparate parts to form a unified whole. Both the character of the philosopher and the true rhetorician, Plato suggests, inform the practical concerns of the statesman's pursuit of the common good.

With this background in mind, when we turn to the writings of Aristotle, we can discover a transformed conception of the character of the rhetorician.[23] Because we do not have Aristotle's dialogues on rhetoric or his works on the sophist and the statesman, we do not know the contours of Aristotle's treatment of these characters, or the similarities and differences of his arguments regarding the rhetorician, the sophist, and the statesman in comparison to Plato's account. In Aristotle's book *On Sophistical Refutations*, he aims to distinguish genuine reasoning from fallacious arguments that he calls sophistical; among those who used such deceptive forms of persuasion, he mentions Gorgias, referring to him as one of the "paid professors" who impart "not the art but its products."[24]

In Aristotle's book on *Rhetoric*, the sophistical rhetoric of Gorgias and others like him is quickly dismissed.[25] Aristotle's intended audience is future *politikos*, those who will be charged with planning, leading, and organizing the community. To take up that role, they will need to become artful rhetoricians, not sophists. "Sophistry is present not in the power, but in the intention."[26] Aristotle's *Rhetoric* completes, as it were, the call that we find in Plato's dialogues for a true art of rhetoric.

The true art of rhetoric, according to Aristotle, must focus on the means of persuasion "that are intrinsic to the art."[27] Aristotle dismisses previous efforts to provide an account of the art of rhetoric because such efforts misconstrued rhetoric by treating it solely in terms of the given end of persuasion; for that reason, earlier rhetoricians such as Gorgias focused on "things that are extraneous to the matter at hand" such as prejudice and passions; to win, such rhetoricians were willing to warp their audience by unfairly appealing to pity or anger.[28]

One might ask, if the outcome of persuasion is not the matter at hand, then what is the "matter at hand" that Aristotle considers to be intrinsic to the art of rhetoric? Aristotle considers rhetoric to be a productive activity that involves seeing the means of persuasion available on each matter; rhetoric is artful insofar as it is guided by ends internal to the activity of persuasive public speaking. What are the constituents of the activity of rhetoric? Every such instance involves a speaker, a speech, and an audience. Accordingly, there are three guiding ends: the *ethos* of the speaker, the *logos* of the speech, and the *pathos* of the audience. In order to progress toward mastery in the art of persuasive speaking, according to Aristotle, one must gain a command of one's character (*ethos*), the body of one's speech (*logos*), and the mood of one's audience (*pathos*). These are not three discreet goals; to the contrary, they are tightly interconnected. To present oneself as a trustworthy character, a speaker must have a well-organized speech delivered in a manner that is suitable to the mood of one's audience.

Aristotle endorses the practice of learning to present the best available arguments on both sides of a case, "not in order that we might act on both (since one ought not to be persuasive about corrupt things), but so that the way things are might not go unnoticed."[29] Creating the conditions in which arguments from multiple perspectives are advanced allows the truth to come into focus in a clearer and subtler manner. Members of a community who have to deliberate and make decisions about difficult and uncertain matters should see the artful rhetorician as their friend, for in cases when one recognizes that one's perspective is limited, it is helpful to hear the best arguments from those who have come to differing conclusions about a topic. Aristotle has confidence in reason's ability to track the truth. He states, "rhetoric is useful because things that are true and things that are just are by nature stronger than their opposites."[30]

Aristotle's claim that there is an art of rhetoric is akin to his view that there is an art of medicine. Physicians engage in the practice of medicine when they act in an excellent manner according to the standards of their practice. Health is the given end of medicine, but the practice of medicine consists in more than a strong commitment to health. Medical practitioners become attuned to the standards of excellence internal to their activities. These include observational excellence that allows one to take in relevant information, diagnostic excellence that allows one to accurately judge health and sickness, and therapeutic excellence that allows one to propose an appropriate remedy or treatment plan. Mastery in the practice of medicine is, in a sense, located in the manner in which the physician observes, diagnoses, and treats. Excellence in the practice of medicine is possible even in cases where the outcome does not result in the health of the patient. As Aristotle puts it, "The job of the doctor's art is not to make someone healthy, but to bring him along as far as is possible in that direction, because even for people who are not capable of gaining health, it is still possible to do a beautiful job of providing treatment."[31] In this way, the activity of the physician can be measured according to two distinct standards: success in the outcome with regard to the health of the patient or excellence in the activity of realizing the powers of the physician according to the standards internal to the practice of medicine. This is not to say that there is an inherent tension between the external end of health and the internal ends of the practice of medicine; rather, mastery in a practice brings to light the ever-tightening connection between the given end and the guiding ends internal to the activities that constitute the practice. As Eugene Garver puts it, mastery of an activity involves "the emergence of ends in themselves out of external ends."[32]

Aristotle's account of rhetoric rests on this same awareness of "the emergence of ends in themselves." Just as the chess-playing child is first motivated to play chess for some goal external to the activity of chess playing, so too, rhetoricians are almost always drawn to the practice of rhetoric for external purposes: winning, persuasion, prestige, power, money, or pleasure. Mastery as a rhetorician, according to Aristotle, does not reside in one's record of success as a persuader; it consists in developing the power "to see the means of persuasion that are available on each matter."[33]

Aristotle divides speeches into three kinds, according to the purposes of the audience. 1) Earlier teachers of rhetoric had taken the courtroom speech as the model of rhetoric; in such cases, the purpose of the audience is to make a judgment about the guilt or innocence of someone's past action. 2) Gorgias developed his reputation as a rhetorician based on his display speeches. At award ceremonies, openings and closings, funerals and births, weddings and anniversaries, speakers are called upon to mark the occasion by praising an honored member or denouncing someone who is dishonorable. At such rhetorical displays, the speaker's task is to employ narrative to build up a trait or set of traits found in the one who is honored. 3) Aristotle takes as his model the deliberative speech given when a community gathers to listen to advice about whether or not to adopt a future policy or course of action.

In outlining the patterns of reasoning typically employed in deliberative speeches, Aristotle discusses the deliberative excellence and practical wisdom requisite for such speeches. As Aristotle notes, the character of the speaker is "just about the most decisive means of persuasion."[34] When an audience perceives the speaker to be one of sound character who is trustworthy, they are more disposed to find the speaker's argument persuasive. The best way to establish trust is to demonstrate good character – especially as integral to the speech. Audiences tend to consider speakers as trustworthy, Aristotle notes, when the speaker shows good will, good judgment, and good character.[35] Because good judgment, deliberative excellence, and good character are crucial to persuasive speaking, Aristotle devotes a great deal of attention to these topics, especially in the first two books of the *Rhetoric*.

In Book I, Chapters 5–7 of the *Rhetoric*, Aristotle provides a sort of condensed summary of the themes discussed in the *Nicomachean Ethics*: happiness, moral virtue, intellectual virtue, the good life, deliberation, etc. Aristotle's account almost prefigures Maslow's hierarchy of needs: the layers of human happiness include possessions, safety, pleasure, self-sufficiency, or the realization of one's humanity in good activity combined with virtue.[36] Each of these goods might be presumed to be ends worth pursuing. However, members of communities frequently find themselves disputing the relative worth of such ends. Should we acquire and save more or enjoy the goods that have been acquired? What is the right balance between the possession of goods and the need for safety? Countless practical questions such as these require good judgment about the relative worth of various goods, especially in contexts where time and resources are limited. Indeed, Aristotle gives a condensed but intense list of goods about which people dispute and deliberate, along with the reasons some goods seem more fitting in certain circumstances and others are more fitting in other circumstances. Is long-term health better than short-term pleasure?[37] Is that which is scarce better than that which is plentiful?[38] Is gold better than water?[39] Is that which is beautiful but difficult better than that which is immediately beneficial but easy? Is health better than money? As Aristotle gestures toward these and similar disputes in Book 1 of the *Rhetoric*, he brings into focus part of what is needed to deliberate well.

In order to deliberate about competing goods, it is necessary to relativize each, treating each as means to some other more worthwhile good, whether the good of an individual or the common good of a community. For example, while health obviously is the end of medicine, and wealth is the end of household management, both health and wealth can be considered as means that are part of a good life, and a well-ordered community needs to secure both health and wealth in some ways for its members. Deliberating about the relative worth of such ends requires a willingness to treat particular ends as means to another purpose.

To the one who is thirsty, water is a worthwhile end, and practical wisdom is crucial for inquiring, deliberating, judging, and choosing the best way to pursue that end in a concrete circumstance. However, in order to deliberate about the relative worth of water compared to gold, a more complex level of deliberation is required. Water is a means to satisfying thirst and pursuing health, while gold is a very different sort of good; the worth of gold is tied up with its being a scarce and beautiful form of wealth that is desirable in contexts in which many other goods of the body and safety are secure. While water for drinking is a means to a healthy life, once one's thirst is quenched and a reliable source of clean water has been secured, it becomes apparent that water (and even health) are not the highest ends in a good human life. As such, in a certain sense, gold is more valuable than water, but there are conditions under which a particular person might reasonably trade precious gold in order to secure drinking water. In order to answer questions about the relative worth of water and gold, it is necessary to relativize each given end, seeing particular ends as means to another end.

Mastery at the practice of rhetoric, according to Aristotle, involves cultivating in oneself and in one's audience the ability to reason together about practical matters. The master rhetorician, it turns out, is closely related to another character, the *phronimos*, the person of practical wisdom. In this way, we find in the writings of Plato and Aristotle a transformation in the character of the rhetorician, from *sophos* to *politikos*, that is, from sophist to statesman. In order to advance toward mastery in the art of rhetoric, one must become a person of practical wisdom, prepared to participate in leadership in the community.

The character of the artful rhetorician concerned with the common good has been profoundly influential in Western culture. This character is embodied in Cicero's eloquent and ethical concern for the common good and St Augustine's eloquent oration on the deepest longings of the restless heart. Contemporary moral philosophers can learn from these ancient examples an understanding of the humanistic task of character diagnosis and cure to bring about a transformation in understanding what it is to become an excellent manager.

14
The Manager as Wise Steward: Activities, Practice, and Virtue

The manager as wise steward is proposed as a regulative ideal. The wise steward artfully manages a group of people, seeing the available means on each matter, organizing, planning, and leading in a way that moves as near as possible in each circumstance toward a worthwhile goal. Such a manager is guided by standards of excellence internal to managerial activities relative to the practices housed in one's institution. To describe the wise steward, two ancient characters are retrieved: the steward and the person of practical wisdom. As a steward, such a manager holds something in trust, including the practices that are housed in the institution. The activities and practice of the manager are examined in order to reveal virtues needed to excel in managerial activities.

In the previous chapter, I asked, "What can we learn about the manager as wise steward from the character-transforming arguments of Plato and Aristotle with regard to the rhetorician?" My goal in this chapter, and in the remainder of the book, is to work toward an answer to this question by focusing on the manager as wise steward.

The argument I am making, a character-transforming argument akin to those described in the previous three chapters, advances along the following path. The quest toward mastery in an activity (often undertaken unwittingly) involves a movement from initial motivation that is almost inevitably based on ends external to an activity toward a state in which a practitioner allows internal ends to disclose themselves as desirable for their own sake; in the case of productive practices, the change in focus toward guiding ends does not involve an abandonment of concern for the given ends. In the process of the search, in order for the ends internal to an activity to reveal themselves with greater clarity, the character of the one on the quest becomes transformed. In the previous three chapters, I traced this process in the character of the moral philosopher

(Chapter 11), the aesthete (Chapter 12), and the rhetorician (Chapter 13). Now, my goal is to show how the manager as wise steward is the term of such a process with regard to managerial activity.

Plato and Aristotle, as I have shown, were critical of the Gorgias-like rhetorician who conceives of the practice of persuasive public speaking solely in terms of outcomes, especially the given end of success at persuading large, and largely uninformed, audiences. The arguments of Plato and Aristotle, I suggested, have as one of their aims to transform the character of the rhetorician, from sophist to statesman. To do this, both Plato and Aristotle, in various ways, called attention away from the good of success and toward the goods that are internal to the practice of persuasive public speaking. The artful rhetorician is deemed excellent not simply in terms of short-term outcomes, but according to a standard of excellence that emerges from the guiding ends internal to rhetorical activity. Mastery of an activity involves "the emergence of ends in themselves out of external ends."[1]

Are there guiding ends internal to the practice of management that disclose themselves out of the activity of pursuing external ends that first motivate management practitioners? What qualities of character are required to allow those ends to become disclosed? One way in which we can make progress in answering these questions is to attend to what Geoff Moore has called MacIntyre's "practice–institution" schema that I discussed in Chapter 7.[2] Prior to the work of Moore, this "practice–institution" distinction had been almost entirely ignored in the management literature, even though there is extensive discussion of the activities and practice of management. As I explained in Chapter 7, MacIntyre distinguishes between practices and institutions using the example of the *practice* of chess as distinct from the *institution* of a chess club. As Geoff Moore has observed, "MacIntyre's generalised description of institutions and their relationship with practices can be applied in almost any context."[3] In addition to the distinction between the practice of chess and the institution of chess clubs, a similar distinction can be made with regard to other games, the arts, the sciences, and even to productive practices. MacIntyre specifically discusses agriculture, architecture, construction, and fishing.[4] I noted earlier how, drawing on his own experience during the summers of his youth working with fishing crews, MacIntyre describes the complex interrelationship for practitioners between the given end (of catching fish) and the guiding ends internal to the practice, "an understanding of and devotion to excellence in fishing and to excellence in playing one's part as a member of such a crew."[5] As one becomes increasingly proficient as a member of a fishing crew, progressing from outsider through greenhorn apprenticeship toward becoming a "journeyman" or even one with mastery of the practice, one acquires not only the specialized skills required in the practice, but also the traits of character and intellect required for excellence in the practice and the way of life that such a practice requires: stamina, cooperation, situational awareness, the ability to follow directions and safety rules while anticipating what is about to happen, and so forth.

With regard to the activities of fishing crews, a distinction can be drawn between those who aim solely at the good of success and those for whom the practice of the fishing crew becomes a way of life in which the excellences that are internal to the practice of such a crew emerges out of the activity of aiming at the productive end of catching fish. This distinction is analogous to the difference between the Gorgias-like rhetorician willing to do anything to win and the Cicero-like statesman who engages in the practice of rhetoric with an eye to the excellences internal to the practice. To ask which is better, the one who aims at success or the one who aims at excellence, is to bring into focus the incommensurability of the two standards involved. One might be tempted by the oversimplified response that declares that those who aim at success are better when measured in terms of success. Take the example of a fishing crew, the sole aim of which is to catch more and more fish. A fishing crew that pursues such an end, of course, is likely to encounter the problem of over-fishing, which may lead eventually to a lack of success. In other words, one of the shortcomings of the success orientation is that it is a short-term model that always measures success solely in terms of short-term results. In order to adjudicate the dispute between those who prize success and those who prize excellence, it is necessary to understand each from an insider's perspective.

Fishing crews whose activities are guided by excellences internal to the practice continue to aim at and be motivated by the given end of catching fish. However, the pursuit of the given end gives rise to an awareness of the guiding ends that constitute excellence in the practice of the fishing crew, and of the complicated relationship between guiding ends and given ends. Certainly those who are excellent at the activity of fishing tend to be successful at catching fish, but such a crewmember is both excellent at and motivated by the activities that characterize the practice of the fishing crew.

Practices need institutions in order to be sustained.[6] This is true for the practice of chess as well as for productive practices, for example, fishing crews of the sort MacIntyre describes. Because fishing crews are typically small, the institutional structure of such a group frequently is simple: a small-boat captain or skipper manages the vessel and the crew. Behind this, there is almost always a larger and more complicated institutional structure or set of institutions for fishing licenses, safety standards, hiring, pay, contracts, and so forth. In other productive practices that involve a more complicated coordination of large numbers of people, the levels of institutional structures, both internal and external, are frequently even more complicated. For example, in construction, manufacturing, communication, health care, education, transportation, and virtually every form of productive activity where people work together to provide goods or services, a practice or interlocking set of social practices are housed in an institution. Institutions are the "bearers" of practices, and frequently of complex, interrelated practices.[7]

Those who are charged with managing such institutions have the task of acting as stewards of the core practice and the interlocking practices housed in the institution. Institutions need to be administered through the work of the manager. As MacIntyre warns, those charged with planning, organizing, and leading such institutions constantly face the temptation of focusing on the goods of success to the neglect of the goods of the practices housed in the institution. Several questions arise for those charged with administering such institutions. To what extent must an institution's leaders understand that goods internal to the practices are housed in the institution? Are there distinct goods internal to the activities of the one administering the institution?

At the end of Chapter 6, I raised a set of questions about the manager. Are managers of every sort effectively prevented from recognizing the goods internal to social practices and formation in the virtues? Isn't it possible that, just as some athletes become egotistical and brutish while others develop qualities of sound character (and it is these that we consider to be more genuinely "athletes"), some managers become hollow in their quest for measurable success while others discover that internal to the activities of planning, organizing, leading, monitoring, correcting, and celebrating there are standards of excellence, such that the story of a manager who takes up a quest to pursue those activities well would involve the cultivation of the virtues? Is it possible for a moral philosopher and a manager (or future manager) to develop a relationship of trust where together they can investigate the qualities of character and intellect that need to be cultivated in order to become excellent at the activities of managing? Is the task of managing an institution the sort of activity that has its own internal standards of excellence apart from the given, external end that is so much the focus of the manager?

One step toward answering these questions requires coming to see the work of managing an institution as involving stewardship, that is, the manager is the steward of one or more social practices. The notion of stewardship has come to be used widely in discussions of the natural environment; the leadership literature in business has extended the notion of stewardship to "the attitudes and behaviors that place the long-term best interests of a group ahead of personal goals that serve an individual's self-interests."[8] Stewardship is not primarily the result of formal rules; rather, it "is facilitated through organizational structures that help leaders to generate interpersonal and institutional trust, clarity regarding organizational strategy, and intrinsic motivation in followers."[9]

Peter Block writes, "Stewardship is to hold something in trust for another. Historically, stewardship was a means to protect a kingdom while those rightfully in charge were away, or, more often, to govern for the sake of an underage king."[10] In his description of the manager as steward, Block is writing for organizational leaders, challenging them to change their orientation by encouraging them to "choose service over self-interest" and to "reside over the orderly distribution of power."[11] The task of the manager as steward, according to Block, is "to systematically move choice and resources closer to the bottom and edges of the organization."[12] Situating stewardship in the context of managerial leadership, Block writes, "Corporate stewardship has come to mean financial responsibility for both the institution and the community it lives in."[13] Understood this way, stewardship is "the willingess to be accountable to the well-being of the organization by operating in service, rather than in control, of those around us."[14]

Block's notion of the manager-as-steward is influenced in part by Robert Greenleaf's idea of the servant–leader. In his seminal and now classic book, *Servant Leadership: A Journey in the Nature of Legitimate Power and Greatness*, Greenleaf proposed a model of organizational leaders as servants. Servant leaders give priority to others, aiming to build up others and help them flourish by empathically listening to others and helping them draw out their deepest aspirations and purposes. Larry Spears, the longtime successor, President, and CEO of the Robert K. Greenleaf Center for Servant-Leadership, has identified ten characteristics of servant-leaders: listening, empathy, healing, awareness, persuasion, conceptualization, foresight, stewardship, commitment to growth, and building community.[15] As understood by Greenleaf and Spears, stewardship is the recognition that leaders have the task to hold their institution in trust to serve the good of society; in that way, "stewardship and servant-leadership are closely aligned ideas."[16]

The manager's task involves being a steward of the resources of the institution. The chief "resources" of any institution include both the people and the practices "housed" in the institution. So, one part of the manager's task is to take on the role of the servant–leader, cultivating the conditions in which members of the organization deepen their pursuit of excellence in the activities and practices housed in the institution. Excellence in the activity of managing involves making progress in the role of being a steward of resources, careers, and social practices.

James MacGregor Burns, in his seminal 1978 book, *Leadership*, and later Bernard M. Bass in his 1985 book, *Leadership and Performance Beyond Expectations*, drew a distinction that is now well known in leadership literature: they distinguish between transactional and transformational leaders. Transactional leaders motivate workplace performance through a system of rewards and punishments, while transformational leaders provide an inspiring mission, inviting others "to transcend their own self-interests for the good of the group, organization or society; to consider their long-term need for self-development rather than their need of the moment; and to become more aware of what is really important."[17]

Part of the manager's task is to provide an appropriate institutional structure needed to sustain and enhance the practices housed in the institution. Considered a certain way, this is obvious: the task of administrators at health care institutions is to facilitate the practice of medicine; the task of construction supervisors is to manage those engaged in the practices of the various construction trades. With that said, management activities are rarely described in just those terms. What would come from helping managers see that integral to their task is the work of providing the institutional structure needed to house one or more practices, each of which has its own order and internal ends. In that sense, the manager as steward is involved in a sort of practice.

In the next chapter, I consider this in greater detail. For now, it is worth noting that management has been described as a practice, most notably by Peter Drucker in his 1954 classic, *The Practice of Management*. Drucker's goal was "to look at management as a whole" in order "to depict management as a distinct function, managing as specific work, and being a manager as a distinct responsibility."[18] In a certain sense, Drucker's language shadows in quite remarkable ways the lanugage of Plato and Aristotle; he is concerned to understand the manager in terms of a practice, focusing on the role, function, specific work, nature, activities, purposes, operations, and powers of the manager. For those conversant with the grammar and philosophy of the ancient Greeks generally and Aristotle in particular, Drucker's use of these terms is striking. However, it is also quite noticeable that Drucker does not frame questions about the manager's practice in terms of goals that are internal to the activities of the manager's practice or the character traits that are requisite to pursue those goals.

Drucker's description of the manager's practice is a refined extension of the classic account of the manager's functions presented in 1916 by Henri Fayol: planning, organizing, coordinating, commanding, and controlling.[19] In the 1930s, Gulick gave managers one of their early acronyms, POSDCoRB, to describe the manager's function: planning, organizing, staffing, directing, coordinating, reporting, and budgeting.[20] Drucker was writing in the 1950s for a postwar audience of a new generation who, as Drucker saw it, needed systematic knowledge, concepts, and principles in order to map out the "dark continent" of management, a territory previously only partially explored.[21] Drucker's account of the manager's practice is divided into three related aspects. The manager's function involves 1) managing a business, 2) managing managers, and 3) managing workers and work.[22] Drucker further identifies five operations of the manager; the manager 1) sets objectives, 2) organizes, 3) motivates and communicates, 4) measures performance, and 5) develops people.[23]

Many later explorers of the domain of management challenged Drucker's account in various ways. One of the most notable of these, as I mentioned in Chapter 7, is Henry Mintzberg. From the time of his doctoral research in the 1960s to the present, Mintzberg has criticized Drucker, Fayol, and others who provide a theory of "what managers should do" with too little basis in "what it is that managers do."[24]

Accordingly, Mintzberg approaches management through field studies and inductive research focusing on empirical evidence. For his doctoral research, Mintzberg followed five separate managers, each for one week, focusing his observations of their work activities.[25] More recently, he updated his findings, based on his observations of a day in the life of 29 different managers from a range of levels and organizations, big and small, including business, government, health care, and the social sector.[26] Mintzberg's observations reveal what almost every manager knows: managerial work tends to occur at an unrelenting pace throughout the work day; it is characterized by brevity, variety, fragmentation, and a high degree of verbal contact with a wide range of people.[27]

Mintzberg is critical of the "planning, organizing, staffing, directing, coordinating, reporting, budgeting" description of managerial activities in part because this sort of abstract formulation does not capture the shifting roles that are an integral feature of the work activities of managers. In part, Mintzberg's criticism is that such lists "do not, in fact, describe the actual work of managers at all."[28] Based on his field studies, Mintzberg draws from the theater to describe managerial activity in terms of roles.[29] Managers "play roles that are predetermined, although individuals may interpret them in different ways."[30] Mintzberg's observational field studies of managers required him to develop a taxonomy of managerial activities in terms of ten roles: figurehead, liaison, leader, monitor, disseminator, spokesman, entrepreneur, disturbance handler, resource allocator, and negotiator. These interpersonal, informational, and decisional roles, according to Mintzberg, form an integrated whole.[31]

My own experience, both as a manager and as a philosophy professor, points to several challenges in discovering ends in themselves out of the managerial activities of pursuing external ends. For starters, managerial activities, and especially in the context of large corporations, are strongly dominated by instrumental rationality. Further, the intensity of the work leaves little time or opportunity to focus on excellence internal to activities. Certain habits of constantly focusing on external goods, reinforced by institutional forms or an outcome-oriented organizational culture virtually blind some to concern for excellence internal to activities. While Drucker has focused on the practice of management, and Mintzberg on the activities and roles of the manager, neither has framed their investigation in Aristotelian terms of a quest for excellences in managerial activities and practices. Both write as observers of the practice of management rather than as practitioners, and neither is primarily concerned, it seems, to bring into focus the guiding ends internal to managerial practice, even though each provides very suggestive avenues for taking up such an investigation.

The sort of quest I am suggesting is phenomenological in character. It requires consideration of one's own experience, or at least a willingness to take up the perspective of a practitioner while also reflecting on the activities of the practitioner. As such, it requires understanding management activities in terms of an apprenticeship in which one is initiated into a practice, with the activities of the manager as the setting for one's progress toward mastery. Such a perspective poses a range of difficulties. From the perspective of undergraduates preparing for careers in business administration, not only do they frequently come with strong outcome-based motivations, but they frequently have comparatively little experience as managers. From the perspective of MBA students in their mid-20s, especially those who have a mix of ambition and native intellectual ability in verbal or analytic skills, the tendency toward instrumental rationality may be even more pronounced. In the case of mid-career managers, there may be much more experience in the practice of management, even if it has not been problematized in terms of discerning the guiding ends internal to managerial activities. Further, the unrelenting pace and ongoing demands of the managerial role leave little time to reframe one's activities for philosophical reflection. Having taught each of these kinds of students, I have learned that there are differences in what is needed to get people with different levels of experience in managing to investigate the excellences that are internal to the activity of managing.

Inspired by Mintzberg's field studies, I have used job shadowing, both as an assignment for students and in my own research, to bring into focus the activities of managers, the excellences internal to those activities, and the traits requisite to excel in those activities. As an assignment, I have had students choose a manager to "shadow" for part of a workday. After shadowing a manager, a series of interview questions help get at the activities of the manager. What is your job usually like? Was today a typical day? What do you do? What are the duties/functions/responsibilities of your job? What kinds of problems do you deal with? What kinds of decisions do you make? What percentage of your time is spent doing what? Does your work involve planning, organizing, leading, monitoring, correcting, celebrating, or other activities? How would you characterize the core of your job or the shifting roles involved? What goals are you aiming for in your work? Are there goals that are "given" in your position, that is, goals that come with the position? Are there goals that are "given" by the company? Are you able to set, question, or refine those goals? If so, how do you deliberate about the goals you are pursuing in your work?

When assigning students to shadow and interview a manager, I encourage each student, after raising questions about the activity of the work, to ask questions about the position and the background of the person in the managerial role. How did this type of work interest you and how did you get started? What might you say to a student considering this kind of work? What part of this job do you personally find most satisfying? What part of this job do you find most challenging? What is required to work toward mastery or excellence in this role? These sorts of questions lead to an investigation of the traits required to excel in the managerial activities of the position. What personal qualities do you believe contribute most to success in this role? In addition to the skills and talents that are essential to be effective in your job, what character traits do you think are required to do well in this job? Do you think those traits can be acquired? How did you acquire the traits you need for your job? Do you think that those traits can be acquired before entering this job? Do you think those traits can be acquired through a formal training program? How might a student or prospective employee evaluate whether or not one has the personal traits, or at least their beginnings, required in a position such as yours?

To help focus the discussion, I find it helpful to provide a list of virtues, and then to invite reflection on the question of which of these are required in order to excel at the activities of the role in question: patience, perseverance, determination, gentleness, intelligence, friendliness, punctuality, attentiveness, independence, assertiveness, cooperativeness, sensitivity, clarity in expression, creativity, initiative, honesty, bravery, self-discipline, kindness, depth, mildness, compassion, truthfulness, practical wisdom, deliberative ability, ability to execute, resourcefulness, integrity, loyalty, fairness, and civic concern. It is also helpful to invite consideration of other possible traits (e.g., toughness, ambition, and cunning) along with reflection on the question of whether the traits required to excel in the role are also traits that make for a good human life.

In Chapter 7, I discussed Goleman's notion of "emotional intelligence" and "soft skills" along with the language of traits used by Covey and others, noting that most of those who have used such an approach, especially in human resource management, have tended to focus on success in terms of measurable outcomes rather than excellence in activities. I noted that there is wide agreement regarding the traits required for success as a manager: trustworthiness, self-control, empathy, creativity, clarity, persuasiveness, and effectiveness. The question here is slightly different; rather than treating such traits as instrumental qualities that are useful for producing results, I am proposing inquiry into the traits required for and developed in the pursuit of excellence in managerial activities.

For those with relatively limited experience in managerial roles (as is common with many undergraduate students), conducting such an interview puts one in a better position to reflect on the activities of the manager in terms other than an outcome orientation. I have also used a version of this exercise with mid-career managers; rather than asking them to shadow someone else, each is invited both to reflect on and describe their own activities, along with the traits of character and intellect required to excel at those activities.

Part of what emerges from such discussions is that most managers do not have a typical day, even though there are ongoing patterns of responsibility. As managers and those who have interviewed managers discuss managerial activities, it helps to bring into focus the ways in which managers make progress in mastering a very complicated role. In multiple cases, the manager, when invited to reflect on their own activities, reports that it was a new experience to focus attention on their activities, the excellences in those activities, and the character traits required in the pursuit of excellence in those activities. As one such person put it, "I had not previously thought about my work in those terms."

Even for those who have thought of managerial work in light of emotional intelligence, soft skills, and traits needed to do the job well, puzzles arise when different traits suggest contrary acts. For example, managers need to be both reliably trustworthy and creative. I mentioned in Chapter 8 that MacIntyre points to the incompatible and sometimes contradictory demands upon managers; the manager is expected to remain constant in adhering to established routines and policies, but other situations call for initiative and independent quick thinking to realize that a novel circumstance requires an imaginative approach for which going "by the book" or following a procedure is inappropriate. Recall that MacIntyre voiced this criticism in the context of an electrical power company and the tension between the corporation as profit-maximizing organization and as an institution that provides a public good. However, similar tensions can occur in the lives of managers that work at not-for-profit organizations. An administrator at a hospital or a school, as with almost all managers, needs to be both reliable and, at times, creative. Some circumstances call for applying established policies, but other situations demand resourcefulness beyond any manual. Indeed, managers face many such tensions. Does this circumstance call for calm or for persuasive passion? Is this a circumstance in which an excellent manager would respond with empathy, or is this a time to crack the whip, as it were, to make sure everyone focuses on the task at hand to get the job done? In order to be excellent at managerial activities, a complex cluster of dispositions is needed. In addition to trustworthiness, calm self-control, empathy, creativity, clarity, persuasiveness, and effectiveness, an excellent manager needs to know which disposition to draw from in each circumstance.

To resolve such dilemmas, perhaps the most important trait required for achieving excellence in the activity of managing is prudence, that is, wisdom about how to act and what to do. Practical wisdom involves the ability to decide well: listening, assessing, considering alternatives, judging, and carrying out good decisions. Aristotle called the person who possessed this excellence the *phronimos*, that is, the person of practical wisdom. Later, we will investigate this trait in greater detail. For now, we can point to this ancient character, the *phronimos*, and combine this with the role of the accountable caretaker to bring into greater focus the conception of the manager as wise steward.

While there may be contemporary examples, I am treating this character as a regulative ideal. In the case of specific flesh-and-blood managers, development into this character may be either a process of growth involving deepened appropriation through deliberate choices that confirm and consolidate one's character or it may involve a transformation. I am focusing now on this character as both the term of the process of retrieving the qualities of the steward and the person of practical wisdom as well as the goal of becoming the kind of character that is excellent at managing as a domain-relative practice.

This type of manager currently exists outside of the mainstream of contemporary models. The following is the beginning of the sketch of such a character. Such a person has far-sighted concerns that extend beyond short-term quantifiable results. The manager as wise steward may exist in organizations of various sizes and types. The wise steward certainly operates according to traditional standards of ethics, including transparency, honesty, responsibility, and accountability. Such a person is aware of the concrete particularities of one's institution as well as the interlocking practices that are housed in the institution. The wise steward undertakes the activity of managing a group of people as an art; to manage artfully one is able to see the available means on each matter, organizing, planning, and leading in a way that moves as near as possible in each circumstance toward a worthwhile goal. Such a manager recognizes that there are standards of excellence internal to managerial activities and to the practices housed in the institution in which one operates. The wise steward has an appreciation of those practices, recognizing that practitioners are often the ones best suited to provide suggestions about how to arrange aspects of the organization in a manner that promotes the pursuit of such excellences. In addition, the wise steward is aware of both oneself and one's organization as situated in a social context. Accordingly, the wise steward recognizes oneself and one's institution as part of a tradition while linking the organization to other groups of various sorts, including the local community and the wider world, considered both globally and in terms of recalling the past and looking ahead to the future.

The wise steward recognizes that the activities of members of the organization are first and foremost the activities of human persons. Accordingly, coworkers, customers, suppliers, and everyone with whom one comes into contact are treated with the dignity befitting a person. The manager as wise steward provides opportunities for everyone in one's organization to make a personal contribution that develops his or her capacities as a person while also recognizing that each has a life beyond the organization. The wise steward operates with person-based and community-oriented concerns for common goods, including truth and beauty, that transcend the given ends pursued in the near term by the organization. The wise steward is attentive to preserving and improving resources, including those that are financial, natural, and social. Wise stewards create conditions in which members of the organization at times can reason together with others about the ends being pursued by their organization such that the good of financial success is balanced with a range of other human, social, and environmental goods.

With this sketch of the manager as wise steward in hand, let's turn now to investigate whether the activities of such a manager can be practiced in an artful manner, guided by internal standards of excellence that emerge out of the pursuit of external ends.

15
Management Is a Domain-Relative Practice

Extending Geoff Moore's account of MacIntyre's practice–institution schema, focus turns to the question of whether management is a practice. To do so, the conversation between MacIntyre and Joseph Dunne on the question of whether teaching is a practice is examined. To resolve the dispute, the notion of a domain-relative practice is introduced and explained. A domain-relative practice possesses internal standards of excellence identifiable to practitioners while being related to another particular domain. In addition to teaching, other examples are investigated, including coaching, writing, and public speaking. Management is a domain-relative practice with internal standards of excellence. One of the features of the manager's task is that it is always relative to the practice or practices housed in the institution that one is charged with managing.

Let's consider more intensively the manager's activities. As I have noted, MacIntyre's account of the virtues has given rise to debates as to whether managing is a practice with standards of excellence internal to its activities. It is common to speak of the practice of medicine or the practice of law. Is it helpful to encourage managers to think of their activities in terms of a practice? My goal in this chapter is to answer in the affirmative by drawing a distinction, thereby deepening the account of the manager as wise steward.

As an example, let's consider for a moment the activities of a project manager who works for the International Olympic Commission. Fans of the Olympic Games may rarely consider the activities of the many managers working in the background that make possible such an event. The tasks of such a manager include preparing for and carrying out the administrative and logistical responsibilities associated with the Olympic Games. To work as a project manager for the International

Olympic Commission requires excellent organizational skills and planning abilities, the ability to anticipate problems and propose solutions with precision, speed, and accuracy in stressful situations. In addition to the work of planning events and preparing policy guidelines for those participating as athletes, support staff, fans, dignitaries, and media, such a person would need excellent communication skills, diplomacy, tact, discretion, and flexibility. Such a role requires both the ability to plan for the future and the ability to make good judgments in urgent situations when the unexpected occurs.

Of course, in a certain sense, the same could be said of almost any management position. As mentioned in earlier chapters, it is these sorts of activities, common to almost all managers, which have been the focus of Weber, Fayol, Drucker, Mintzberg, and many other management writers. At the same time, the work of a project manager for the International Olympic Commission is quite distinctive when compared to other sorts of managerial roles. For example, to achieve excellence in such a role, it would be crucial to have a special knowledge of the world of sports and of international athletic federations. I have chosen the example of a project manager for the International Olympic Commission because it helps bring into focus two social realities discussed earlier: 1) the way that goals internal to an activity emerge from external ends, and 2) the complex relationship between practices and institutions.

Consider for a moment the activity of horseback riding. It is an ancient practice. From antiquity, human beings developed expertise in riding horses to accomplish specific given ends: hunting, agriculture, transportation, and military purposes. Equestrian activity for its own sake has developed as a highly sophisticated practice that has been institutionalized at many levels, including multiple events in the Olympics. In learning to ride a horse, it is crucial to develop skill in mounting and dismounting. As one acquires mastery of these skills, it becomes apparent that these same skills are also useful for increasing physical strength, flexibility, agility, coordination, balance, and health. Mounting and dismounting the horse can be pursued for the sake of health, or even for its own sake – to the point that the ancient Greeks built artificial horses, not only to provide the occasion to master skills at mounting and dismounting, but also as a form of gymnastic exercise using artificial vaulting horses and pommel horses with handles. Such artificial horses have been used continuously at the modern Olympics beginning with the games of 1896 in Athens. As gymnasts and trainers increasingly pursued excellence in gymnastic activity, they developed increased awareness of excellences internal to such activity – apart from the goods of horsemanship or health. Contemporary gymnastics has developed highly sophisticated norms and standards of excellence, and multiple institutions regulate those norms.

During the 2000 Olympics in Sydney, several gymnasts were involved in accidents, ramming into the horse's front end or botching their landings. The crashes were ascribed to a calibration error; the vault had been set two inches too low. In response, the International Gymnastics Federation deliberated about possible changes to the sport. In doing so, they evaluated the worth of various given ends, including safety for the athletes and the desire to facilitate increased gymnastic excellence. After their deliberations, they decided to endorse an equipment change, away from the traditional vaulting horse to an oval-shaped vaulting "table" that athletes have nicknamed "the tongue." Those deliberations involved choosing equipment that balances the goods of safety and health for the athletes with sophisticated acrobatic difficulty.

This example shows that human activity involves a complex order of purposes and motivations. Horsemanship, engaged in as a productive activity in pursuit of a given end, resulted in the discovery of multiple internal ends. Equestrian activity engaged in for an external end such as hunting, transportation, or military victory, disclosed itself as an activity with its own internal ends; indeed, the activity of vaulting onto the horse in various styles of mounts and dismounts itself emerged as a practice. As the practice of gymnastic vaulting emerged out of the activity of mounting horses, it gave rise to a set of institutions that serve to house the practice of vaulting while sustaining and extending the activities of gymnasts.

Is one who works as a project manager for the International Olympic Committee engaged in a social practice according to MacIntyre's stipulative definition? Are there goods internal to the activities of such a manager? On the one hand, such a manager obviously is charged with organizing people to efficiently and effectively pursue a specific given end. In that sense, such a manager seems little different from the Weberian office executive. On the other hand, the activity of managing, like the activity of mounting and dismounting a horse, seems to disclose itself as a complicated ordered activity that involves its own internal standards of excellence. Just as mounting and dismounting might at first seem to be merely instrumental activities, is there a similar level of complexity with regard to managerial activity? Is there an art to managing? Are there standards of excellence internal to the activity of managing, such that practitioners can recognize excellence in the activity, even apart from measurable outcomes?

To puzzle through this question, let's trace the debate that emerged in the published conversation between Alasdair MacIntyre and Joseph Dunne with regard to teaching. Early in the conversation, Dunne asked MacIntyre to comment on a government report in Ireland that recommends that in schools, the headmaster or principal "should be replaced by a 'chief executive.'"[1] Striking a polemical note, MacIntyre criticized the tendency to conceive of the school as "a machine whose activities are to be understood as transforming input into measurable output."[2] It's a regrettably familiar picture: the teacher is thought of as one with technical expertise in raising test scores and producing outcomes for assessment. Instead of conceiving of the purpose of the school in terms of developing the powers and abilities of the student, i.e., "the whole cultural formation of the student," the ideal teacher in such a system is the one who can produce the highest measurable outcome at the lowest cost. Unsurprisingly, MacIntyre criticizes this model of education. He calls instead for an approach where each teacher "is engaged in initiating his or her students into some practice."[3]

Dunne asked MacIntyre, "Can we helpfully construe teaching as itself a practice and see the curriculum itself as a set of practices into which students are to be initiated?"[4] MacIntyre provided a long, somewhat wandering answer, portions of which were quite surprising to Dunne. Specifically, MacIntyre stated, "Teaching itself is not a practice, but a set of skills and habits put to the service of a variety of practices."[5] The heart of MacIntyre's proposal was that teachers should think of themselves in terms of the disciplines they teach, "as a mathematician, a reader of poetry, an historian or whatever, engaged in communicating craft and knowledge to apprentices."[6] Included in his answer, MacIntyre emphatically denied that teaching is itself a practice. Dunne later pressed this point, but MacIntyre dug in his heels, claiming that teaching "is never more than a means, that it has no point and purpose except for the point and purpose of the activities to which it introduces students."[7]

Dunne later challenged MacIntyre's claim, conceding that teaching is not a sort of "domain-neutral expertise,"[8] but suggesting teaching is a practice according to MacIntyre's well-known definition. Specifically, Dunne suggested that teaching is a complex form of socially established cooperative human activity, that it contains its own internal standards of excellence, that it is the good of a certain kind of life, and that the dialectic between practice and institution is reflected in the case of teaching and school.[9] Further, as Dunne points out, in their conversation, MacIntyre made several relaxed comments that support the claim that teaching is a practice; MacIntyre refers to the "ends of teaching" and "the practice or practices of teaching."[10] In addition, Dunne draws from other works by MacIntyre, especially *Dependent Rational Animals*, which make reference to the goods of teaching.

On the whole, it seems to me that Dunne and the others who agree with him get the better of this debate, but there is certainly room for further reflection.[11] My goal here is to advance the conversation by proposing the notion of a "domain-relative practice," and then to think of both teaching and managing in those terms. Doing so concedes MacIntyre's criticism of those who claim a supposed domain-neutral expertise while also granting Dunne that teaching is an activity with its own set of excellences, one that can be made into a form of life, and that the practice of teaching is housed in relevant institutions such as schools, colleges, and universities.

In coining this phrase, "domain-relative practices," I am pointing to activities that 1) *possess internal standards of excellence identifiable to practitioners,* and 2) *are always related to another particular domain.* In each such case, familiarity with the particularities of the other related domain is an integral feature of the activity. By a "domain-relative practice," I mean more than the simple insight that each social practice is relative to its own particular domain. Obviously, the practice of medicine is related to the domain of health care, and the practice of mathematics is related to the domain of numbers, etc. Instead, I am drawing on a suggestion, made by MacIntyre in a number of places, that social practices can interlock such that we can refer to "a set of interlocking social practices."[12] I am proposing that "domain-relative practices" always interlock with other practices.

In a way, I'm extending a remark made by MacIntyre about the virtue of patience. MacIntyre notes that patience is the virtue of "waiting attentively without complaint, but not of waiting for anything at all. To treat patience as a virtue presupposes some adequate answer to the question: waiting for what? With the contexts of practices a partial, though for many purposes adequate answer may be given: the patience of a craftsman with refractory materials, of a teacher with a slow pupil, of a politician in negotiations."[13]

So, the virtue of patience is relative to various domains; just as the attentive waiting without complaint that characterizes the virtue of patience varies with different domains, in an analogous way, the activity of teaching is relative to various domains, including the subject matter and the teacher's ability to cultivate a relationship in light of the particularities of each student or group of students.

To explore the notion of a "domain-relative practice," let's focus for a moment not just on teaching or managing, but also on writing, speaking, and coaching: each of these is a social activity that has internal standards of excellence identifiable to practitioners, and each is also always relative to a particular domain: one teaches a subject, writes or speaks on a topic, coaches a sport, and so forth. There is no detached, pure, abstract, "Platonic form" of coaching. Similarly, teaching, public speaking, and writing are each socially embodied in two senses. Each of these is a social activity, discoverable always and only in a social context where the one engaging in the activity is related to other human persons. Additionally, each of these activities always has an interlocking relationship with some specific social context. In athletics, there are basketball coaches, baseball coaches, and so forth, but there are no coaches "in general."[14]

Let me turn now to consider the practice of coaching in athletics to illuminate similar points.[15] Take the example of an excellent basketball coach. On the one hand, many of the qualities that make for an excellent basketball coach are the same qualities found in an excellent coach from any sport: abilities to motivate, communicate, carry out well-designed practice routines with appropriate training and drills for skills instruction and game preparation, adeptness at in-game coaching, and so forth. On the other hand, excellence at coaching basketball is specifically related to the game of basketball; an excellent basketball coach needs to have a great deal of skill that is specific to basketball: aiding one's athletes in improving the particular skills needed in basketball, stressing defense and teamwork, diagnosing opponent strategies, creating opportunities for open shots while limiting these in the opposing team, etc. If someone is very good as a basketball coach, it does not follow that the same person would be very good as the coach of a golf squad or a swimming team. Excellence as a coach is intimately tied to the coach's familiarity with the particular sport one is coaching.

As a brief aside, it will help to apply MacIntyre's distinction between success and excellence to the case of a basketball coach. Success is measurable in terms of outcomes while excellence is embodied in activities. Success at coaching is typically measured by counting the victories of a coach's team; excellence at coaching is subtler, and is revealed in the activity of coaching and is recognizable to fellow practitioners or those familiar with the standards of the practice. Consider the case of Brad Stevens, the young basketball coach of the Butler University team that lost in the NCAA men's basketball championship game in 2010 and 2011. Butler is a comparatively small school (then) from a small conference. As such, it was a great success for the team to advance to the championship game two years in a row, but they ultimately failed to win the championship: their record in championship games is 0–2. Let's focus especially on their 2010 game against Duke. In the final moments of the game, Butler's star player, Gordon Hayward, missed a long shot at the buzzer that would have completed a thrilling David-over-Goliath victory. Should Butler's loss in the 2010 championship game be considered a success or a failure? How should we evaluate the performance of Butler's coach in that game? Measured in terms of success, Butler lost the game. However, when evaluated according to standards internal to the practice of coaching, even in Butler's defeat, it is possible to see the excellence in the performance of their coach, Brad Stevens: his ability to devise a successful strategy against an opponent with arguably superior athletes; his diagnostic abilities in pre-game preparation; his ability to motivate his athletes, communicating distinct roles to each and unifying them toward a common purpose; his calm focus during in-game decision-making; his ability to coach his team to remain within striking distance in the final seconds; and so forth. The artful coach excels at discovering the means of coming as near to victory as the circumstances of each particular case allow. Coaching, then, is a practice with its own internal excellences even as it is always related to a particular domain, such as basketball.

Suppose that Butler's basketball coach, Brad Stevens, were suddenly thrust into the role of coaching a different sport, for example, a baseball team. What would it take for him to excel at coaching in baseball? Certainly, he could draw from many of the same excellences that are involved in coaching basketball, but he would also need to attend to the many ways in which the practice of baseball is different from basketball.

Someone might object that competitive sports such as basketball do not have internal standards of excellence, or that focusing on those is foolish. Wouldn't a basketball coach that pursues internal standards of excellence or the development of positive character traits (over and above winning) have a very short career? In response, I want to acknowledge that there is a complicated relationship between the goods of excellence and the goods of success. Excellent coaches usually have winning records, but the coach with the most wins is not always the most excellent coach. What if the coach inherited a team with superior athletes? What if the victories were secured by cheating or by encouraging one's athletes to cheat? These strategies may make a coach successful in terms of victories, but not excellent *qua* coach. At the same time, a coach that is excellent at strategy, diagnosis, communication, motivation, decision-making, and so forth, may or may not produce victories in particular situations, such as the case of the Butler men's basketball team in the 2010 NCAA championship game. Coaching, as with any social practice that is artful, may be measured in terms other than a simple appeal to success such as counting victories. In this sense, excellence in coaching involves discovering the means of coming as near to victory as the circumstances of each particular case allow. Pursuing those excellences involves acquiring a set of character traits: determination, honesty, fairness, and so forth.

Coaching, like teaching, is an activity that is both a task and an achievement. In certain cases, the coach or the teacher might have done everything one could do to accomplish the given task without yielding a successful achievement. For that reason, John Dewey seemed to get things not quite right when he compared teaching to selling commodities. "No one can sell unless someone buys. We should ridicule a merchant who said that he had sold a great many goods although no one had bought any. But perhaps there are teachers who think that they have done a good day's teaching irrespective of what pupils have learned."[16] Dewey goes so far as to claim, "the same exact equation between teaching and learning that there is between selling and buying."[17] Of course, Dewey's central point is that teaching is a social activity, and success at teaching has to correspond in some way with the student having learned. But there are several ways in which Dewey's comparison between teaching and selling is unhelpful. For starters, it seems deeply confused to think of the relationship between teachers and learners in terms of "the same exact equation" as that between sellers and buyers. Of course, what is right about Dewey's point is that there is some relationship between the activity of teaching and the outcome of learning; obviously, a teacher whose entire class fails to learn is probably not a good teacher. At the same time, the relationship between teaching and learning is as complicated as the relationship between coaching and victories or between public speaking and persuasion. Just as some courtroom cases are easy to win, and some athletes given specific competition make it easy for a coach to achieve victory, so too, some students learn easily. Learning outcomes are not always an indicator of teaching excellence.

However, this is not the reasoning behind MacIntyre's criticism of Dunne's suggestion that teaching is a practice. Instead, MacIntyre is extending his criticism of the Weberian manager. He is warning us to beware of that character who, based on a supposed domain-neutral expertise in social organization, claims proficiency at organizing any social group to pursue a given end: increasing agricultural efficiency, making fishing operations more profitable, or knowing how to make the trains run on time. MacIntyre is not proposing that locomotive engineers and switchmen can run the railroad without anyone managing operations. Neither can athletes run the Olympic Games without managers. As I showed earlier, MacIntyre's criticism is directed at the supposition that the manager can develop expert knowledge of an abstract rational method employing supposedly disinterested principles that can be applied to every social domain without regard for the particularities of specific practices and traditions.

MacIntyre's comments about teaching in his conversation with Dunne strike me as an extension of this criticism. He is critical not only of the tendency to conceive of the schoolmaster as a chief executive, but also of teachers who "devote themselves to ... and presuppose the input/output model."[18] However, MacIntyre does not go far enough, it seems to me, in thinking through his own notion of a practice with reference to teaching or other similar activities.

A series of distinctions might help sort through the contentious features of the debate. First, notice this difference. Dunne is a teacher of teachers, helping to prepare those who will spend their lives as teachers, especially in the primary grades. In contrast, MacIntyre's career as a teacher has been almost always focused on university settings, especially within the discipline and practice of philosophy. Obviously there is a significant difference in the excellences required to teach seven-year-olds or ten-year-olds compared with those who are twenty or older. The degree to which a teacher needs to be a practitioner of a particular field of study varies considerably with the age of one's students. For those of us who teach philosophy in university settings, it comes rather easily for us to think of ourselves (as MacIntyre proposes) as philosophers charged with teaching. MacIntyre's claim that each teacher should think of "her or himself as a mathematician, a reader of poetry, a historian or whatever, engaged in communicating craft and knowledge to apprentices" seems more sensible at the university level – or even perhaps secondary and middle-school levels, but less so at primary levels or younger. So, one point that needs to be clarified is that teaching is always relative to particular students – their age, aptitude, background, etc., – and excellence in the activity of teaching requires a teacher that is attentive to the particular students in one's care.

As his conversation with Dunne unfolded, MacIntyre stated, "It's not clear to me how far we disagree. You say that teaching is itself a practice. I say that teachers are involved in a variety of practices and that teaching is an ingredient in every practice. And perhaps the two claims amount to the same thing; but perhaps not."[19] MacIntyre went on to state that, "All teaching is for the sake of something else and so teaching does not have its own goods. The life of a teacher is therefore not a specific kind of life."[20]

If MacIntyre's point is that it is just as mistaken to think that one can be an expert in "teaching" as it is to think that one could be an expert in writing, coaching, or managing, then his point is well taken. Each of these is always relative to a particular domain. But MacIntyre seems to go too far in certain respects, or to express himself in this conversation in a manner that is not complicated enough to capture the subtlety involved in good teaching. In particular, MacIntyre seems to overlook certain goods that arise in the relational context of teaching. Part of the task of any teacher is, as Nel Noddings put it in her response to the Dunne/MacIntyre conversation, to cultivate relationships of care and trust, both as an end in itself and in order to develop a feeling of safety where teacher and students together can engage the material in a shared quest; as such, each teacher is called to guide students in the apprenticeship of a discipline, while also, as Noddings puts it, to "share some responsibility for the development of students as whole persons."[21] No matter the academic discipline, Noddings points out that teachers "affect the lives of students not just in what we teach them by way of subject matter but in how we relate to them as persons."[22] Regardless of the subject, "the teacher sets an example with her whole self – her intellect, her responsiveness, her humor, her curiosity...her care."[23] So it strikes me as not quite right when MacIntyre states that the life of a teacher is "not a specific kind of life" and that teaching always is "for the sake of something else."

In a parallel manner, I am proposing that it is helpful to conceive of management as a domain-relative practice. I am focusing here on one aspect of MacIntyre's criticism of the manager as office executive: the supposition that the manager can develop expert knowledge of an abstract rational method employing supposedly disinterested principles that can be applied to every social domain without regard for the particularities of specific practices and traditions.

This aspect of MacIntyre's criticism runs as follows. The character of the bureaucratic manager rests on a false set of metaphysical assumptions about the self; in pretending to take up a detached, disengaged perspective that applies supposedly atemporal principles to particular social contexts, such a manager is engaged in a metaphysical self-contradiction. This does not mean that there are no universal moral standards, nor is it reducible to a simple rejection of principles in ethics. As MacIntyre puts it in *After Virtue*, the contradiction lies in the manager's claim to simultaneously "pass judgment from a purely universal and abstract point of view" where "anyone and everyone can thus be a moral agent, since it is in the self and not in social roles or practices that moral agency has to be located" while at the same time, the manager claims expert authority, enjoying "their status in virtue of their membership within hierarchies of imputed skill and knowledge."[24] The heart of the contradiction lies in a failure to recognize adequately the relationship between an abstract, atemporal realm of thought and the concrete, space-and-time setting of each circumstance. MacIntyre suggests that the managerial type he has in mind tends to make decisions by abstracting each situation and then treating it as an atemporal problem considered primarily in terms of efficiency and effectiveness. Doing so allows one to focus on certain features of the context while other aspects of the situation are neglected as nonrational, private values not subject to consideration. However, the claim that one can methodically identify and solve problems by solely attending to abstract concerns directs attention away from other features of a particular context that may be crucial: the particularities of place or tradition, the intentions and dispositions of those involved in the situation, or the impact of the decision on various stakeholders such as the workers, the suppliers, the consumers, the natural environment, and the broader society.

Just as a basketball coach can be evaluated either in terms of success (typically measured in terms of victories) or excellence (according to the standards internal to coaching), so, too, a manager can be evaluated either according to some measurable outcome or by attending to the excellence internal to the activities of administering and leading. Management is done artfully insofar as it accords with internal standards of excellence.

At the same time, the manager's task involves administering and leading in an institutional setting where another practice or set of practices are housed. Just as there are no coaches or teachers *per se* (only coaches of one or more particular sports and teachers of one or more particular disciplines), so, too, management is a domain-relative practice. So, excellence in management always involves attending to the excellences of those practices housed in the institution that one is charged with managing. And, as with other practices, it is the virtues that make possible the pursuit of the excellences internal to managing.

Earlier I noted Whetstone's suggestion, that ethicists could focus more intently on the way practicing managers use virtue language, "listening to what managers themselves say when discussing excellent managers."[25] In Whetstone's studies of the language used by managers and those who are managed to describe the excellences involved in managing well, Whetstone showed that contemporary managers, while certainly not schooled in the classical and medieval tradition of the virtues, employ with considerable articulation a moral language that "is essentially one of virtues and vices."[26] The traits reported in Whetstone's study correspond to a rather traditional list of moral virtues: honesty, trustworthiness, dedication, fairness, integrity, self-control, politeness, compassion, and loyalty.[27] Whetstone also reported that those he studied listed several other traits: flexibility, good judgment, the ability to show perspective, and the ability to be innovative.[28] As I discuss in the next chapter, excellent managers need especially to practice the virtue of practical wisdom.

To summarize the argument of this chapter, just as Aristotle proposed that excellent rhetoric, while always relative to one's subject and one's audience, is an activity that has its own internal standards of excellence, the same is true of other domain-relative practices, such as managing. Returning to the example of the program manager who works for the International Olympic Commission, certainly the manager's task shares much with other managers: organizing people and resources in an efficient manner to accomplish a given purpose. However, such a manager's given purpose involves more than a quantifiable outcome. The same is true of management generally; whether one is managing events at the Olympic Games, a fishing crew, a hospital, a construction firm, a transportation company, a communication firm, or virtually any organization, the manager's task is relative to the practice or practices housed in the institution that one is charged with managing.

So, who is the manager as wise steward? In Chapter 14, I provided a sketch of this character as a regulative ideal. In this chapter, I argued that management is a domain-relative practice. Understanding managerial activities in these terms shows that the manager as wise steward is guided by standards of excellence internal to managerial activities, even as those activities are relative to the practice or practices of which the institution is the bearer. Next, let's examine more intensively practical wisdom, the central virtue required of such a manager, investigating what it is, how it relates to other human traits, its constituent parts, and its place in a good human life.

16

The Dispositions of the Wise Steward and the Parts of Practical Wisdom

What virtues must the wise steward embody in order to manage in an excel-
lent manner? Many lists of traits have been developed to identify personal
qualities needed by those in managerial roles, but determining which such
traits to draw from in a particular circumstance requires practical wisdom.
This chapter focuses on the virtue of practical wisdom, investigating what it
is, how it relates to other human traits, its constituent parts, its role in mana-
gerial activities, and its place in a good human life. The account draws from
the wisdom tradition, especially as expressed in the writings of Aristotle and
Thomas Aquinas, as well as contemporary authors who have revived concern
for practical wisdom. Practical wisdom is the central virtue for the manager
as wise steward.

What traits are needed to excel as a manager? As noted earlier, this
question is addressed in various ways in several strands of recent
management literature.[1] Many lists identify characteristics considered
crucial for managers such as these: dependability, a calm demeanor,
empathy for others, creativity, the ability to multitask and return to
task after interruption, a persuasive ability to motivate, and an ability
to get things accomplished. What can a moral philosopher, drawing
from contemporary virtue ethics and the revived interest in the ancient
and medieval tradition of the virtues, bring to this conversation about
managerial traits?

In addition to the excellent traits included on any such list, a manager
must be able to make good judgments in each particular circumstance
to determine which trait should be called upon here and now. Does
this situation call for reliability (by applying established policies) or

independent initiative (by creatively transcending the past in a novel manner)? My focus in this chapter is on practical wisdom as the central disposition required to excel in managerial activities. To examine practical wisdom more intensively, my goal is to investigate what it is, how it relates to other human traits, its constituent parts, its role in managerial activities, and its place in a good human life. To begin this inquiry, let's bring into focus the nature of the sort of friendship on offer between the moral philosopher and the manager.

On the face of it, the first movements of the moral philosopher's entrance into conversation with the manager might perhaps seem threatening and alien, especially when compared to the proposals of management gurus who promise to help managers "win." To a new manager, advice on how to win, especially coming from someone who has all the marks of a winner, might quite reasonably seem like an attractive offer. In contrast, the Socratic moral philosopher might seem to begin in a combative mode with stinging attacks that call into question the worth of the manager's given purpose.

The task of the moral philosopher, as I have suggested, involves constantly shifting focus from the goods of success toward the goods of excellence, not in order to abandon the pursuit of given outcomes, but to relativize such a quest while coming to recognize that excellence in activities involves the ability to give an account of the worth of the given end in light of other goals.

I hope by this point in the argument to have reached a place of trust where we can see that the task of the moral philosopher must go beyond the sting of the gadfly. The moral philosopher and the manager, I hope, might participate together in a dialogue in pursuit of excellence investigating the goods internal to the manager's activities while cultivating the traits needed to undertake such a pursuit.

One way to advance that inquiry is to retrieve insights from the ancient Greeks about the dispositions needed to excel as human beings and as citizen leaders. Chief among these is the meta-disposition involved in the realization that wisdom is a goal, not a possession. Wisdom is not acquired from buying a book. It cannot be taught; it must be earned in making it one's quest. With that said, an important step in advancing toward the disposition of wisdom involves investigating what it is and how it relates to other excellent dispositions.

The classic descriptions of the virtue of practical wisdom can be found in Book VI of Aristotle's *Nicomachean Ethics* and in questions 47–56 of the *Secunda Secundae* of St Thomas Aquinas's *Summa Theologiae*.[2] In sum, practical wisdom is the virtue whereby one acquires a disposition of intellect such that, in each action, one is excellent at 1) deliberating about what to do while attending to relevant particularities, 2) making in each instance a good judgment, and 3) carrying out such decisions in action.[3] As such, the person of practical wisdom has actively developed excellence at taking in information for deliberation, judgment, and execution. In short, the person of practical wisdom has cultivated excellence in the realization of one's human powers to *see*, *judge*, and *act*. These constitute the key parts of the virtue of practical wisdom.

Because this virtue involves a sort of foresight, Cicero translated Aristotle's Greek term, *phronesis*, with the Latin, *providentia*, denoting a kind of divine foresight. This Latin term was later contracted, so that the medievals used the term *prudentia* to denote wisdom in human action, especially the ability to foresee the consequences of action in each case. Centuries later, the term prudence took on negative connotations, so that a "prude" or prudish person came to be thought of as one who is unduly cautious, overly concerned with social decorum, or uneasy with normal human desires as they relate to sexuality, alcohol, or other potential sorts of mischief. The classical and medieval notion of practical wisdom is quite different from the modern sense of prudishness. At the heart of practical wisdom is the ability to reason well about action, bringing together sound principles with what is known about the past and the present to make good decisions, choosing an appropriate means toward achieving a worthwhile goal.

In the traditional list of cardinal virtues, practical wisdom has held a primary place (even more important than courage, temperance, and justice) on the grounds that being precedes goodness.[4] In order to make fitting and appropriate decisions, one must be disposed with a sort of "openness to being," that is, a willingness to receive and understand each situation as it is. This involves being rightly disposed to the reality of each circumstance in terms of the past, present, and future. In order to cultivate this disposition, the medievals pointed to *memoria* (an openness to the past that is free from falsification), *docilitas* (an ability to practice silence in order that one might listen to the fullness of each present moment), and *solertia* (an openness to the unexpected future).[5]

Practical wisdom requires knowledge of both abstract, universal truths and awareness of the concrete particularities of each action. Correct judgments are frequently based on experience without scientific understanding. In instances where someone has a great deal of experience, experiential knowledge of particulars may be quite reliable. As Aristotle notes, a person who has practical experience but an inability to articulate that sort of knowledge in theoretical terms is a more reliable guide to good decisions than a person who has theoretical understanding but an inability to recognize the way those abstract truths are embodied in a particular instance. "If a man knew that light meats are digestible and wholesome, but did not know which sorts of meat are light, he would not produce health, but the man who knows that chicken is wholesome is likely to produce health."[6]

Decisions that call for practical wisdom frequently require experiential knowledge of particulars. Aristotle and St Thomas Aquinas referred to this kind of knowing as "particular reason." Because this kind of knowing is developed through experience, it is common for people with a great deal of experience in a certain domain to have such knowledge. While it is possible for this kind of knowledge to be organized and systematized, it need not be. It is common for people with experience to be immersed in a set of practices and a tradition that makes them attentive to relevant particularities needed for good decision-making. Although it is a dictum of Aristotelian philosophy that "the senses know particulars while the intellect knows universals," this actually oversimplifies Aristotle's considered view. In addition to sense awareness and intellectual knowledge, Aristotle describes a sort of experiential knowledge of particulars that is distinct from the external senses and the intellect. The medievals had several names for this knowledge of particulars; they sometimes called it discursive, collative, estimative or cogitative.[7] This cogitative power involves a pre-reflective ability to attend to an organized whole, perceiving it as harmful or beneficial while also seeing it as connected to other realities. In practical matters, it attends to the particularities of each instance, for every action involves something unique.

Malcom Gladwell's popular book, *Blink*, has encouraged increased interest in and debate about a phenomenon that Gladwell calls "thinking without thinking." Gladwell's book begins with the story of a statue purportedly made in ancient Greece recently purchased by a prominent museum. When suspicions were raised about the sculpture's authenticity, art appraisers with years of experience in ancient Greek sculpture were asked to evaluate the statue. Almost immediately, each expressed with confidence that the statue was a forgery. With a brief look, the appraisers judged that something was "just wrong" about the statue. Without giving a scientific account, the appraisers described their judgments using terms more commonly associated with the senses: the sculpture "stinks" or it leaves "a bad taste." Eighteen months later, through careful chemical testing of the stone, it was verified that the statue indeed was a forgery.[8]

What is the nature of the sort of knowledge that the art appraisers had? In what sense did they "know" that the statue was not authentic? What is this phenomenon that Gladwell aptly names "thinking without thinking," and how is it different from "real thinking," in which one can provide good reasons or evidence to support one's conclusions? In the case of the fake statue, we can distinguish between the sort of knowledge provided by the appraisers and the scientific evidence based on chemical analysis of the stone. For the appraisers, judgment was based on experience with particular authentic statues. For the scientists, judgment was based on their ability to measure evidence against universal standards. This distinction can be used to explain the kind of information that managers frequently use to make decisions. It goes without saying that managers are sometimes required to make time-sensitive decisions and that they frequently do not have the time or resources to gather scientifically verifiable information to support a particular decision. Further, the uniqueness of a particular case may be such that it is impossible, or nearly impossible, to gain scientific evidence to support a required decision. Part of what is needed to excel in the activities of managing involves the realization of one's powers of "particular reason," that is, this discursive power that makes it possible to attend to the appropriate features of a concrete context in order that one can make good judgments.

One way in which philosophers and theologians in the virtue tradition articulated the virtue of practical wisdom involved contrasting it with several corresponding vices. Practical wisdom involves a disposition toward excellence in seeing, judging, and acting; one might be deficient in any of those parts. One might be hasty, blind to the concrete realities that surround a particular situation, inconsistent, indecisive, thoughtless, negligent, or completely remiss in decision, cunning, crafty, small-minded, insidious, fraudulent, filled with guile, or covetous.[9]

In summary, in the tradition of the virtues, practical wisdom is characterized as the excellent disposition of intellect that perfects seeing, judging, and acting in a manner such that one finds fitting means to accomplish an appropriate goal in a manner that goes beyond tactical cunning. As Aristotle puts it, practical wisdom involves "calculating well toward some specific worthy end on matters where no exact technique applies."[10]

In his 2006 Presidential Address to the Society for Business Ethics, Dennis Moberg observed that the virtue of practical wisdom "has received scant attention in business ethics."[11] In a similar way, Gary Weaver has written that among those concerned with business ethics and organizations, more attention "needs to be paid to the notion of practical wisdom."[12] In the 1990s, philosophers such as Robert Solomon and Thomas Morris began to draw from Aristotle's virtue ethics, including his emphasis on practical wisdom, to frame questions about business organizations.[13] During the same time, a number of contemporary psychologists returned to the cognitive roots of their discipline, drawing from the virtue tradition to study human wisdom, which in turn inspired psychological studies of character, executive wisdom, and virtuous leadership.[14] Alejo Sison, in his recent survey of the literature of the virtues in business ethics journals shows a pattern of significantly increased interest in virtue ethics and practical wisdom.[15] Attending to these discussions brings into focus several ways in which the virtue of practical wisdom might inform contemporary managerial activities.

Schwartz and Sharpe note that it is difficult to define practical wisdom without offering a formula that is "too precise to capture this expansive concept or too vague to be of much use."[16] Nonetheless, several recent writers offer updated Aristotelian accounts that helpfully define and explain this virtue.[17] Moberg begins his account of practical wisdom with a dictionary definition: "the ability to judge rightly in matters relating to life and conduct."[18] He immediately refines that definition: "Inspired mostly by the work of Aristotle, I define practical wisdom as *a disposition toward cleverness in crafting morally excellent responses to, or in anticipation of challenging particularities.*"[19] Moberg goes on to explain the various parts of this definition. As a disposition, it is an active, stable trait. It has an intellectual element insofar as it involves ingenuity in crafting responses. It has to do with forming good judgments about actions, that is, with finding morally excellent responses. It involves excellence that is both reactive and proactive, that is, both crafting morally excellent responses and being able to anticipate. It deals with cases that are challenging, that is, where the best decision is not obvious. It entails an ability to make excellent decisions in light of the particularities of each context and circumstance.

Moberg identifies four contexts that frequently arise for managers that call for the exercise of the virtue of practical wisdom.[20]

1) *Information Uncertainties and Ambiguities.* Mangers frequently find themselves faced with a difficult decision because key information is lacking or incomplete, especially information about the intentions of one or more of the people involved in a situation. The person of practical wisdom is able to recognize the need for more information and to know how to gather what is needed to decide well.

2) *Execution Binds.* Managers sometimes encounter circumstances in which the most ethical alternative seems to involve significant cost. Practical wisdom encourages one to consider whether there is a way to execute the best option in precisely the right manner, while diminishing the foreseen harm, so the action is done at the right time toward the right person for the right reason in the right way.

3) *Moral Dilemmas.* Managers find themselves in situations where it seems that choosing one good thing will require a trade-off that diminishes another good: Self-interest or the good of the group? Justice or mercy? Truth or loyalty? Short-term profit or long-term sustainability? Practical wisdom rarely reduces these dilemmas to a simple ranking system; attentive to the specifics of each case, the person of practical wisdom seeks to craft an imaginative decision well suited to the circumstance.

4) *Ethical Leadership Predicaments.* Managers are frequently called upon to lead a social unit and to develop new policies in a context in which some of the people who will be affected by the policy may be opposed to the proposed direction. The person of practical wisdom is attuned so that decisions are made in an appropriate manner, attending to the concerns of those who may disagree without producing a stalemate, undue distrust, or disgruntlement.

To advance the conversation in business ethics and to deepen the pursuit of the virtue of practical wisdom and its role in managerial activities, three things might be done.

First, as I have tried to suggest throughout this book, it is fruitful to shift the framework in ethics, away from arguments about competing ethical standards that might be used as side constraints to limit an otherwise unbridled pursuit of given ends, and toward questions of character. Practical wisdom is an intellectual disposition. The person of practical wisdom, along with the character that I have proposed – the wise steward – is a regulative ideal. Describing and imagining such a character helps shape aspirations and serves as a goal to be pursued, appropriated, and embodied in one's personal quest to realize one's human powers to the full. Understood this way, practical wisdom is not an impersonal, detached standard; rather, it is a virtue that can be realized to a greater or lesser extent in the lives of individual human persons. Further, any human person who claims to have realized this excellence to the fullest shows his or her own lack of wisdom. One sign of wisdom is the recognition that one is, at most, on the way toward cultivating the virtue of practical wisdom.

Second, emphasizing practical wisdom as a personal, intellectual virtue can be a helpful way of reframing the case study approach in business ethics. As is well known, the case study approach to learning is widespread in business education, including business ethics. Framing inquiry into case studies in terms of the manager as wise steward is a helpful way to build on much that is beneficial in the use of case studies. As Moberg has noted, practical wisdom is required in four common kinds of cases encountered by managers: information uncertainties, execution binds, dilemmas, and leadership predicaments. For example, consider the well-known case frequently studied in business ethics courses of the Tylenol crisis faced by Johnson & Johnson in 1982.[21] What does this case teach students? One textbook approach uses the case as an example to show that "Johnson & Johnson managers faced ethical issues that were inextricably bound to practical business concerns."[22] However, this way of describing the case, as if managers have to learn two different modes of reasoning, one ethical and the other practical, seems inadequate. According to this widely held view, reason consists in impersonal, neutral, universal theories, and the Tylenol case is helpful for showing that the cost–benefit analysis of practical profit maximization is inadequate if it is not balanced against appeals to an entirely different set of rational standards, that is, standards of ethical duty that are also presumed to be impersonal, neutral, and universal. A shortcoming with this way of framing the issue is that it leaves the students, future managers, and managers without a principled way to balance competing standards.

In contrast, when the Tylenol case is framed as an occasion to make progress in cultivating the virtue of practical wisdom, it encourages us to investigate the actions and activities of James Burke, the CEO of Johnson & Johnson in 1982 when the crisis occurred. What were Burke's guiding purposes? What informed his deliberations, judgment, and action? What was he able to see about the situation? When information was missing, what did he do to gather appropriate information needed to make a good decision? What did he do to deliberate about the case? What did he do to demonstrate that he was a person of good moral character? How did he show that he was a person with good judgment? How did he indicate that he had good will toward others? How did the practical wisdom of Burke in his role as CEO demonstrate trustworthiness and good judgment? In what ways did James Burke exemplify the characteristics of a wise steward?

A third way in which emphasizing the virtue of practical wisdom might advance business ethics involves deepening understanding with regard to the ways in which we debate the relative worth of various ends. How does one make good decisions in a concrete situation while balancing a range of competing goods. Let's return for a moment to consider a debater's dispute that Aristotle mentions in the *Rhetoric*. Which is better: water or gold? Thinking through the dispute can bring into focus similar sorts of deliberations required of managers and executives. For example, in the Tylenol crisis, the CEO had to balance several goods and potential dangers: the safety of those who use Tylenol, the company's reputation, trust in pharmaceutical capsules, company profits in the short-term, the risk of permanent loss of market share, the profits of distributors and stores that had purchased the product, and the possibility of permanent damage to the product line or to Johnson & Johnson.

How does practical wisdom provide guidance to determine what is the best course of action in a concrete circumstance? One way to work toward an answer to this question is to consider the following well-known apparent contradiction in Aristotle's *Nicomachean Ethics*. In Book III, Aristotle seems to insist quite forcefully that deliberation is always about means. However, in Book VI, Aristotle seems to suggest that practical wisdom involves evaluating whether particular ends are worthwhile.

Let's examine these apparently contradictory texts. Book III, Chapter 3 of the *Nicomachean Ethics* begins with Aristotle asking, "Do people deliberate about everything, and is everything an object of deliberation, or are there some things about which there is no deliberation?"[23] Aristotle's answer seems to be quite clear: "We deliberate, not about ends, but about what forwards those ends."[24] Humans deliberate in a range of spheres; Aristotle lists several: medicine, business, navigation, large-scale political projects, and many similar sorts of human pursuits where the end is given but where it is unclear what is the best way to reach the given end. "A doctor does not deliberate about whether he'll make his patients healthy, nor a public speaker about whether he will persuade his audience."[25] In all such pursuits, Aristotle emphasizes that ends are taken as given. Humans do not deliberate about ends, "but rather they take the end for granted and examine how and by what means it will come about; and if it appears as coming about by more than one means, they look to see through which of them it will happen most easily and best."[26] Indeed, Aristotle repeats this conclusion multiple times in this chapter. In some cases, humans deliberate about what is the best tool for the job, or what is the best way to use a tool, or "how it is to be done or by what means."[27] Of course, the result of deliberation, when it goes well, is a definite decision: "What we decide about are the things that forward our ends."[28]

However, in Book VI, where Aristotle provides his account of the intellectual virtues, and especially the virtue of practical wisdom, his description of deliberation seems rather different. This tension emerges with his description (in Book VI, Chapter 5) of *phronesis*, the virtue of practical wisdom. The person with this excellence is "able to deliberate well about the things that are good."[29] So excellence in deliberation seems to involve more than simply an ability to deliberate well toward a given end. Indeed, Aristotle next states that the person with practical wisdom is needed in cases where "no exact technique applies."[30] Practical wisdom involves "calculating well towards some specific worthy end."[31] The puzzle shows itself in Aristotle's account of practical wisdom as "a disposition accompanied by rational prescription, true, in the sphere of human goods, relating to action."[32] After all, isn't it quite common for humans to deliberate about "what is good and bad for human beings?"[33] Indeed, isn't this the heart of moral philosophy: to deliberate and engage in debate about what actions are good for human beings?

As Aristotle deepens his account of practical wisdom, he returns again to deliberation, but this time (in Book VI, Chapter 9), his account seems more complicated. Deliberation is a sort of inquiry, not just about the best means to accomplish any given end, but with regard to a fitting and worthwhile end. Aristotle states, "Deliberative excellence is correctness as to what one should achieve and the way in which, and when, all in accordance with what is beneficial."[34] This view, that deliberation has to do with both means and ends, seems to be in tension, perhaps even in contradiction, with Aristotle's earlier account.

Several things will help us puzzle through the apparent contradiction. First, let's consider this question. What has changed between Book III and Book VI of the *Nicomachean Ethics*? The answer is that in those intervening chapters and books, Aristotle has provided a fine-grained account of the character virtues. This is relevant to the issue at hand in the following way. At the end of Book VI, Aristotle notes that it is possible to possess the intellectual excellence of deliberating about and deciding upon the best means to accomplish a given end even without virtue of character. Such a person, Aristotle insists, may be clever, but lacking in practical wisdom. Cleverness is a sort of *faux phronesis*. Authentic practical wisdom, according to Aristotle, involves excellence with regard to both means and the end. "By calculation the person without self-control, or the one with a bad character, will achieve what his project requires, thereby having 'deliberated correctly,' although he will have got himself a great evil."[35] Such a person may possess the *faux* excellence of cleverness while lacking the authentic excellence of practical wisdom, but the object chosen is not really good, and practical wisdom involves "correctness of deliberation that is deliberative excellence, i.e. the sort that enables one to achieve what is good."[36]

Bringing the puzzle into deeper focus, we might ask, "How is it possible to deliberate about ends in order to determine if a given end is in fact good in a concrete circumstance?" Returning to Aristotle's *Rhetoric*, we can recall that Aristotle advocates learning how to advance the best arguments on both sides of an issue, "not in order that we might act on both (since one ought not to be persuasive about corrupt things), but so that the way things are might not go unnoticed."[37] In other words, excellence at making the best decision in a concrete circumstance involves a willingness to consider the situation from multiple perspectives. Doing so allows one to move toward a more refined, sophisticated, and subtle awareness of the relevant particularities informing a situation.

In order to deliberate about competing goods, it is necessary to relativize each, treating each as means to some other more worthwhile good, whether the good of an individual or the common good of a community. For example, while health obviously is the end of medicine, and wealth is the end of household management, both health and wealth can be considered as means that are part of a good life, and a well-ordered community needs to secure both health and wealth in some ways for its members. Deliberating about the relative worth of such ends requires a willingness to treat particular ends as means to another purpose.

Returning to the dispute about the relative worth of water compared to gold, the solution to the dispute is not so simple as determining a single metric for measuring the worth of each. Water is a means to satisfying thirst and pursuing health; gold is a very different sort of good. The worth of gold is tied up with its being a scarce and beautiful form of wealth that is desirable in contexts in which many other goods of the body and safety are secure. While water for drinking is a means to a healthy life, once one's thirst is quenched and a reliable source of clean water has been secured, it becomes apparent that water (and even health) are not the highest ends in a good human life. As such, in a certain sense, gold is more valuable than water, but there are conditions under which a particular person might reasonably trade precious gold in order to secure drinking water. As such, in order to answer questions about the relative worth of water and gold, it is necessary to relativize each given end, seeing particular ends as means to another end.

This insight is particularly important for managers who are charged with planning, organizing, and leading an institution in light of the practices housed within that institution. In concrete circumstances, managers constantly find themselves weighing and evaluating the relative worth of incommensurable goods. In the Tylenol case, the good of safety for one's customers is incommensurable with the good of profit or reputation. Indeed, the well-known case of the Ford Pinto gas tank reveals the foolishness of treating human safety and profit according to a shared metric.

In a certain sense, practical wisdom involves the ability to reason well with regard to finding appropriate means to realize a particular goal. However, in a fuller and deeper sense, practical wisdom involves the ability to reason well about human affairs generally. For example, it takes a sort of wisdom in military affairs to know what is required to bring about victory in a particular case. However, in the case of a Pyhrric victory, where devastating and irreplaceable casualties accompany success, the intellectual acumen of the strategist clouds the ability to reflect on the broader social and political purposes for seeking to win.

In the context of contemporary management, I have suggested that excellence at the activities that are internal to managing as a domain-relative practice requires the development and exercise of the virtue of practical wisdom. This involves calculating well toward some specific end by finding an appropriate course of action suitable to the concrete particularities of the situation. It also involves a willingness to question whether the given ends that one is pursuing are worthwhile, both for oneself and for others. Practical wisdom, understood this way, involves a willingness to allow given ends to be called into question such that alternatives are treated as more than nonrational preferences. In this way, practical wisdom involves crafting morally excellent responses not only to particular decisions, but also to large questions. How might short-term profit be balanced with long-term sustainability? How might the goals of one's firm or unit be balanced with the well-being of the community or geographical region in which one's firm operates? How might the concerns of one's unit for efficiency and effectiveness be balanced with the recognition that the members of one's unit are persons with capacities and gifts, many of which go well beyond those that are realized through their work? How might those impacted by the activities of one's unit be invited at times to participate in common deliberation about the ends being pursued by the enterprise?

Understood this way, reason is not simply an abstract, disengaged, detached instrument. Reasoning about ends and evaluating given purposes is a personal excellence that occurs within a community and between communities, especially when objections are raised and considered. For such reasoning to go well, the interlocutors need to be willing to listen to alternative proposals and the concerns that give rise to them on their own terms.

An objector might complain that this adventure amounts to little more than a call for philosopher–managers! In Plato's *Republic*, Socrates declares that, "Unless the philosophers rule as kings or those now called kings and chiefs genuinely and adequately philosophize, and political power and philosophy coincide in the same place, while the many natures now making their way to either apart from the other are by necessity excluded, there is no rest from ills for the cities."[38] The objector might question whether the book's entire argument amounts to a call for managers to become philosophers. Isn't it foolish to think that managers must become philosophical in order to excel as managers? After all, the tasks and concerns of the manager are really different from those of the philosopher. The philosopher has the luxury of contemplating grand ideas while the manager has to focus on the task at hand, organizing people and resources to solve a particular problem.

One way to respond to this sort of honest objection involves following Aristotle in the way he drew a distinction between different kinds of activities and the wisdom appropriate to each. Noting that there is a difference between making (*poesis*), thinking (*theoria*), and doing (*praxis*), Aristotle distinguished between three corresponding sorts of wisdom. These three sorts of wisdom can reside in three characters: 1) the person with technical expertise knows how to produce a given outcome; 2) the person with theoretical understanding knows how to understand unchanging principles; and 3) the person with practical wisdom knows how to act in a given circumstance.[39] At first, it might seem that the manager possesses a value-neutral expertise while the philosopher is concerned with abstractions. However, the situation is actually a bit more complicated; one of the central aims of this book is to show that the mastery in managerial technical expertise to organize a group of people to accomplish a given end involves practical wisdom, including the wisdom to create the conditions for the shared pursuit of the truth about the appropriate place of those given ends in terms of a larger framework. In order to advance toward mastery in any technical expertise, one needs to cultivate practical wisdom, including the wisdom to know how, when, and in what manner to use one's technical expertise. Part of the answer to understanding the relation between the manager and the moral philosopher comes from seeing that the expertise of the manager in organizing people and resources to accomplish a given end inevitably gives rise to questions that require practical wisdom.

Another part of the answer comes from understanding more clearly the philosopher's task. An Aristotelian might state, "It is the business of the wise person to order." [40] It is the characteristic mark of reason to know order, but order is related to the work of reason in four ways: 1) reason beholds the order of things in nature; 2) reason arranges and discerns order in things through language and thought; 3) reason establishes order in deliberate human actions chosen for their own sake; and 4) reason establishes order in external things through productive activities. Among these four, there is a strong tendency to associate the work of the philosopher, especially the metaphysician, with the first two, while the work of the manager seems concerned with the fourth. However, there is a sort of common ground between the moral philosopher and the manager when it comes to the third of these, the exercise of reason in deliberate human actions chosen for their own sake. Both the moral philosopher and the manager are concerned with this sort of practical wisdom, even though both may come to that concern from a different path. So we can concede that the manager need not be a moral philosopher, and moral philosophers need not aspire to be managers, even as we recognize that both are concerned with cultivating practical wisdom. The main way that moral philosophers engage in the activity of cultivating practical wisdom is by puzzling through questions and apparent inconsistencies and contradictions that arise regarding what it is, how it relates to other human traits, its constituent parts, and its place in a good human life.

I am not suggesting that managers must become philosophers – at least not in the sense that managers must give themselves over completely to the task of deliberating about questions of human purpose. However, I am suggesting that it is worthwhile at times to evaluate the given ends of one's organization and to engage with others about such questions, seeking to reason together with others about the kinds of lives we want to lead and about the kinds of communities we want to shape. Further, I am suggesting (with MacIntyre) that the tendency to think that reason is merely an instrument for efficiently and effectively bringing about a chosen end is diminished and hollow. So, I am suggesting that managers need practical wisdom, both in the sense that they need to attend to relevant particularities in order to accomplish given purposes and in the sense that they need to evaluate whether the ends proposed in their planning and organizing are conducive to a good life.

Another way to explain this point is to note that the virtue of practical wisdom involves two sorts of reasoning that are not widely recognized in modern contexts. Earlier, I mentioned the Aristotelian notion of particular reason; a great deal more could be said about this aspect of rationality. In a similar way, more could be said about the substantive reasoning needed in order to take up a rational evaluation of purposes. For now, suffice it to say that the virtue of practical wisdom, as practiced by the manager as wise steward, involves the ability to craft morally excellent responses to, or in anticipation of challenging particularities while evaluating in an excellent manner the ends that one is pursuing in order to judge with others whether they are worthwhile and conducive to a good human life, both for oneself and for others.

Conclusion

The purpose of this book is to do the groundwork to encourage managers, future managers, and moral philosophers who engage in dialectical conversation with them to achieve a transformed understanding of the character the manager as wise steward. The metanoia *I have in mind is primarily personal. Characters and the character traits of humans are embodied primarily in individual human persons. Virtues are confirmed and consolidated through personal deliberate choices. In a secondary way, character traits are embodied in cultures and institutions. At this broader social and institutional level, the transformation in the character of the manager may take generations. To carry it through will require the work of many, and it likely will involve deliberate choices to make numerous institutional changes.*

I began in Chapter 1 with the story of the students in my course on Business Ethics. I contrasted their career aspirations and motivations with those of pre-med students hoping to gain admittance to medical school. Future physicians almost always explain their motivations in terms of service to others. "I want to be the kind of physician that offers care to others, my patients as well as my coworkers, regardless of their station in life, their abilities, or their disabilities." The sense that the role of the physician is to serve as community helper is very deeply ingrained; a widely held intuition about the physician's role guides our sense of excellence in the practice of medicine. Young people aiming to pursue the practice of medicine readily recognize that such a life requires the cultivation of a set traits of character and intellect. In contrast, students from the school of business, as I recounted, explained to me their career aspirations in a comparatively shallow manner: "I want to make money. Lots of it."

211

If we were to track the character arc of some of these bright, ambitious business administration students, we might find them years later in a corner office, having developed expertise in organizing people effectively and efficiently to accomplish some given end, compensated with considerable bonuses, but having to pass on their way into the office through a gauntlet of protesters aiming to bring attention to corporate greed and its corrosive effects on society. My argument has been that we need a transformation in the character of the manager, and that moral philosophy can play a role, admittedly rather limited, in bringing about that transformation. I have proposed that the power of moral imagination be employed to envision as attractive a different understanding of the managerial role. The sort of managerial character I have proposed is, I hope, taking shape on the horizon.

The manager as wise steward has a self-understanding that involves being charged with holding something in trust while choosing service over self-interest. The wise steward has responsibilities to plan, organize, and lead an institution; such an institution is understood as the bearer of one or more social practices. The wise steward understands one's work to be guided by excellences internal to the domain-relative practice of one's managerial activities along with the disposition of being on the way toward practical wisdom. The wise steward manages artfully, seeing in each circumstance the available means to organize a given group of people to come as near as possible to achieve a worthwhile goal. In communion with others in friendship, this sort of manager asks a series of questions, over and over again. What would the person of practical wisdom do in this situation? How can I organize, plan, and lead in a wise manner this group with which I have been tasked with managing? How can I better understand the complexities and relevant particularities of this circumstance? How might I improve my abilities to deliberate and use good judgment? What is the dwelling place of wisdom in this situation? What would it be to act, here and now, in the way in which a wise person would? Developing the disposition to ask these kinds of questions requires cultivating a distinct outlook with its own motivations and passions.

If I have laid the groundwork to encourage managers, future managers, and moral philosophers who engage in dialectical conversation with them to begin to think of the character of the manager in terms of the wise steward, then I have accomplished my task. The sort of transformation for which I have argued involves changing our social understanding of what it means to be a manager. The *metanoia* I have in mind may occur in an individual person, but I also envision a cultural change that may take more time, perhaps generations. To carry it through will require the work of many, and it likely will involve changes in institutions, too.

The argument that I have advanced is based on the insight that dispositions are, first and foremost, human, personal qualities. Character and the character traits of humans are embodied primarily in individual human persons. One's traits are certainly shaped and influenced in many ways: by physiological factors, one's family and local community, language, culture, and the social organizations and institutions in which one participates or with which one encounters. Virtues are confirmed and consolidated through the deliberate choices of individual human persons, even as the social nexus in which one dwells shapes the way a virtue is embodied in a particular human person.

Those primarily concerned with organizations, institutional structures, and issues of governance of organizations are working on a parallel track when they focus on institutional traits and organizational culture. Indeed, some go so far as to use the language of "organizational virtues." In doing so, the language of virtues is used, it seems to me, in a secondary sense. In a qualified manner, virtues and vices can be embodied in organizations. In a manner analogous to the way that individual humans have personality traits, organizations have traits, that is, a culture. An organization's culture consists in a shared perception of how the organization's members describe and perceive the way things are done. Organizational culture is sometimes described in terms of various dimensions, each of which is admitting of degrees. A common list of such dimensions includes attention to detail, outcome orientation, people orientation, team orientation, aggressiveness, stability, innovation, and risk taking. Strong organizational cultures are those in which the key values are intensely held and widely shared. Organizational culture is established and maintained by the vision of the founders, practices that judge candidates that join the organization based on "fit," the ongoing actions and decisions of organizational leaders, and socialization, that is, the process of helping employees learn the culture, especially through stories, rituals, and symbols.

The account of the character of the manager that I have provided proposes that the virtues of the wise steward are primarily personal. Virtues and vices are personal qualities developed through the concrete decisions of one's life, including the ways in which one participates in, or challenges participation in the social structures in which one finds oneself. In a secondary way, the transformation in the character of the manager might come about in a culture, whether that of an organization or a larger culture. So, the argument that I have made is primarily for a transformation in character to be adopted by individual persons, and secondarily for a transformation in institutions and culture.

The character of the manager increasingly comes into existence through the concrete decisions of individual managers to conduct themselves in these terms. As more and more do so, especially in particular organizations, we can hope for a shift in the cultural understanding of what it means to be a good manager. In this way, there is a complex dialectic between an individual human person's dispositions and the social nexus in which one finds oneself.

An objector might counter that the entire account of the manager as wise steward that I have proposed may be, in certain instances, not just foolishly idealistic, but perhaps illegal. After all, in a for-profit institution where a manager is hired to serve to advance the purposes of the owner, placing priority on the good of the workers and their practices, or the clients, the suppliers of various elements of production, the community of reference, the natural environment, the common good of the broader society, or future generations could be, in some instances, against the law. The objector might point out that in many institutions where managers work, there are laws and policies that have been established requiring managers to prioritize shareholder interest above other concerns. In that case, the character I have proposed may seem not just foolish, but criminal.

My response to this sort of objection is that the situation is likely more complicated than that described by the objector. Certainly there are some institutions with policies that inhibit managers from acting in a virtuous manner or with a concern for the common good; some institutions may be irremediably disordered in such a way that those in managerial roles are practically barred from practicing the virtues or acting as a wise steward. It may be most prudent not to participate in such institutions; if one does choose to participate in such institutions, practical wisdom may point to the necessity of working to bring about change in the governance structures of such organizations. Most situations, however, it seems are more complicated. Instances where institutional policies prevent exercising good judgment about the wisdom of a specific course of action seem rare. In many of the sorts of institutions that the objector has in mind, there is an organizational mission statement. In such cases, the good of seeking shareholder value is invariably one goal among several. In such a context, there is space to seek ways to craft an imaginative response balancing the various goods being pursued in a particular circumstance.

The aftermath of the recent economic crisis offers an opportunity to examine other kinds of institutional structures and governance models for organizations. In the wake of the crisis, we find ourselves in a period where it seems reasonable to consider unwinding some of the command-and-control policies that have been put in place that blind people to the use of good judgment and responsible wisdom. Are there different models for organizing and institutionalizing productive activities? For example, the Mondragon Cooperatives, the largest employer in the Basque region of Spain, use a worker–ownership model. In those sorts of corporations, managers are accountable to the worker–owners. Alternatively, credit unions provide another sort of institutional structure; in most credit unions, the task of the manager is described in terms of "serving the members." These sorts of institutional structures are perhaps more conducive to a humanistic model in which the manager can excel as a wise steward.

Managers who work in the not-for-profit sector, for example, in schools, hospitals, and social service organizations, might do more to study these sorts of alternative models of governance and accountability to gain insight regarding institutional structures. Are the governance structures of the institution wise with regard to accountability? Institutions based on the shareholder model tend to promote systems of accountability that aim up and away from those whom the manager serves, and the accountability tends to be based on short-term, measurable outcomes. In contrast, the institutional structures and governance models of worker cooperatives and credit unions merit fuller examination as models conducive to a wider and deeper sort of accountability.

One of the chief differences between the manager as office executive and the manager as wise steward involves the way each understands command and control. For the office executive, command and control are crucial. For the wise steward, while there certainly are moments when a situation calls for firm directions, practical wisdom suggests that it is important to develop trust in the ability of individuals and small groups to act in a responsible, self-directed manner. Certainly, in a crisis situation or a medical emergency, it may be necessary for someone to take a leadership role to organize an appropriate response by giving orders: go do this now. However, most situations in which managers organize, plan, and lead a social group do not call for commands and controls. The wise steward needs to exercise the virtue of practical wisdom to determine when the command and control approach is appropriate while also learning to recognize opportunities for intentionally and systematically moving resources and responsibility closer to those engaged in the core practices of the institution. The principle of subsidiarity can serve as a practical guide: personal decisions are best made by individual persons, and decisions are made best when they are made by the smallest, lowest, or least centralized authority appropriate to the matter, with higher and larger authorities intervening only in case of need, and then only to restore responsibility back to the appropriate level.

Beyond the organization, the wise steward recognizes that one's institution or unit relates to other groups in complex ways. In some instances, a market relationship is helpful, with prices serving as indicators or signs that provide information about goods or services on offer from others. At the same time, not every human relationship is reducible to market terms. Further, within one's institution, the wise steward recognizes that relationships are more complicated than mere market relationships. So, part of the wisdom required of the wise steward is the ability to determine the suitability of market relationships in concrete circumstances.

Finally, the wise steward acts with an eye on the common good. This involves recognizing that the common good is more than a collection of individual preference–satisfactions. Human beings engage in social practices both to be productive and for the sake of excellence in practical activities. The goods and services that result from productive activities are finite. A context of scarce resources gives rise to questions about the distribution of such goods and services. Is the logic of markets the most sensible way to distribute the limited goods and services that are the outcomes of productive activities? Is there a role for the logic of gift with regard to questions of distribution? Should the dominant concern that guides distribution be efficiency, justice, love, or something else? How do the activities of the wise steward promote not only the well-being of the social unit in question, but also the common good? These and many similar questions must continue to be investigated in order to encourage cultivation and growth in the character of the manager as wise steward.

Notes

Introduction

1. See for example, see D. Schoen (2011) "Polling the Occupy Wall Street Crowd," *Wall Street Journal*, October 18. http://online.wsj.com/article/SB10 001424052970204479504576637082965745362.html
2. A. MacIntyre (1977a) "Utilitarianism and Cost–Benefit Analysis: An Essay on the Relevance of Moral Philosophy to Bureaucratic Theory," in *Values in the Electric Power Industry*, edited by K. Goodpaster and K. Sayre. Notre Dame, IN: University of Notre Dame Press, 218.
3. R. Beadle (2001) "MacIntyre and the Amorality of Management, presented at the Second International Conference of Critical Management Studies, July 2001, available online at http://www.mngt.waikato.ac.nz/ejrot/ cmsconference/2001/Papers/Management and Goodness/Beadle.pdf, accessed on 5 May 2013.
4. For example, see A. MacIntyre (1984a) "Does Applied Ethics Rest on a Mistake?," *The Monist*, 67, 598–613.
5. See the "Guide to Further Reading" in K. Knight (1998) *The MacIntyre Reader* (Notre Dame, IN: University of Notre Dame Press), 284.
6. For examples, see the special (2008) edition of *Philosophy of Management* devoted to "MacIntyre, Empirics and Organisation": R. Beadle and G. Moore (2008b) *Philosophy of Management*, 7; G. Moore (2012a) "The Virtue of Governance, the Governance of Virtue," *Business Ethics Quarterly* 22, 293–318; G. Beabout (2012) "Management as a Domain-Relative Practice that Requires and Develops Practical Wisdom, *Business Ethics Quarterly* 22, 405–432; R. Beadle and K. Knight (2012) "Virtue and Meaningful Work," *Business Ethics Quarterly* 22, 433–450; M. Schwartz (2010) "Moral Vision: Iris Murdoch and Alasdair MacIntyre," *Journal of Business Ethics* 90, 315–327; J. Dobson (2009) "Alasdair Macintyre's Aristotelian Business Ethics: A Critique," *Journal of Business Ethics*, 86, 43–50; G. Moore (2008) "Re-Imagining the Morality of Management: A Modern Virtue Ethics Approach," *Business Ethics Quarterly*, 18, 483–511; J. Hine (2007) "The Shadow of MacIntyre's Manager in the Kingdom of Conscience Constrained," *Business Ethics*, 16, 357–371; G. Moore (2002) "On the Implications of the Practice–Institution Distinction: MacIntyre and the Application of Modern Virtue Ethics to Business," *Business Ethics Quarterly*, 12, 19–32; R. Beadle and G. Moore (2006) "MacIntyre on Virtue and Organization," *Organization Studies*, 27, 323–340; D. Dawson and C. Bartholomew (2003) "Virtues, Managers and Business People: Finding a Place for MacIntyre in a Business Context," *Journal of Business Ethics*, 48, 127–138; P. du Gay (1998) "Alasdair MacIntyre and the Christian Genealogy of Management Critique," *Cultural Values*, 2, 421–444; K. Balstad Brewer (1997) "Management as a Practice: A Response to Alasdair MacIntyre," *Journal of Business Ethics*, 16, 825–833; I. Mangham (1995) "MacIntyre and the Manager," *Organization*, 2, 181–204;

L. Nash (1995) "Whose Character? A Response to Mangham's 'MacIntyre and the Manager,'" *Organization*, 2, 226–232; C. Horvath (1995) "Excellence v. Effectiveness: MacIntyre's Critique of Business," *Business Ethics Quarterly*, 5, 499–532; D. McCann and M. Brownsberger (1990) "Management as a Social Practice: Rethinking Business Ethics After MacIntyre," in M. Stackhouse, et al. (eds) *On Moral Business* (Grand Rapids, MI: Eerdmans), 508–514; P. Santilli (1984) "Moral Fictions and Scientific Management," *Journal of Business Ethics*, 3, 279–286.

7. J. Dobson (1996) "The Feminist Firm: A Comment," *Business Ethics Quarterly*, 6, 227–232 (sparking debate); A.C. Wicks (1996) "Reflections on the Practical Relevance of Feminist Thought to Business," *Business Ethics Quarterly*, 6, 523–532 (responding to Dobson); J. Dobson (1997) "MacIntyre's Position on Business: A Response to Wicks," *Business Ethics Quarterly*, 7, 125–132; A.C. Wicks (1997) "On MacIntyre, Modernity and the Virtues: A Response to Dobson," *Business Ethics Quarterly*, 7, 133–135.

8. Balstad Brewer (1997), 825.

9. Ron Beadle has argued that Brewer's reasoning is spurious. See (Beadle) 2001.

10. G. Moore (2012a), 294.

11. G. Moore (2012a), 303.

12. J. Bakan (2004) *The Corporation*. New York: Free Press.

13. Bakan (2004), 35.

14. Bakan (2004), 56.

15. Bakan (2004), 57.

16. Bakan (2004), 57.

17. Bakan (2004), 58.

18. Bakan (2004), 59.

19. The primary solution proposed by Bakan is an improved regulatory system, especially "government regulation." See Bakan (2004), 161.

20. T. Wright and J. Goodstein (2007) "Character is not 'Dead' in Management Literature: A Review of Individual Character and Organizational-Level Virtue," *Journal of Management December*, 33:6, 928–958.

21. T. Wright and J. Goodstein (2007), 939.

22. T. Wright and J. Goodstein (2007), 942.

23. M. McLuhan and B. Powers (1992) *The Global Village* (Oxford: Oxford University Press), 6.

24. L. Rohrer (2009) "Can Business Managers Be Virtuous?," MacIntyre Conference Proceedings, Lincoln University, October.

1   The Dreams of Future Managers

1. See the Saint Louis University web site, www.slu.edu.

2. For well-known examples from popular and academic writers, see: M. Friedman (1970) "The Social Responsibility of Business Is to Increase Its Profits," *The New York Times Magazine*, 13 September, 122–126; M. C. Jensen and W. H. Meckling (1976) "Theory of the Firm: Managerial Behavior, Agency Costs and Ownership, *Journal of Financial Economics*, 3:4, 305–360. For criticisms, see L. Stout (2012) *The Shareholder Value Myth* (San Francisco: Berrett-Koehler).

3. Robert G. Kennedy examines this point in more detail in his little book, (2006) *The Good that Business Does* (Grand Rapids: Acton Institute Christian Thought Series). I made a similar argument in my article, (1999) "Business or Medicine: Challenging the Stereotypes," *National Catholic Register*, 1 August, 9.

4. R. Beadle (2001). The substance of that paper was published as (2002) "The Misappropriation of MacIntyre," *Reason in Practice*, 2:2, 45–54. (This journal is now called *Philosophy of Management*.).

5. P. Drucker (2002) *The Essential Drucker* (New York: Harper Business), 15.

6. F. Taylor (1903) *Shop Management* (New York: Harper and Row), 3.

7. G. Hamel (2007) *The Future of Management* (Boston, MA: Harvard Business School Press), 9.

8. Hamel (2007), 9.

9. For a detailed treatment of moral imagination as it relates to management, see P. Werhane (1999) *Moral Imagination and Management Decision-Making* (Oxford: Oxford University Press).

10. For a fuller treatment of the political, economic, financial, and systematic reasons for the 2008 crises, see the essays in (2009) *Critical Review*, 21: 2–3; for an account that focuses on epistemological and philosophical issues related to the 2008 financial crisis, see C. Dierksmeier (2011) "The Freedom–Responsibility Nexus in Management Philosophy and Business Ethics," *Journal of Business Ethics*, 101, 263–283.

11. S. Datar, et al. (2010) *Rethinking the MBA* (Boston: Harvard Business Press); A. Colby, et al. (2011) *Rethinking Undergraduate Business Education* (New Jersey: Jossey-Bass); H. Spitzeck, et al. (eds) (2009) *Humanism in Business* (Cambridge: Cambridge University Press); E. Von Kimakowitz, et al. (eds) (2011) *Humanistic Management in Practice* (New York: Palgrave Macmillan).

12. Servant leadership has been explored and defended for decades, especially by Robert Greenleaf and many others influenced by Greenleaf's vision of the leader as servant. For a classic expression of servant leadership, see R. Greenleaf (1977) *Servant Leadership: A Journey into the Nature of Legitimate Power and Greatness* (New York: Paulist Press). Also see www.greenleaf.org and www.spearscenter.org.

13. This claim is developed more fully in a book I coauthored with several colleagues: G. Beabout, et al. (2002) *Beyond Self-Interest: A Personalist Account of Human Action* (Lanham, MD: Rowman and Littlefield). In particular, see Chapter 2.

14. For treatments of the contributions of virtue ethics and the common good to management, see D. Koehn (1995) "A Role of Virtue Ethics in the Analysis of Business Practice," *Business Ethics Quarterly*, 5, 533–539; A. Sison, (2003) *The Moral Capital of Leaders: Why Virtue Matters* (Cheltenham, UK: Edward Elgar); and the special issue edited by A. Sison, E. Hartman, and J. Fontrodona, "Reviving Tradition: Virtue and the Common Good in Business and Management," (2012) *Business Ethics Quarterly* 22.

15. J. Lantos (1999) *Do We Still Need Doctors? A Physician's Personal Account of Practicing Medicine Today* (New York: Routledge).

16. J. Cornwall and M. Naughton (2008) *Bringing Your Business to Life: The Four Virtues that Will Help You Build a Better Business and a Better Life* (Ventura, CA: Regal).

17. C. Dierksmeier and D. Mele (2012) *Human Development in Business: Values and Humanistic Management in the Encyclical Caritas in Veritate* (New York: Palgrave Macmillan).
18. MacIntyre examines the character of the manager in Chapter 3 of his (1981) *After Virtue* (Notre Dame: University of Notre Dame Press). The three editions of *After Virtue* (1981, 1984, 2007), each uses the same pagination, though the second and third editions contain additional material. See also Utilitarianism and Cost–Benefit Analysis: An Essay on the Relevance of Moral Philosophy to Bureaucratic Theory" in K. Sayre (ed.) *Values in the Electric Power Industry* (Notre Dame: University of Notre Dame Press), 217–237; (1979) "Corporate Modernity and Moral Judgment: Are They Mutually Exclusive?" in K. E. Goodpaster and K. M. Sayre (eds) *Ethics and Problems of the 21st Century* (Notre Dame: University of Notre Dame Press), 122–135; (1982) "Why are the Problems of Business Ethics Insoluble" in B. Baumrin and B. Friedman (eds) *Moral Responsibility and the Professions* (New York: Haven Publishing), 99–107; (1984a) "Does Applied Ethics Rest on a Mistake?", *The Monist*, 67, 598–613; (1999b) "Social Structures and Their Threat to Moral Agency", *Philosophy*, 74, 311–329.

2 Moral Philosophy and the Manager

1. Joseph Sachs points out that ancient warriors, at least as depicted by Homer, also engaged in persuasive speaking. See the editor's "Introduction" in J. Sachs (2009) *Plato's Gorgias and Aristotle's Rhetoric: Translation, Glossary and Introductory Essay* (Newburyport, MA: Focus Publishing), 2–3.
2. Plato, *Theaetetus* 174. In general, the references that I make in this book to ancient and medieval texts do not rely on a specific translation. For that reason, I have provided the Stephanus pagination widely used in modern translations for references to Plato's dialogues, while I typically have drawn from (1961) *The Collected Dialogues of Plato* ed. E. Hamilton and H. Cairns (Princeton: Princeton University Press).
3. The conversation that Socrates has with Phaedrus about the nature of rhetoric occurs away from the crowds of Athens, in the shade of a tree along the river outside the city. See *Phaedrus* 229b.
4. The conversation that Plato records between Socrates and the famed rhetorician Gorgias occurs within the city, at the house of Callicles. Callicles is a man of the city, a property owner who admires Gorgias' promise that his expertise can yield increased money and power.
5. For summaries of business ethics as an academic field, see G. Enderle (1996) "Towards Business Ethics as an Academic Discipline," *Business Ethics Quarterly*, 6, 43–65; P. Werhane and R. Freeman (1999) "Business Ethics: The State of the Art," *International Journal of Management Review*, 1, 1–16; C. Cowton (2008) "On Setting the Agenda for Business Ethics Research," in C. Cowton and M. Haase (eds) *Trends in Business and Economic Ethics* (New York: Springer), 11–30.
6. R. Hare (1992) "One Philosopher's Approach to Business and Professional Ethics," *Business and Professional Ethics Journal*, 11, 3, 3–19, emphasis in the original.
7. Hare, 1992, 3.

8. For examples of moral philosophers in business ethics who see their task in similar terms, see R. DeGeorge (1982) *Business Ethics* (New York: MacMillan); M. Velasquez (1982) *Business Ethics: Concepts and Cases* (Englewood Cliffs, NJ: Prentice Hall); N. Bowie (1999) *Business Ethics: A Kantian Perspective* (Oxford: Blackwell); T. Donaldson and T.W. Dunfee (1999) *Ties that Bind: A Social Contracts Approach to Business Ethics* (Boston, MA: Harvard University Press). In contrast, for an approach to ethics and business management that places less emphasis on debates about principles and their application and more emphasis on character and culture, see K. Goodpaster (2006) *Conscience and Corporate Culture* (Malden, MA: Wiley-Blackwell).
9. R. Hare (1992), 17.
10. R. Hare (1992), 9.
11. R. Hare (1992), 19.
12. R. Hare (1992), 13.
13. G. Marino (2001) "Avoiding Moral Choices: Call in the Ethics Experts," *Commonweal*, March 23, 11–15.
14. R. Rorty (1979) *Philosophy and the Mirror of Nature* (Princeton, NJ: Princeton University Press), 365–372.
15. R. Rorty (1979), 370.
16. R. Rorty (1979), 370.
17. R. Rorty (1979), 372.
18. R. Rorty (1998) *Achieving Our Country* (Boston: Harvard University Press).
19. M. Horkheimer (1992, originally 1939) "The Social Function of Philosophy," in *Critical Theory. Selected Essays* (New York: Continuum), 264.
20. See J. Nicholas (2012) *Reason, Tradition, and the Good: MacIntyre's Tradition Constituted Reason and Frankfurt School Critical Theory* (Notre Dame, IN: University of Notre Dame Press).
21. I see as exemplars in this approach especially Socrates, Plato, Aristotle, and Kierkegaard. My argument draws from each of these.
22. P. Hadot (1995) *Philosophy as a Way of Life* trans. M. Chase (Oxford: Blackwell), 265.
23. A. Whitehead (1979) *Process and Reality* (New York: Free Press), 39.
24. G. Press (2007) *Plato: A Guide for the Perplexed* (London: Continuum), 5.
25. "If Plato had wanted to speak directly to the audience, to give his own views and his own arguments for them, the treatise form of writing was available to him, but he did not choose it." G. Press (2007), 6.
26. G. Press (2007), 55.
27. G. Press (2007), 67.
28. G. Press (2007), 67.
29. For a very helpful account of Plato's dialogues, see J. Sallis (1996) *Being and Logos: Reading the Platonic Dialogues*. Third edition (Bloomington, IN: Indiana University Press). For a chart summarizing a range of forms of life, from hunters and anglers to merchants, sophists, and the philosopher, see 470–471.

3   MacIntyre, Our Gadfly

1. From *Newsweek*, quoted on the back cover of the third edition of *After Virtue* (2007).

2. Quoted on the back cover of J. Horton and S. Mendus (eds) (1994) *After MacIntyre: Critical Perspectives on the Work of Alasdair MacIntyre* (Notre Dame, IN: University of Notre Dame Press).

3. S. Hauerwas (2007) "The Virtues of Alasdair MacIntyre," *First Things*, 37 October.

4. Quoted on the back cover of A. MacIntyre (1999a) *Dependent Rational Animals: Why Human Beings Need the Virtues* (Chicago: Open Court).

5. See the back cover of the Third Edition of *After Virtue*. Of course, the superlatives used to describe MacIntyre, displayed so prominently on the back cover of his books, may be little more than the standard process of marketing. If viewed this way, the irony is rich; the content of MacIntyre's books warns against the hollowness of consumer culture while the back covers of his books contain the tools of marketing to increase sales! The heaps of strong praise likely embarrass the professor in certain ways.

6. Plato, *Apology* 30e.

7. T. D'Andrea (2006) *Tradition, Rationality, and Virtue* (London: Ashgate), 397.

8. For critical perspectives on MacIntyre's interpretations of other thinkers, see J. Horton and S. Mendus (eds) (1994) and J. Davenport and A. Rudd (eds) (2001) *Kierkegaard After MacIntyre* (Chicago: Open Court). For critical perspectives on MacIntyre's treatment of the natural moral law, see L. Cunningham (ed.) (2009) *Intractable Disputes about the Natural Law* (Notre Dame, IN: University of Notre Dame); for essays more sympathetic with MacIntyre's contributions to moral and political philosophy, see P. Blackledge and K. Knight (eds) (2011) *Virtue and Politics: Alasdair MacIntyre's Revolutionary Aristotelianism* (Notre Dame, IN: University of Notre Dame Press).

9. For example, in his interview with Giovanna Borradori, MacIntyre concedes that the history that he provides in his *Short History of Ethics* is flawed (see K. Knight (ed.) (1998), 260), and on p. x of *Dependent Rational Animals*, MacIntyre concedes that the account of the virtues that he provided in *After Virtue* (along with his insistence that the virtues need not involve issues of metaphysical biology) was inadequate.

10. A number of helpful book-length works engage MacIntyre's work. In addition to Thomas D'Andrea (2006), see P. McMylor (1994) *Alasdair MacIntyre: Critic of Modernity* (New York: Routledge); B. Ballard (2000) *Understanding MacIntyre* (Lanham, MD: University Press of America); C. Lutz (2004) *Tradition in the Ethics of Alasdair MacIntyre: Relativism, Thomism, and Philosophy* (Lanham, MD: Lexington Books); and C. Lutz (2012) *Reading Alasdair MacIntyre's After Virtue* (London: Continuum).

11. J. Cornwell (2010) "MacIntyre on Money," *Prospect*, 176, 58–61.

12. A. MacIntyre (1981), especially Chapter 3, arguing that the bureaucratic manager is a contemporary embodiment of the philosophy of emotivism.

13. See A. MacIntyre (1977a), 217–237 (arguing that the cost–benefit analysis of the bureaucratic manager is utilitarian in character, is not value-neutral, and rests on the shortcomings and presuppositions of utilitarian practical reasoning); A. MacIntyre (1979a), 122–135 (arguing that corporations require executives to embody incompatible traits); A. MacIntyre (1979b) "Social Science Methodology as the Ideology of Bureacratic Authority," in M. J. Falco (ed.) *Through the Looking Glass: Epistemology and the Conduct of Enquiry. An Anthology* (Washington, DC: University Press of America), 42–58

(arguing that social scientific theorists and bureaucratic managers mask in similar ways their shared inability to predict social outcomes in a rational manner).

14. A. MacIntyre (1990a) *Three Rival Versions of Moral Inquiry: Encyclopedia, Geneaology, Tradition* (Notre Dame, IN: University of Notre Dame Press).

15. For a sobering and perhaps too dark account of the apparent decline of the influence of the "tradition" at Catholic universities, see J. Burtchaell (1998) *The Dying of the Light* (Grand Rapids: Eerdmans), 563–633.

16. It might help some readers to understand another feature of my formation. Many of my teachers held that the moral life is "caught" as much as it is "taught." In answer to Meno's question ("Whether virtue can be taught?"), my teachers would have given an answer that was qualified and subtle: learning to practice the virtues comes as much from *imitating* the example of those who are wise as it does from learning their arguments, although careful analytical thinking certainly is important. As Aristotle taught, the human being is "the most imitative of living creatures," (Aristotle, *Poetics*, 1448b7) and it is through imitation that we learn. (In general, the references that I make in this book to the writings of Aristotle do not rely on a specific translation. For that reason, I have provided the Bekker pagination widely used in modern translations for references to Plato's dialogues, while I typically have drawn from *The Basic Works of Aristotle*, edited by R. McKeon. New York: Random House, 1941.) The teachers I have in mind were influenced by the *Ratio Studiorum*, the 1599 Jesuit document that outlines a plan of studies that places special emphasis on Aristotle, Cicero, and St Thomas Aquinas. In the contemporary context, the traditional Jesuit curriculum has been modified significantly at most Jesuit schools, but many of the traditional elements remain even today. Of course, the period of my education – the 1970s and 1980s – was full of tumult and confusion in the broader culture, and this impact was felt on the campuses with which I am most familiar. As a student, I lived through "Animal House" food fights in the cafeteria, but I also sensed the tradition of the virtues. My adult life has been spent with many professors and colleagues who exuded the instruction of the *Ratio*: "Members of our Society shall expressly follow the teaching of St. Thomas... They should consider him their own teacher and make every effort to have their students hold him in the highest possible esteem." (A. P. Farrell 1970, S.J. (trans.) "The Jesuit *Ratio Studiorum* of 1599," available online at: http://www.bc.edu/bc_org/avp/ulib/digi/ratio/ratio1599.pdf. For a more recent translation with commentary, see C. Pavur (2005) *The Ratio Studiorum: The Official Plan for Jesuit Education* (The Institute of Jesuit Sources), available online at: http://www.slu.edu/colleges/AS/languages/classical/latin/tchmat/pedagogy/rs/rs1.html). While studying the texts of St Thomas and his teachers (especially Plato, Aristotle, and St Augustine), the aim is both to engage their arguments and to *imitate* their excellences. The moral philosopher who takes seriously the task of proposing models for imitation will face almost immediately a difficult challenge. Some in one's audience may not have firmly developed habits of intellectual and moral excellence. Those in whom the virtues are underdeveloped will not be disposed to perceive the acquisition of the virtues as personally desirable. For this reason, it is sometimes best for a teacher or writer seeking to build up virtue in one's student or reader (and in oneself) to proceed by way of indirection. Accordingly, many of my favorite writers

proceed with a literary and poetic sensibility as well as a subtle awareness of the dispositional tendencies of various readers. In addition to Plato, my favorite authors who employ this sort of indirection include St Augustine, Pascal, Soren Kierkegaard, and Walker Percy, among others.

17. A. MacIntyre (1981), 191.

18. MacIntyre provides a detailed account of the virtues in Chapters 10–17 of *After Virtue*, including a discussion that points to both the cardinal virtues (fortitude, temperance, justice, and wisdom) and the theological virtues (faith, hope, and love).

19. A. MacIntyre (1981), 162–163.

20. The "function argument" may be summarized as follows. 1) Goodness is the fulfillment of a thing's proper function. 2) A thing's proper function can be determined by identifying what makes it a specific kind of thing. 3) Rational activity makes the human animal specifically different from the other animals. So, goodness for a human being consists in acquiring those habits of intellect and of character that make for a life of excellent rational activity; in other words, the happy life, according to Aristotle, is the life of intellectual and moral virtue. Aristotle, *Nicomachean Ethics*, 1197b25–1198a18. As mentioned previously, my references to the writings of Aristotle do not typically rely on a specific translation. I have benefitted from reading many translations of the *Nicomachean Ethics*, and I have a particular fondness for the translation of Christopher Rowe, Oxford: Oxford University Press, 2002.

21. Aristotle, *Nicomachean Ethics*, 1094a1–1094a2.

22. Aristotle, *Nicomachean Ethics*, 1094a3.

23. The story is found in Chapter 14 of *After Virtue*. David Solomon, during a panel presentation at the University College Dublin on March 6, 2009, suggested that a 100 years from now, philosophers will continue to discuss MacIntyre's story of the chess-playing child. In a private conversation on that weekend, Solomon (in his role as the Director of the Center for Ethics and Culture at the University of Notre Dame where MacIntyre held a chair) stated to me that MacIntyre has said on multiple occasions that he considers this to be his own most important contribution to moral philosophy.

24. A. MacIntyre (1981), 188.

25. A. MacIntyre (1981), 188.

26. A. MacIntyre (1981), 188.

27. A. MacIntyre (1981), 188.

28. A. MacIntyre (1981), 191.

29. In the Postscript to the Second Edition of *After Virtue*, MacIntyre clarifies this example further in response to objections raised by Samuel Scheffler. See pp. 272–275.

30. MacIntyre outlines and responds to several challenges in his Postscript to the Second Edition of *After Virtue* (1984). For a further sample of challenges, see the essays collected in the J. Horton and S. Mendus (eds) (1994).

31. See A. MacIntyre (1984) "Postscript to the Second Edition," in *After Virtue*, 273–278. Also see J. Haldane, "MacIntyre's Thomist Revival: What Next?" in J. Horton and S. Mendus (eds) (1994) *After MacIntyre*, especially pp. 96–99.

32. MacIntyre uses Eichmann as an example of the moral deficiency of bureaucratic rationality, so it is somewhat ironic that MacIntyre's virtue ethics has

been viewed as susceptible to a similar criticism. See A. MacIntyre (1997) *A Short History of Ethics* (London: Routledge), 133.

33. It is a curiosity that MacIntyre's virtue ethic has seemed susceptible to an objection based on the example of Eichmann because, as we will see, MacIntyre used Eichmann as an example both before and after the publication of *After Virtue*. See MacIntyre, *A Short History of Ethics*, 207–208, and A. MacIntyre (1999b) "Social Structures and Their Threat to Moral Agency," *Philosophy*, 74, 311ff.

34. I see two main responses that MacIntyre offers, prior to *Dependent Rational Animals*. In both *Whose Justice? Which Rationality?* and *Three Rival Versions*, MacIntyre argues that the Aristotelian–Thomistic tradition has the resources to engage with and consider objections from rival moral traditions in a way that its main competitor traditions lack. The other strategy is to show that virtue ethics is accompanied by, and part of, the natural law tradition, and thus to emphasize first principles (which are not relative in themselves, although there is an element of relativity in the way that the first principles of the natural law are known by and appropriated by each human person). See for example the Marquette Aquinas lecture, A. MacIntyre (1990b) *First Principles, Final Ends, and Contemporary Philosophical Issues* (Milwaukee, WI: Marquette University Press).

35. A. MacIntyre (1999a), x.
36. See the Prologue to the Third Edition of *After Virtue*, especially pp. x–xi.
37. A. MacIntyre (2007) "Prologue to the Third Edition," in *After Virtue*, ix.

4 The Manager as Office Executive: Emotivism Embodied in a Character

1. A. MacIntyre (1981), 25.
2. Cited by G. Moore (2008), 483–511. Moore is citing S. Hauerwas (2001) *The Hauerwas Reader* (Durham, NC: Duke University Press), 214.
3. A. MacIntyre (1981), 27.
4. "The 'administrative man' takes his place alongside the classical 'economic man.'" H. Simon (1947) *Administrative Behavior: A Study of Decision-Making Processes in Administrative Organization*, (New York: Macmillan), 39.
5. H. Simon (1955) "A Behavioral Model of Rational Choice," *Quarterly Journal of Economics*, 69, 99–118.
6. S. Robbins, et al. (2005) *Management*, Eighth edition (Englewood Cliffs, NJ: Prentice Hall), 19.
7. L. Mises (1944) *Bureaucracy* (New Haven, CT: Yale University Press).
8. For Mises, the manager-as-entrepreneur is a sort of hero, completely distinct from the manager-as-bureaucrat.
9. Mises (1944), 14 (From the Introduction, "The Opprobrious Connotation of the Term Bureaucracy").
10. Mises (1944), 14.
11. T. D'Andrea (2006), xvii.
12. These have been collected in P. Blackledge and N. Davidson (eds) (2006) *Alasdair MacIntyre's Engagement with Marxism* (Leiden: Brill).

13. MacIntyre (1981), *After Virtue*, 252.
14. *Matthew* 25:37–40, New American Bible, Revised Edition.
15. I have drawn this helpful five-point summary from P. McMylor (1994), 7. Also see D'Andrea (2006), 88.
16. D'Andrea (2006) summarizes these three. See p. 89.
17. A. MacIntyre (1984b) *Marxism and Christianity* (Notre Dame, IN: University of Notre Dame), 143.
18. MacIntyre (1984b), 102.
19. See the collection of MacIntyre's Marxists writings, which contains a very helpful overview essay: P. Blackledge and N. Davidson (eds) (2006).
20. A. MacIntyre (1958–1959) "Notes from the Moral Wilderness," *The New Reasoner*, 7 and 8; reprinted in K. Knight (1998), 31–49.
21. MacIntyre (1984b), 101.
22. MacIntyre (1984b), 139.
23. According to MacIntyre (1984b), this deficiency in Marxism has "weakened understanding of the bureaucratic neo-capitalism of the West," 139.
24. A. MacIntyre (1994) "A Partial Response to My Critics," in J. Horton and S. Mendus (eds) *After MacIntyre* (Notre Dame: University of Notre Dame Press), 285.
25. MacIntyre (1994), 285.
26. MacIntyre (1984b), 41.
27. From the Preface of MacIntyre (1984b), ix.
28. A. MacIntyre (1970) *Herbert Marcuse* (New York, Viking Press), 7.
29. MacIntyre (1984b), 124.
30. MacIntyre (1984b), 124.
31. MacIntyre (1981), 11.
32. MacIntyre (1981), 12.
33. A. J. Ayer (1936) *Language, Truth, and Logic* (New York: Dover), 107.
34. D'Andrea (2006), 3.
35. MacIntyre (1981), 21.
36. MacIntyre (1981), 21.
37. MacIntyre (1981), 23.
38. S. Hauerwas (2007), 35–40.
39. MacIntyre (1981), 23.
40. MacIntyre (1981), 23.
41. MacIntyre (1981), 23.
42. MacIntyre (1981), 24.
43. MacIntyre (1981), 25.
44. MacIntyre (1981), 25.
45. MacIntyre (1981), 21.
46. See M. Weber (1947) *The Theory of Social and Economic Organization*, trans. A. M. Henderson and T. Parsons (New York: The Free Press).
47. G. Hamel (2007), 14.
48. See T. Parsons' introductory essay, "Weber's Economic Sociology," in M. Weber (1947).
49. M. Weber (1997) *The Methodology of the Social Sciences*, in E. A. Shils and H. A. Finch (trans. and eds) (New York: Free Press), 88.
50. Weber (1947), 341–358.

51. Weber (1947), 328.
52. Weber (1947), 358–363.
53. Weber (1947), 328.
54. Weber (1947), 364.
55. Weber (1947), 331–332.
56. Weber (1947), 333–334.
57. Weber (1947), 337.
58. Weber (1947), 338.
59. Weber (1947), 338.
60. M. Friedman (1970), 122–126. For a parallel treatment of Friedman's concept of the manager, see M. Calkins and J. B. Wight (2008) "The Ethical Lacunae in Friedman's Concept of the Manager," *The Journal of Markets and Morality*, 11, 2, 221–238.
61. Friedman (1970), 122.

5 Strengths and Weaknesses of Treating the Manager as a Stock Character

1. A. MacIntyre (1981), 27.
2. MacIntyre (1981) explains that he has chosen the word character "precisely because of the way it links dramatic and moral associations" (p. 27).
3. A. MacIntyre (1981), 28.
4. A. MacIntyre (1981), 27 ff.
5. Aristotle introduces many of these characters in the *Nicomachean Ethics*, Book II, 1107a32ff., and he describes them more fully especially in the second half of Book III and throughout Book IV and beyond. Once this way of thinking of stock characters comes into focus, it becomes apparent that this approach to character permeates Aristotle's writing, including for example his *Rhetoric* (where speakers are encouraged to think of their audiences in terms of various stock characters) and even in the *History of Animals* where Aristotle distinguishes between species of animals in part by making reference to various character types.
6. Aristotle, *Nicomachean Ethics* 1123b1.
7. For a contemporary example, see V. Schmidt (2001) *45 Master Characters: Mythic Models for Creating Original Characters* (Cincinnati, OH: Writer's Digest Books).
8. See L. Cooper (2009) *An Aristotelian Theory of Comedy: With an Adaptation of the Poetics, and a Translation of the "Tractatus Coislinianus"* (Ithaca, NY: Cornell University Press). See especially p. 226: "The characters of comedy are 1) the buffoonish, 2) the ironical, and 3) those of the impostor." Aristotle describes these three characters, the *alazôn* (the boaster) and the *eirôn* (the self-deprecator), and the *bômolochus* (the buffoon), in the *Nicomachean Ethics*, Book IV, Chapters 7 and 8. For a discussion of the *alazôn* and the *eirôn*, see P. W. Gooch (1987) "Socratic Irony and Aristotle's 'Eiron': Some Puzzles," *Phoenix*, 41, 2, 95–104.
9. Theophrastus (2003) *Characters*, J. Rusten and I. C. Cunningham (eds and trans.), Third Edition (London: Loeb Classical Library).

10. For the influence of Theophrastus on Chaucer's *Canterbury Tales*, see G. Chaucer and W. Skeat (eds) (1912) *The Complete Works of Geoffrey Chaucer*, Volume 5 (London: Oxford University Press), 298, note 235. For the influence of Theophrastus on Sir Thomas Overbury, see T. Overbury (1614) *New and Choise Characters, of Seuerall Authors* (London: Thomas Creede).
11. F. P. Wilson (1969) *The English Drama, 1485–1585* (Oxford: Oxford University Press), 59.
12. MacIntyre wants to show us that the manager is a hollow character. The manager is a villain in a sense quite distinct from many modern antiheroes, diabolical agents who willfully use their intelligence and power to self-consciously choose a path of darkness and vice.
13. M. Weber (1947), 89.
14. M. Weber (1947), 88.
15. M. Weber (1947), 89.
16. M. Weber (1947), 110.
17. M. Weber (1947), 110.
18. M. Weber (1947), 329.
19. M. Weber (1947), 328.
20. A. MacIntyre (1981), 31–32.
21. A. MacIntyre (2008) "How Aristotelianism Can Become Revolutionary: Ethics, Resistance, and Utopia," *Philosophy of Management*, 7, 1, 3.
22. MacIntyre (1981) presents this argument in Chapter 15, especially pp. 207–211.
23. A. MacIntyre (1981), 213.
24. A. MacIntyre (1981), 216.
25. A. MacIntyre (1981), 216.
26. A. MacIntyre (1981), 216.
27. A. MacIntyre (1981), 222.
28. A. MacIntyre (1981), 219.
29. K. Brewer (1997), 826.
30. T. Whetstone (2003) "The Language of Managerial Excellence: Virtues as Understood and Applied," *Journal of Business Ethics*, 44, 4, 343–357.
31. Whetstone (2003), 344.
32. R. Bellah, et al. (2007) *Habits of the Heart: Individualism and Commitment in American Life*, Third Edition (Berkeley, CA: University of California Press).
33. A half dozen years after the publication of *Habits*, I asked Bellah (while he was making a presentation at Washington University in Saint Louis) about these four people – and about how their lives have changed since the publication of his book. He spoke about them, and especially about Wayne Bauer, with genuine concern, treating them not as "mere types," but with a kind of cordiality due fellow citizens.
34. R. Bellah, et al. (2007), Chapter 1.
35. A. MacIntyre (1981), 31. MacIntyre advances this criticism against "Neo-Weberian organization theorists and the heirs of the Frankfurt School," but his own descriptions of the character of the manager might be susceptible to the same criticism.
36. Writing in the 1790s, Friedrich Schiller composed a series of letters on aesthetic education in which he decried the empty formalism of Kant's moral philosophy. Schiller was disenchanted with the outcomes of both

Kant's emphasis on treating humans as rational ends and the noble ideals of the French Revolution. Each promised an age of enlightenment, but Schiller saw a tendency in each to collapse into violent revolution without a stable social structure. Schiller argued that the problem lies at the level of the human heart. Kant seemed to think that formal rational argumentation was adequate as a basis for the moral life; Schiller argued that focusing on abstract argumentation ignores the need to educate human passions and appetites. Drawing from the Greeks, Schiller argued that art and literature have the noble task of shaping appetite and emotion, of transforming the given inclinations of human nature into those befitting a rational person. See F. Schiller (2004) *On the Aesthetic Education of Man*, trans. R. Snell (New York: Dover Publications), especially the third letter. Also see F. C. Beiser (2005) *Schiller as Philosopher: A Re-Examination* (Oxford: Oxford University Press), especially pp. 129 ff. For that reason, Schiller devoted himself not only to providing an account of the role of art and literature in building up the moral life, but also to the task of composing literary works. To elevate the moral character of a people, Schiller suggested that one must first touch their souls with beauty.
37. V. Schmidt (2001), 8.
38. V. Schmidt (2001), 9.
39. V. Schmidt (2001), 9.
40. Aristotle, *Poetics*, Chapter 10.
41. Aristotle, *Poetics*, Chapter 11.
42. M. Gladwell (2008) *Outliers: The Story of Success* (New York: Little Brown).
43. For examples, see H. Brody (2002) *Stories of Sickness*, Second Edition (Oxford: Oxford University Press); R. Charon and M. Montello (2002) *Stories Matter: The Role of Narrative in Medical Ethics* (New York: Routledge); K. M. Hunter (1993) *Doctor's Stories* (Princeton, NJ: Princeton University Press); T. Chambers (1999) *The Fiction of Bioethics* (New York: Routledge).
44. Authors whose stories involve physicians and health care workers as characters are seemingly without limit, from early English authors (Chaucer, Shakespeare), Russian writers (Dostoevsky, Tolstoy, Chekhov), Irish and British writers (Coleridge, Dickens, Joyce), writers on the continent (Kafka, Flaubert, Balzac), women writers (Jane Austen, Emily Bronte, George Eliot), American writers (Ernest Hemingway, Walker Percy), and non-Western writers (Salmon Rushdie, Sawako Ariyoshi). For more, see N. Cousins (1982) *The Physician in Literature* (Philadelphia, PA: WB Saunders); S. Posen (2005) *The Doctor in Literature: Satisfaction of Disappointment?* (Oxford: Oxford University Press); R. Reynolds and J. Stone (2010) *On Doctoring*, Third Edition (New York: Simon & Schuster); R. S. Downie (2000) *The Healing Arts* (Oxford: Oxford University Press); J. Salinsky (2004) *Medicine and Literature: The Doctor's Companion to the Classics* (Oxford: Radcliffe Medical Press); C. Helman (2003) *Doctors and Patients: An Anthology* (Oxford: Radcliffe Medical Press).
45. For an excellent description of this phenomenon tracing the transformation from the engagement in a productive activity for the sake of an outcome to a transformed motivation where the goods internal to the activity inform in a much deeper way, see E. Garver (1984) "Aristotle's Genealogy of Morals," *Philosophy and Phenomenological Research*, 44, 4, 471–492.
46. S. Lewis (1922) *Babbitt* (New York: Grosset & Dunlap), 29.

47. B. Burrough and J. Helyar (2009) *Barbarians at the Gate: The Fall of RJR Nabisco* (New York: HarperBusiness).

48. B. McLean and P. Elkind (2004) *The Smartest Guys in the Room: The Amazing Rise and Scandalous Fall of Enron* (New York: Penguin).

49. My colleague at Saint Louis University, Vincent Casaregola, teaches a course in which he investigates the way that the business sector has been portrayed in cinema. He focuses on the following films: *Metropolis, Modern Times, You Can't Take It With You, Meet John Doe, Citizen Kane, Death of a Salesman, Executive Suite, The Man in the Grey Flannel Suit, Asphalt Jungle, The Desk Set, The Apartment, The Music Man, How to Succeed in Business without Really Trying, Catch-22, Network, Tucker, Save the Tiger, Wall Street, Glengarry, Glen Ross, The Hudsucker Proxy, Working Girl, The Smartest Guys in the Room,* and *Powaqqatsi.*

50. One could also point to the fiction of Ayn Rand for examples of works of literature with business managers as protagonists. See R. Beadle (2008a) "Rand and MacIntyre on Moral Agency," *The Journal of Ayn Rand Studies,* 9, 2, 221–243. Also, one might explore: T. Prindle (trans. and ed.) (1991) *Made in Japan: And Other Japanese Business Novels* (New York: Sharpe); S. M. Puffer (2004) *International Management: Insights from Fiction and Practice* (New York: Sharpe). In addition, one might consider the fictional character Binx Bolling, the protagonist in Walker Percy's novel, *The Moviegoer.* Binx is a manager at a New Orleans branch office of a brokerage firm. The novel is a beautifully told story of Binx's transformation from detached observer to engaged participant. In his moment of transformation, Binx decides to abandon his life as a "moviegoer" in which life is a collection of diversions, a life where females are mere objects for entertainment. Turning from the hollowness of that life, Binx decides to become married. In the novel's epilogue, the reader is forced to imagine a "missing chapter" where Binx walks away from his job as a manager to become a husband and enroll in medical school. Does Percy's story suggest that it is impossible to live a meaningful life that is morally and spiritually significant while working as a manager?

51. J. Badaracco (2006) *Questions of Character: Illuminating the Heart of Leadership Through Literature* (Boston, MA: Harvard Business Review Press), 3. Badaracco begins his book by describing a class session in which he assigned executives to read a little-known short story by Joseph Conrad titled "The Secret Sharer." It is the tale of a sea captain's first voyage and his decision to let a stranger come on board after the man tells him that he has escaped from another ship where he was unjustly accused of murder. Conrad's short story, according to Badaracco, encourages his students to enter into moral reflection in a wide-ranging conversation. "Was the new captain ready to take on his responsibilities? What did his actions reveal about his character? How do leaders learn from their mistakes?" According to Badaracco, he has used this approach successfully for a decade in the business school at Harvard. What is the secret to his success? "The executives had been induced to treat a work of fiction like a business school case study." Even more, Badaracco claims that literature has the power to pull people into the story so they can reflect upon their roles as business leaders and upon their lives. However, most of the characters Badaracco uses as examples are not business executives. In addition to the short story by Conrad, he uses Chinua Achebe's *Things Fall Apart,* Allan Gurganu's

"Blessed Assurance: A Moral Tale," Louis Auchincloss's *I Come as a Thief,* Robert Bolt's *A Man for All Seasons,* and Sophocles' *Antigone.* Each of these stories has well-drawn characters with a strong character arc – but none of them is a manager.

52. Dennis Samson suggested this to me during a delightful conversation at a conference at Baylor University in 2008.
53. L. Tolstoy, Constance Garnett (trans.) (2003) *Anna Karenina* (New York: Barnes and Noble), 729–730. I am grateful to my colleague, David Muphy, for our discussions of this text and his knowledge of Russian literature and the life of virtue.
54. L. Tolstoy (2003), 733.
55. L. Tolstoy (2003), 734.
56. One might object that it is not his role as manager that brings about Levin's transformation, or that the kind of manager that Levin has become is not at all the same as the Weberian bureaucrat. Levin recognized that he needs to take economic considerations into account when hiring laborers, but the transformed Levin was also aware that he must *not* hire people at unduly low wages "even though he knew that it was very profitable" (Tolstoy [2003], 731). He learned that concerns of economic viability and profit were part of a good life, not the whole of it.
57. L. Tolstoy (2003), 730.

6 Plot and Perspective: Character Traits and Their Cultivation

1. In addition to MacIntyre's contribution to the revival of virtue ethics in the world of English language professional academic philosophy, Elizabeth Anscombe's famous 1958 essay, "Modern Moral Philosophy," *Philosophy,* 33, 1–19, is rightly considered groundbreaking. In addition to the work of MacIntyre, other works in this movement include P. Geach (1977) *The Virtues* (Cambridge: Cambridge University Press); P. Foot (1978) *Virtues and Vices* (Oxford: Blackwell); M. Slote (1992) *From Morality to Virtue* (Oxford: Oxford University Press); R. Hursthouse (1999) *On Virtue Ethics* (Oxford: Oxford University Press). Philosophers who have argued that virtue ethics is a helpful way to approach business include R. Solomon (1992) *Ethics and Excellence: Cooperation and Integrity in Business* (Oxford: Oxford University Press); D. Koehn (1995), 533–539; A. Sison (2003). See also the April 2012 special edition of *Business Ethics Quarterly,* "Reviving Tradition: Virtue and the Common Good in Business and Management." As noted previously, there is a lively discussion applying MacIntyre's virtue ethics to business corporations. For example, see G. Moore (2005a) "Corporate Character: Modern Virtue Ethics and the Virtuous Corporation," *Business Ethics Quarterly* 15:4, 659–685.
2. A. MacIntyre (1981), 204.
3. See Chapter 3.
4. Aristotle, *Nicomachean Ethics* 1105b19–1105b21.
5. Aristotle, *Nicomachean Ethics* 1105b18–1105b 29.
6. Thomas Aquinas, *Summa Theologiae* I–II, trans. Fathers of the English Dominican Province (New York: Benziger Brothers), 49, 1.

7. Aristotle, *Categories* 8b27–8b32.
8. Aristotle, *Categories* 8b27.
9. As noted in Chapter 3 earlier, MacIntyre provides in *After Virtue* a three-stage account of the virtues; he adds a fourth element in *Dependent Rational Animals*.
10. A. MacIntyre (1981), 162–163.
11. A. MacIntyre (1999a), p. x; A. MacIntyre (2007) *After Virtue*, Third Edition (Notre Dame, IN: University of Notre Dame Press), p. xi.
12. A. MacIntyre (1981), 191.
13. A. MacIntyre (1981), 219.
14. A. MacIntyre (1981), 223.
15. Aristotle, *Categories* 9b35.
16. See for example M. Rothbart (2007) "Temperament, Development, and Personality," *Current Directions in Psychological Science*, 16:4, 207–212.
17. M. Rothbart (2007), 207.
18. Rothbart's article provides an overview of the contemporary literature from psychology on temperament.
19. The Meyers-Briggs typology is a popular and widely used account of various deep-seated traits that are given, not acquired. See I. Briggs-Meyers (1995) *Gifts Differing: Understanding Personality Type* (Palo Alto, CA: Davies-Black).
20. Aristotle, *Nicomachean Ethics* 1103a33.
21. Aristotle, *Nicomachean Ethics* 1103b15–1103b18.
22. Aristotle, *Poetics* 1448b8.
23. A. MacIntyre (1981), 31–32.
24. A. MacIntyre (1981), 217.
25. A. MacIntyre (1981), 216.
26. A. MacIntyre (1990a), 60.
27. Plato (1961), *Meno* 70a.
28. See especially *Meno* 86c–86d.
29. Contemporary personalist authors have called this openness the trait of "active receptivity." Norris Clarke has described this character trait as a welcoming openness. Normally, when we think of receiving, it involves a lack or an emptiness; a cup is able to receive liquid because it is empty. But the virtue of active receptivity is a fullness by which one hospitably receives the gift of another. N. Clarke (1993) *Person and Being* (Milwaukee, WI: Marquette University Press). See especially pp. 20–24 and pp. 82–93. Clarke gives credit in part to Hans Urs von Balthasar for his insights about "active receptivity." For further discussion of the theme of "active receptivity," see D. Schindler (1993) "Norris Clarke on Person, Being, and St. Thomas," *Communio*, 20, 580–598. Schindler's discussion of active receptivity is developed more fully in D. Schindler (1996) *Heart of the World, Center of the Church: Communio Ecclesiology, Liberalism, and Liberation* (Grand Rapids: Eerdman's). Also see G. Beabout (2007) "The Silent Lily and Bird as Exemplars of the Virtue of Active Receptivity," in R. Perkins (ed.) *Without Authority: International Kierkegaard Commentary*, Volume 18 (Macon, GA: Mercer University Press), 127–146.
30. Thomas Aquinas, *Summa Theologiae*, I–II, see questions 52, 121, and 139. In general, the references that I make in this book to the work of Thomas Aquinas do not rely on a specific translation. For that reason, I have used a widely used notation procedure to provide references to the *Summa Theologiae*

of Thomas Aquinas; I have typically relied upon the translation of the Fathers of the English Dominican Province, New York: Benziger Brothers, 1948.
31. Thomas Aquinas, *Summa Theologiae*, I–II, 139, 1.
32. Thomas Aquinas, *Summa Theologiae*, I–II, 139, 1.
33. See Aristotle, *Nicomachean Ethics* Book VI, Chapter 13, and Thomas Aquinas' *Commentary on the Nicomachean Ethics*, Book VI, Lecture ##1275–1288.
34. Plato follows this pattern in the *Republic*, and Aristotle follows the same pattern in the *Nicomachean Ethics*, moving from the purgation of vices, the development of moral virtues, and then the development of intellectual virtue, especially wisdom with regard to human action.
35. In later chapters, I examine more deeply the complicated relationship between intellectual excellence (especially knowing how to act) and the character excellences (especially the possession of one's desires and passions such that they are well ordered), especially in light of Book VI of Aristotle's *Nicomachean Ethics*.
36. See R. Bodéüs (1993) *The Political Dimensions of Aristotle's Ethics* trans. J. Garrett (Albany: State University of New York Press), especially Chapter 5, "The Audience of the Political Discourses," 97–122.
37. For a thoughtful reflection on athletics and the development of virtue, see M. Edmundson (2012) "Do Sports Build Character or Damage It?" *The Chronicle of Higher Education*. Retrieved from http://chronicle.com/article/Do-Sports-Build-Character-or/130286/
38. A. MacIntyre (1981), 26.
39. J. Cornwell (2010), 58.

7 The Setting: Institutional Social Structures, Success, and Excellence

1. This lecture was published as the 11th essay in A. MacIntyre (2006a) *Ethics and Politics, Selected Essays, Volume 2* (Cambridge: Cambridge University Press), 186–204. All references are to this published version. It originally appeared in MacIntyre (1999b).
2. A. MacIntyre (1999b), 311.
3. H. Arendt (1992) *Eichmann in Jerusalem: A Report on the Banality of Evil* (New York: Penguin). This is not the first time that MacIntyre had drawn on the Eichmann case. In 1966 (just a few years after Eichmann's trial and Arendt's description in her book), MacIntyre published his *Short History of Ethics*. MacIntyre voiced then a criticism of "specialists such as Eichmann." He wrote, "Whether the cargo was sheep or Jews, whether points X and Y were farm and butcher's slaughterhouse or ghetto and gas chamber was no concern." A. MacIntyre (1966) *A Short History of Ethics* (New York: Macmillan).
4. A. MacIntyre (1999b), 314.
5. A. MacIntyre (1999b), 311.
6. These examples refer to thought experiments widely discussed in the literature of professional philosophers who work in the analytic tradition.
7. H. Arendt (1992), 287.
8. C. Taylor (1989) *Sources of the Self: The Making of the Modern Identity* (Harvard, MA: Harvard University Press); C. Taylor (2007) *A Secular Age* (Harvard, MA: Harvard University Press).

9. A. MacIntyre (1981), 31–32.
10. D. Blagg and S. Young (2001) "What Makes a Good Leader?" *Harvard Business School Bulletin* (available at: <www.alumni.hbs.edu/bulletin/2001/february/leader.html>, accessed 5 May 2013.).
11. H. Fayol (1916) C. Storrs (trans.) (1949) *General and Industrial Management* (London: Sir Isaac Pitman and Sons).
12. For examples of management textbooks reproduced in multiple editions that borrow their basic framework from Fayol, see S. Robbins and M. Coulter (2011) *Management* (Saddle River, NJ: Prentice Hall); R. Daft (2011) *Management* (Mason, OH: Southwestern).
13. H. Mintzberg (1973) *The Nature of Managerial Work* (New York: Harper & Row), 93–94.
14. H. Mintzberg (2009) *Managing* (San Francisco, CA: Berrett-Koehler Publishers).
15. For examples, see S. Covey (1989) *Seven Habits of Highly Effective People Management: Traits of Successful Business Leaders* (New York: Free Press); L. Segil (2002) *Ten Essential Traits for Managers* (Somerset, NJ: Wiley); G. Kaupins (2006) "The Characteristics and Traits of Successful Managers and Supervisors," *Academy of Business and Public Administration Proceedings*, Dallas, TX, April; D. Amaral-Phillips (2001) "Traits of Successful Managers" (available at: <http://www2.ca.uky.edu/afsdairy-files/extension/nutrition/Traits_of_Successful_Managers.pdf>, accessed on May 5, 2013.).
16. In particular, the concern with (and debate about) soft skills was sparked by Daniel Goleman's 1995 best seller, *Emotional Intelligence*. Originally written to persuade educators about the effectiveness and importance of school-based social and emotional learning programs, Goleman discovered that he had a larger audience in business managers quite interested in what he had to say about the importance of "soft skills" for success. So, he followed up his best seller on emotional intelligence with a book titled *Working with Emotional Intelligence* that he aimed at an audience of managers. In that book, he tells his readers about a "new yardstick" being used by organizations in hiring and promotion decisions. He claims that there is research that distills "with unprecedented precision which qualities mark a star performer." D. Goleman (2000) *Working with Emotional Intelligence* (New York: Bantam), 3.
17. In his popular best seller, Covey describes the qualities needed to be "highly effective" both in terms of "habits" and in terms of "character traits": S. Covey (1989) *Seven Habits of Highly Effective People* (New York: Free Press) especially 21–22, 217, and 219.
18. MacIntyre's definition of a social practice is widely discussed: "By a 'practice' I am going to mean any coherent and complex form of socially established co-operative human activity through which goods internal to that form of activity are realized in the course of trying to achieve those standards of excellence which are appropriate to, and partially definitive of, that form of activity, with the result that human powers to achieve excellence, and human conceptions of the ends and goods involved, are systematically extended'" (*After Virtue* 187). This definition is stipulative; he claims it "does not completely agree with current ordinary usage" including his "own previous use" of the word (187). MacIntyre's definition has become widely quoted and debated in the scholarly literature. See D. Miller (1994) "Virtues,

Practices, and Justice" in J. Horton and S. Mendus (eds) *After MacIntyre* (Notre Dame, IN: University of Notre Dame Press); R. Keat (2000) *Cultural Goods and the Limits of the Market* (New York: Palgrave Macmillan). In order to explain his stipulative definition, MacIntyre begins by listing examples and then ruling some out while including others. Tic-tac-toe is not a practice; presumably it is not complicated enough. Football, architecture, and farming are practices, but MacIntyre rules out activities that are merely parts of those practices: throwing a football with skill, brick-laying and turnip-planting. In response, scholars in a range of disciplines and professions have debated various activities. See D. Sellman (2000) "Alasdair MacIntyre and the Professional Practice of Nursing," *Nursing Philosophy* 1, 26–33; N. Noddings (2003) "Is Teaching a Practice?," *Journal of Philosophy of Education*, 37, 2, 241–251; J. Dunne (2003) "Arguing for Teaching as a Practice: A Reply to Alasdair MacIntyre," *Journal of Philosophy of Education* 37, 2, 353–369; E. B. Lambeth (1990) "Waiting for a New St. Benedict: Alasdair MacIntyre and the Theory and Practice of Journalism," *Journal of Mass Media Ethics*, 5, 2, 75–87; K. Balstad Brewer (1997); R. Beadle (2008a) "Why Business Cannot Be a Practice," *Analyse und Kritik*, 30, 1, 227–241; Beadle is responding especially to G. Moore (2001) "On the Implications of the Practice–Institution Distinction: MacIntyre and the Application of Modern Virtue Ethics to Business," *Business Ethics Quarterly*, 12, 1, 483–511. MacIntyre is not *primarily* interested in questions about whether or not some activity is (or is not) a practice. Even in his comments about teaching not being a practice, MacIntyre's central point is that teachers should see their task as helping to initiate their students into a discipline. "The teacher should think of her or himself as a mathematician, a reader of poetry, a historian or whatever, engaged in communicating craft and knowledge to apprentices" (A. MacIntyre and J. Dunne [2002] "Alasdair MacIntyre on Education: In Dialogue with Joseph Dunne," *Journal of Philosophy of Education*, 36, 1, 1–19). In *After Virtue*, he states explicitly that he wants to steer away from such debates: "the question of the precise range of practices is not at this stage of the first importance" (188).MacIntyre does not provide a history of the notion of a practice, and it is not always clear how MacIntyre's stipulative definition both draws from and departs from the way other thinkers, especially Aristotle and Karl Marx, used this notion. Kelvin Knight provides a very helpful account of MacIntyre's understanding of practices and institutions in K. Knight (2007) *Aristotelian Philosophy: Ethics and Politics from Aristotle to MacIntyre* (Cambridge: Polity), especially pp. 156–160. MacIntyre does not invoke Karl Marx often in *After Virtue*. While MacIntyre does make mention of Marx's *Theses on Feuerbach* on p. 84, he does not do so when he explains what he means by a practice. The case was different in MacIntyre's earlier writings. For example, *Marxism and Christianity* includes a chapter titled, "From Philosophy to Practice: Marx." So, it is sensible that one might turn to Marx to deepen one's understanding of MacIntyre's notion of practice.Karl Marx, writing in a bold and compact style, began his short essay on Feuerbach with this critique: "The main deficiency, up to now, in all materialism – including that of Feuerbach – is that the external object, reality and sensibility are conceived only in the form of the object and of our contemplation of it, rather than as sensuous human activity and as practice – as something non-subjective" (K. Marx, "Eleven Theses on Feuerbach." Thesis 1. Translated by Carl Manchester. Available at www. carlmanchester.net/marx/index.html.) Marx goes on to object that Feuerbach and others have not gone far enough to emphasize concrete social practices. "The question whether objective truth can be attributed to human thinking is not a question of theory but a practical question." Marx complains that when thinking is "isolated from practice," then the pursuit of truth devolves into controversies and debates that are "purely scholastic" (Karl Marx, "Eleven Theses on Feuerbach." Thesis 2). Marx famously concludes, "Philosophers have only interpreted the world in different ways. What is crucial, however, is to change it" Karl Marx, "Eleven Theses on Feuerbach." Thesis 11). MacIntyre learned from Marx to engage in philosophy while being attentive to concrete social practices. Just as Marx was critical of his contemporaries for engaging in philosophizing that resulted in pointless academic abstractions, MacIntyre's turn to social practices and a concrete social context is part of his criticism of a tendency in professional philosophy toward disengaged abstractions.Of course, Marx draws this concern with *praxis* in part from Aristotle, so it should not be surprising that there is an Aristotelian backdrop to MacIntyre's notion of practice. However, when we turn to the texts of Aristotle, we notice that he used the term *praxis* in a way that is significantly narrower than MacIntyre's notion of a practice. Aristotle, within his account of intellectual virtues, distinguished between three kinds of knowing: *theoria*, *praxis*, and *techne*. See especially Book VI, Chapter 2 of Aristotle's *Nicomachean Ethics*. For Aristotle, *theoria* is thinking aimed at the activity of contemplating eternal truths, especially the enquiries of natural philosophy, mathematics, and philosophical wisdom; *praxis* is thinking aimed at practical activity, especially life in a political community and the practical wisdom needed to make good decisions; and *techne* is thinking aimed at productive activity, such as architecture, medicine, rhetoric, or poetics. It might at first appear that MacIntyre uses the term "practice" as an equivalent for Aristotle's notion of *praxis*. After all, MacIntyre states that one of the practices he has in mind is "politics in the Aristotelian sense" (188). However, MacIntyre's notion of a practice is actually much wider than Aristotle's notion of *praxis*.MacIntyre lists "the enquiries of physics, chemistry and biology" as practices; Aristotle would consider each of these inquiries to be a *theoria*, not a *praxis*. Also, MacIntyre considers games (football, chess), artistic pursuits (painting and music), productive activities (farming, architecture, medicine), while Aristotle would consider each of these to be a *techne*, not a *praxis*. MacIntyre lists communal activities, such as the making and sustaining of a family or a social community, as practices, but questions abound with regard to these. Isn't "making" a family in some sense a productive activity on Aristotle's schema? Isn't family life and political life integrally tied into metaphysical biology in the Aristotelian schema? Leaving these questions to the side for now, my point is that MacIntyre's notion of a "practice" is Aristotelian in the sense that it rests on an Aristotelian distinction between internal and external goods, but MacIntyre explains and employs that distinction in a way that is slightly different from Aristotle.

19. A. MacIntyre (1981), 194–195.

20. A. MacIntyre (1981), 188–189.
21. A. MacIntyre (1981), 190.
22. MacIntyre describes a tradition as a "historically extended, socially embodied argument, and an argument precisely in part about the goods which constitute that tradition" (1981, 222).
23. MacIntyre writes, "It is characteristic of what I have called external goods that when achieved they are always some individual's property and possession. Moreover characteristically they are such that the more someone has of them, the less there is for other people. This is sometimes necessarily the case, as with power and fame, and sometimes the case by reason of contingent circumstance as with money. External goods are therefore characteristically objects of competition in which there must be losers as well as winners" A. MacIntyre (1981), 190.
24. For Aristotle, external goods are that at which one who practices a *techne* aims to produce. Aristotle uses many examples to illustrate this. For the bridle maker, the external good is the bridle. For the carpenter, the external good is the building. For the sculptor, the external good is a statue. For the physician, the external good is health. For the rhetorician, the external good is persuasion. For the one who practices household management, the external good is wealth. For the military leader, the external good is victory. Some of these, such as buildings, statues, and wealth, are objects that can be possessed as property, and some of these, such as military victory, might be part of a zero-sum game where one side winning necessitates another side losing. Aristotle does not consider that it is characteristic of external goods that they can be possessed as property. For example, the goods of health or persuasion, which are external to the activities of the physician and the rhetorician respectively, cannot be possessed as property. Further, Aristotle does not hold that external goods are goals in a zero-sum game. For example, there is no reason bridles, statues, buildings, health, or persuasion have to be part of a contest where one side's victory requires another side's loss. The activity of a sculptor results in the external good of statues, but it does not have to result in someone else losing anything.
25. G. Moore (2002), 19–32. In addition to Moore's work applying MacIntyre's schema to study organizations, I have been intrigued by and benefitted from conference presentations (at the 2008 meeting of the International Society for MacIntyrian Philosophy) by Ron Beadle, Carter Crockett, and Samantha Coe. Each has used MacIntyre's practice–institution distinction for empirical research regarding organizations.
26. A. MacIntyre (1981), 194.
27. A. MacIntyre (1981), 194.
28. A. MacIntyre (1981), 194.
29. A. MacIntyre (1981), 194.
30. A. MacIntyre (1981), 194.
31. A. MacIntyre (1981), 194.
32. A. MacIntyre (1981), 196.
33. A. MacIntyre (1981), 194.
34. A. MacIntyre (1981), 196.
35. A. MacIntyre (1981), 194.
36. A. MacIntyre (1981), 194–195.

37. A. MacIntyre (1981), 195.
38. A. Clark and J. Treanor (2008) "Greenspan – I Was Wrong about the Economy. Sort of," *The Guardian*. Available at: <http://www.guardian.co.uk/business/2008/oct/24/economics-creditcrunch-federal-reserve-greenspan>), accessed on July 11, 2012.
39. It might help here to indicate that MacIntyre's practice–institution has been qualified and clarified by later discussion, both by MacIntyre and by scholars in organizational studies seeking to apply this schema. In a 1994 essay titled, "A Partial Response to My Critics," MacIntyre makes several crucial concessions and clarifications regarding his practice–institution schema. He concedes that some of the misunderstandings from his critics (such as David Miller) are the result of his own "lack of attention to productive practices" (in J. Horton and S. Mendus (eds) [1994], 284). MacIntyre next provides an example (which has become widely quoted by commentators) of two fishing crews. One is a modern crew organized for the sake of profits; the other is a more traditional crew. We are asked to imagine someone who joins the crew, motivated at first perhaps initially by the pursuit of a wage, but who later acquired from the crew "an understanding of and devotion to excellence in fishing and to excellence in playing one's part as a member of such a crew" (285). MacIntyre concedes that the goal of such a crew is to catch fish and to provide economic support to the crew's members, but as evidence that their goals also include the excellences internal to the practice of fishing, he points to the way such crews support one another in times of personal difficulties and exhibit a continuing allegiance to the crew and the fishing village through periods of economic hardship. MacIntyre's point in this example is to show that it is possible for the participants in a productive practice (such as the fishing crew) to be concerned with external goods while continuing allegiance to the internal goods of the practice. "The subordination of economic goods to goods of practice can be a rewarding reality" (285).MacIntyre's fishing-crew example shows some things about productive practices, but it raises other questions. For example, given that it is difficult for practices to survive for any length of time unsustained by institutions, what sort of institution might support the fishing crew's practice? Can this same schema be applied to other sorts of productive activities? Farming? Mining? Manufacturing? Railroading? Retailing? Could an airline or an electric utility be understood using this schema? Could one apply MacIntyre's practice–institution schema to these businesses? Is it possible to conceive of corporations as institutions that house practices?Geoff Moore, in a series of papers, has suggested, "MacIntyre's schema can be applied directly to business as a practice and to corporations as institutions" (G. Moore [2002], 23). Moore extends this analysis in several later essays. Also see Moore's (2005b) "Humanizing Business: A Modern Virtue Ethics Approach," *Business Ethics Quarterly*,15, 2, 237–255 and his (2005c) "Corporate Character: Modern Virtue Ethics and the Virtuous Corporation," *Business Ethics Quarterly*, 15, 4, 659–685. Moore claims that it is the special function of management to provide administrative support to the "core-practice" housed in the institution and to protect the practice from the corrupting tendencies of institutions. Ron Beadle (2008) has challenged Moore's claim that business is (or can be) a practice. Beadle argues that Moore has failed to distinguish between the "business-of-a-craft" and "business-qua-business." This is a friendly debate between Beadle and

Moore. Together, they recently coedited a volume of the journal *Philosophy of Management* devoted to the topic: R. Beadle and G. Moore (2008). I address this debate more fully later. For now, it is worth noting that there are ongoing efforts to understand and apply MacIntyre's practice–institution schema.

40. A. MacIntyre (1981), 195.
41. R. Solomon (1993) "Corporate Roles, Personal Virtues: An Aristotelean Approach to Business Ethics," *Business Ethics Quarterly*, 2, 337. See also R. Solomon (1992).
42. R. Solomon (1993), 327.
43. For example, these may involve procedures and protocol for records, job descriptions, employee manuals, accounting policies, customer service procedures, disaster and emergency plans, design and development manuals, environmental policies, finance formulas, quality control and audit procedures, personnel policies, marketing plans, security operations, inventory control, and so forth.
44. MacIntyre presents this criticism in his essay, A. MacIntyre (1979a), 219–237.
45. A. MacIntyre (1981), 194.

8 MacIntyre against the Manager

1. For a summary that helpfully connects the arguments from MacIntyre's early writings to his "After Virtue Project," see T. D'Andrea (2006).
2. A. MacIntyre (1981), 30.
3. A. MacIntyre (1981), 30.
4. A. MacIntyre (1981), 30.
5. Also see F. Sejersted (1996) "Managers and Consultants as Manipulators: Reflections on the Suspension of Ethics," *Business Ethics Quarterly*, 6, 1, 67–86.
6. T. D'Andrea (2006), Chapter 4.
7. T. D'Andrea (2006), 245.
8. At the end of Chapter 7 of *After Virtue*, MacIntyre intimates but leaves undeveloped something like the thesis I am arguing later in this book, that is, that there might be a different and better way to conceive of what it means to be a manager. He hints that this non-bureaucratic manager would "allow for individual initiative, a flexible response to changes in knowledge, and the multiplication of centers of problem solving and decision-making." See A. MacIntyre (1981), 106.
9. A. MacIntyre (1981), 76–77.
10. A. MacIntyre (1981), 107.
11. A. MacIntyre (1981), 187–188.
12. K. Balstad Brewer (1997), 832. G. Moore points to and extends the debate in his essay (2008), 483–511.
13. This debate is summarized well in Ron Beadle's essay (2008b), 227–241. Beadle is responding especially to G. Moore (2001).
14. R. Beadle (2008b).
15. A. MacIntyre (1981), 31–32.
16. B. Taylor (2003) *Management Science*, Eighth Edition (Englewood Cliffs, NJ: Prentice Hall), 2.

17. A. MacIntyre (1981), 204.
18. A. MacIntyre (1981), 204.
19. See R. Beadle and G. Moore (2008a) "MacIntyre on Virtue and Organization, *Organization Studies*, 27:3, 323–340. Moore and Beadle write, "In private correspondence MacIntyre has confirmed to us that his thinking was in part developed through empirical work in which hypothetical scenarios were put to the power company executives (October 6, 2005)." See A. MacIntyre (1979), 124.
20. A. MacIntyre (1979), 124.
21. A. MacIntyre (1979), 123.
22. A. MacIntyre (1979), 123.
23. A. MacIntyre (1979), 124.
24. A. MacIntyre (1979), 126.
25. A. MacIntyre (1981), 254–255.
26. A. MacIntyre (1981), 227.
27. J. S. Mill (1859) *On Liberty* (London: Parker and Son), 141.
28. A. MacIntyre (1981), 137.
29. A. MacIntyre (1981), 137.
30. A. MacIntyre (1981), 137.
31. A. MacIntyre (2006), 149.
32. T. D'Andrea (2006), 395.
33. A. MacIntyre (1981), 263.

9   The Virtuous Manager, the Art of Character, and Business Humanities

1. W. Shaw (2011) *Business Ethics*, Eighth Edition (Boston, MA: Cengage).
2. Shaw (2011), 19.
3. Shaw (2011), 20.
4. A. MacIntyre (1990a), 266.
5. Plato, *Symposium*, 206–210.
6. D. McGregor (1960) *The Human Side of Enterprise* (New York: McGraw Hill). McGregor's argument is compressed in his classic article, "The Human Side of Enterprise," reprinted in (1966) *Leadership and Motivation, Essays of Douglas McGregor*, in W. Bennis and E. Schein (eds) (Cambridge, MA: MIT Press), 3–20.
7. P. Drucker (1954) *The Practice of Management* (New York: Harper & Row).
8. R. Arum and J. Roksa (2011) *Academically Adrift: Limited Learning on College Campuses* (Chicago: University of Chicago Press), 81.
9. R. Arum and J. Roksa (2011), 121–122.
10. S. Datar, et al. (2010), 322.
11. S. Datar, et al. (2010), 322.
12. S. Datar, et al. (2010), 323
13. A. Colby, et al. (2011), 51.
14. A. Colby, et al. (2011), 51.
15. A. Colby, et al. (2011), 60.
16. A. Colby, et al. (2011), 60.
17. A. Colby, et al. (2011), 60.
18. H. Spitzeck, et al. (2009), xxix.

19. The Humanism in Business series includes E. von Kimakowitz, et al. (eds) (2010); C. Dierksmeier (2011b) *Humanistic Ethics in the Age of Globality* (London: Palgrave Macmillan); W. Amann, et al. (eds) (2011) *Business Schools Under Fire: Humanistic Management as the Way Forward* (London Palgrave Macmillan); H. Spitzeck, et al. (eds) (2011) *Banking with Integrity* (London: Palgrave Macmillan); C. Dierksmeier and D. Melé (eds) (2012); W. Amann and A. Stachowicz-Stanusch (eds) (2012) *Integrity in Organizations: Building the Foundations for Humanistic Management* (London: Palgrave Macmillan).
20. M. Evans and D. Greaves (2010) "Ten Years of Medical Humanities," *Medical Humanities*, 36, 1, 66–68.
21. H. Cook (2010) "Borderlands: A Historian's Perspective on Medical Humanities in the U.S. and the U.K.," *Medical Humanities*, 36, 1, 3–4.
22. M. Evans and D. Greaves (2000) "Medical Humanities," *Medical Humanities*, 26, 1, 1–2.
23. For a directory of programs that support degrees and certificates in medical humanities, http://medhum.med.nyu.edu/directory.html.
24. M. Evans and D. Greaves (2010), 66.
25. See for example, R. Charon and M. Montello (2002).
26. J. Weichert and M. Pirson "The Role and Development of the Aspen Institute," in W. Amann, et al. (2011), 390–396.
27. For a very helpful and extensive collection, see M. Stackhouse, et al. (1995).
28. The tradition of Catholic social thought includes extensive interdisciplinary reflections on the economic sector. For an overview, see C. Dierksmeier and D. Melé (eds) (2012). The John A. Ryan Institute for Catholic Social Thought maintains an excellent Web site with extensive resources for research and curriculum development relating Catholic social thought to business education, including many creative ways to incorporate the Catholic social tradition into many disciplines related to business education: http://www.stthomas.edu/cathstudies/cst/default.html.
29. O. Williams (ed.) (1998) *The Moral Imagination* (Notre Dame, IN: University of Notre Dame Press).
30. At Saint Louis University, Vincent Casaregola offers the course "English 318" called "Film: The Culture of Business."
31. J. Badaracco (2006), 2.
32. J. Badaracco (2006), 2.
33. Ernest Pierucci raised this friendly objection in his response to my paper, "A New Humanistic Synthesis? Toward a Business Humanities Approach," at the meeting of the Eighth International Conference on Catholic Social Thought and Management Education at the University of Dayton, June 18, 2012.

10 Character Transformation in the Friendship of Readers and Writers

1. G. Hamel (2012) *What Matters Now: How to Win in a World of Relentless Change, Ferocious Competition, and Unstoppable Innovation* (San Francisco, CA: Jossey-Bass), 3.
2. G. Hamel (2007), xi.
3. G. Hamel (2007), 151–179.

4. H. Mintzberg (2005) *Managers, not MBAs* (San Francisco, CA: Berrett Koehler).
5. S. Sanghera (2003) "You Should Be Bonkers in a Bonkers' Time," *Financial Times* September 23.
6. T. Peters (2003) *Re-Imagine: Business Excellence in a Disruptive Age* (London: Dorling Kindersle), 13.
7. P. Senge (1990) *The Fifth Discipline: The Art and Practice of the Learning Organization* (New York: Doubleday), especially Chapter 18, "The Leader's New Work."
8. P. Senge (1990), 340.
9. The subtitle of Hamel's 2012 book reveals his goal: "*How to Win...*" In a similar way, Peters, despite his frequent use of an almost postmodern style and appeals to a new kind of leader for a new context, seems to leave the old answer to the manager's purpose unchallenged; like Hamel, Peters describes the manager's purpose in terms of winning. T. Peters (2003), 29.
10. A. MacIntyre (2006), 128 (Vol. 2).
11. R. Scholes and R. Kellogg (1966) *The Nature of Narrative* (Oxford: Oxford University Press), 4. Alternatively, see the 40th-anniversary republication of this text; it contains an excellent essay by James Phelan that covers the development of literary criticism pertaining to narrative over the last 40 years, pointing especially to the work of Wayne C. Booth.
12. Scholes and Kellogg include oral narrative in their account of narrative. For an excellent account of the distinctive features of oral culture, see W. Ong (2002) *Orality and Literacy* (New York: Routledge).
13. W. Ong (1975) "The Writer's Audience is Always a Fiction," *PMLA*, 90, 1, 9–21.
14. In a personal conversation with May Sim and Ken Casey (both of whom were students of MacIntyre's during the 1980s while he was on the faculty at Vanderbilt) I was told that MacIntyre, in his teaching, would stress the importance of students learning to write for an "ideal reader." (This conversation occurred on March 9, 2009 at the Third Annual Conference of the International Society for MacIntyrean Enquiry held at University College Dublin.) In his published work, I am not familiar with any place where MacIntyre discusses the importance of writer–narrators imagining an implied audience. The closest that he comes, to my knowledge, is in his essay, "The Ends of Life, the Ends of Philosophical Writing," 128–132.
15. W. Ong (1975), 9.
16. Booth uses the example of Aesop's fable of the goose who laid the golden egg to illustrate the distinction between "nonce beliefs" (beliefs suspended for the sake of the story) and fixed norms. See W. C. Booth (1989) *The Company We Keep: An Ethics of Fiction* (Berkeley, CA: University of California Press), 142–146.
17. For a particularly engaging account of Twain's biography that focuses on the religious influences in his life and in his writing, I warmly recommend H. Bush (2008) *Mark Twain and the Spiritual Crisis of His Age* (Tuscaloosa, AL: University of Alabama).
18. Of course, much more could be said about the precise nature of the transformation that Twain wants to bring about in his reader. See Booth's very rich discussion of Twain's novel throughout his *The Company We Keep*. My point here is simply to draw on the example of Twain's novel to explain what I mean by an "implied narrative."

19. See R. Scholes and R. Kellogg (1966), Chapter 7.
20. Aristotle, *Nicomachean Ethics*, Book XIII, Chapters 3–4, 1156a7–1157b6.
21. Aristotle, in Book VIII of the *Nicomachean Ethics*, famously draws a distinction between three sorts of friendship: those based on 1) utility, 2) pleasure, and 3) "the friendship between good people, those resembling each other in excellence, that is complete; for each alike wishes good things for the other in so far as he is good, and he is good in himself" *NE* 1156b7–1156b10. Booth uses Aristotle's taxonomy of these three kinds of friendship to suggest a way that we, as readers and writers, might evaluate the moral features of the friendship cultivated in various author–reader relationships.
22. Quoted by W. C. Booth (1989), 135.
23. A. MacIntyre (1990a), 233.
24. J. Pieper (1966) *The Four Cardinal Virtues* (Notre Dame, IN: University of Notre Dame Press), 29.
25. J. Pieper (1966), 29.
26. Practical wisdom involves "calculating well toward some specific worthy end on matters where no exact technique applies" (Aristotle *Nicomachean Ethics* 1140a28). In order to determine whether a particular end is worthwhile (such as money or physical health), it is necessary for one's perceptions to be shaped by good character traits and to be able to relativize the given end, viewing it as subordinate to some other higher end (such as the goal of a flourishing, unified human life or the common good of a flourishing community).
27. Plato, *Phaedrus*, 274–277, and the *Seventh Letter*, 341–344.

11   Transforming the Character of the Moral Philosopher

1. A. MacIntyre (2000) "Theories of Natural Law in the Culture of Advanced Modernity," in E. B. McLean (ed.) *Common Truths: New Perspectives on Natural Law* (Wilmington, DE: Intercollegiate Studies Institute).
2. A. MacIntyre (1958) "On not Misrepresenting Philosophy," *Universities and Left Review*, 4, 72.
3. A. MacIntyre (1979c) "Why Is the Search for the Foundations of Ethics so Frustrating?," *Hastings Center Report*, 9, 4, 22.
4. S. Soames (2003) *Philosophical Analysis in the Twentieth Century* (Princeton: Princeton University Press), 2, 463; quoted by MacIntyre in *God, Philosophy. Universities*, 17–18.
5. A. MacIntyre (1990a), 136, 139, and 175; MacIntyre gives a detailed description of the "everyday plain person" in A. MacIntyre (1992) "Plain Persons and Moral Philosophy: Rules, Virtues and Goods," *American Catholic Philosophical Quarterly*, 66, 1, 3–7. This character is prefigured in the "ordinary agent" in A. MacIntyre (1977b) "Epistemological Crises, Dramatic Narrative, and the Philosophy of Science," *The Monist*, 60, 4, 453–472. After his 1992 essay, MacIntyre makes reference to the "plain person" frequently. For example, see Volumes 1 and 2 of MacIntyre (2006a), especially Chapters 6, 7, and 9 in Volume 1, *The Tasks of Philosophy*, and Chapters 3, 7, and 10 in Volume 2, *Ethics and Politics*.
6. A. MacIntyre (1992), 3–7.

7. A. MacIntyre (1977b), 453. This important essay has been republished in various collections.
8. A. MacIntyre (2006a), 185 (Vol. 2).
9. During his interview with Giovanna Borradori, when asked about his life prior to the publication of *After Virtue* and his apparent existential inquietude, he stated, "When I look back on my asserted beliefs during that period, I see my thinking as having been a clumsily patched together collection of fragments" ("An Interview with Giovanna Borradori" in K. Knight (ed.) (1998).
10. A. MacIntyre (2006a), 128–132 (Vol. 2).
11. A. MacIntyre (2006a), 131 (Vol. 2).
12. A. MacIntyre (2006a), 127 (Vol. 2).
13. A. MacIntyre (2006a), 131 (Vol. 2).
14. A. MacIntyre (2006a), 131 (Vol. 2).
15. A. MacIntyre (2006a), 132 (Vol. 2).
16. A. MacIntyre (2006a), 128 (Vol. 2).
17. A. MacIntyre (2006a), 182 (Vol. 1).
18. A. MacIntyre (2006a), 130 (Vol. 2).
19. A. MacIntyre (2006a), 130–131 (Vol. 2).
20. A. MacIntyre (2006a), 131 (Vol. 2).
21. A. MacIntyre, "Philosophy Recalled to Its Tasks," 181 (Vol. 1).
22. A. MacIntyre (2006a), 180 (Vol. 1).
23. A. MacIntyre (2006b) *Edith Stein: A Philosophical Prologue* (London: Rowman and Littlefield), vii.
24. A. MacIntyre (2006a), 132 (Vol. 2).
25. MacIntyre presumes that his reader is familiar with both Heidegger's philosophy and biography. Heidegger, who is considered by many to be one of the most important philosophers of the 20th century, was also a student of Husserl. Heidegger became a member of the Nazi party and seemingly distanced himself from his mentor.
26. A. MacIntyre (2006a), 180 (Vol. 1).
27. A. MacIntyre (2011) *God, Philosophy, Universities: A Selective History of the Catholic Philosophical Tradition* (London: Rowman and Littlefield), 10.
28. A. MacIntyre (2011), 11.
29. MacIntyre hints (on rare occasions) that there may be an alternative way to conceive of what it means to be a manager. For example, see A. MacIntyre (1981), 106.

12   Transforming Character: The Manager and the Aesthete

1. A. MacIntyre (1981), 24–35.
2. C. Taylor (2007), 473.
3. C. Taylor (2007), 477.
4. A. MacIntyre (1981), 25.
5. For interpretations that emphasize literary aspects of his work, in addition to the work of E. Mooney, see E. Ziolkowski (2011) *The Literary Kierkegaard* (Evanston, IL.: Northwestern University Press); L. Mackey (1971) *Kierkegaard: A Kind of Poet* (Philadelphia, PA: Univeristy of Pennsylvania Press).

6. For a helpful and complete survey, see A. Rudd (2012) "Alasdair MacIntyre: A Continuing Conversation," in J. Stewart (ed.) *Kierkegaard's Influence on Philosophy: Anglophone Philosophy* (London: Ashgate), 117–134.
7. Rudd (2012), 122.
8. A. MacIntyre (1981), 40.
9. A. MacIntyre (1981), 42.
10. A. MacIntyre (1981), 41.
11. As noted earlier, Rudd (2012) traces the conversation in detail. A range of responses by Kierkegaardians to MacIntyre is found in the volume edited by J. Davenport and A. Rudd (2001). That conversation continued in various ways; see, for example, J. Lippitt (2007) "Getting the Story Straight: Kierkegaard, MacIntyre, and Some Problems with Narrative," *Inquiry* 50:1, 34–69; E. Mooney (2007) *On Søren Kierkegaard: Dialogue, Polemics, Lost Intimacy, and Time* (London: Ashgate), 120ff. I criticized MacIntyre's interpretation of Kierkegaard in (1996) *Freedom and Its Misuses: Kierkegaard on Anxiety and Despair* (Milwaukee: Marquette University Press). In the "Preface to the Second Edition," (2009), I qualified my comments about MacIntyre on p. 17.
12. A. MacIntyre (2001) "Once More on Kierkegaard," in J. Davenport and A. Rudd (2001), 339 ff.
13. E. Mooney (2001) "The Perils of Polarity: Kierkegaard and MacIntyre in Search of Moral Truth," in J. Davenport and A. Rudd (2001), 234.
14. G. Beabout (2007), 129.
15. S. Kierkegaard (2001) *The Essential Kierkegaard* (Princeton: Princeton University Press), 3–7.
16. See Sylvia Walsh's helpful summary in (1994) *Living Poetically: Kierkegaard's Existential Aesthetics* (University Park, PA: Pennsylvania State University Press). In Chapter 1, Walsh summarizes Kierkegaard's arguments against the romanticism of Hans Christian Andersen. In Chapter 2, she summarizes Kierkegaard's arguments against German romanticism.
17. Walsh (1994), 35.
18. "By failing to separate himself from his writings, thereby creating an aesthetic distance in relation to them, Andersen in particular is guilty of infusing his novels with his own unreflected life experiences. His poetic productions thus merely narrate in their details the misfortunes, bitterness, and discontent with the actual world that characterize his own life. At the same time, by so closely identifying with the characters of his novels, his own personality becomes lost or evaporated in his poetic productions." See Walsh (1994), 35.
19. J. Garff (2005) *Søren Kierkegaard: A Biography*, trans. Bruce H. Kirmmse (Princeton: Princeton University Press), 88–95; A. Hannay (2001) *Kierkegaard: A Biography* (Cambridge: Cambridge University Press), 48; G. Beabout (2007), 127–146; F. Jensen (2009) "Poul Martin Møller: Kierkegaard and the Confidant of Socrates," in J. Stewart (ed.) *Kierkegaard and His Danish Contemporaries – Philosophy, Politics and Social Theory*, Vol. 7 (Farnham: Ashgate), 101–168.
20. As recounted by Kierkegaard's biographers, Kierkegaard attended Møller's lectures on Greek moral philosophy and on Aristotle's psychology. Although Møller was 19 years Kierkegaard's elder, the two became close. We know relatively little about the details of the relationship between student and mentor, but Kierkegaard's biographers describe a kind of heart-to-heart intimacy felt between them, despite the difference in age. In a letter from Hans Brøchner, we are told that the mentor's strongest influence on Kierkegaard was Møller's

character and the way he lived his philosophy. Møller taught Kierkegaard to be attentive to the manner in which one is disposed to others and to the world, to concretize philosophical truths in one's mode of existing, and to depict philosophical issues through literary dramatization, thereby capturing the way that habits of character shape one's personality. See J. Garff (2005), 88–95; A. Hannay (2001), 48.

21. Schlegel captured this when he wrote, "As his artistic ability developed and he was able to achieve with ease what he had been unable to accomplish with all his powers of exertion and hard work before, so too his life now came to be a work of art for him." F. Schlegel (1971) *Friedrich Schlegel's Lucinde and the Fragments*, trans. Peter Firchow (Minneapolis: University of Minnesota Press), 102, quoted in Walsh (1994), 52.

22. Walsh develops this point throughout her work. For example, see Walsh (1994), 244.

23. S. Kierkegaard (1992), 276.

24. S. Kierkegaard (1992), 270.

25. S. Kierkegaard (1992), 279.

26. S. Kierkegaard (1992), 301.

27. S. Kierkegaard (1992), 300.

28. S. Kierkegaard (1992), 280.

29. S. Kierkegaard (1987) *Either/Or*, Vol. 2, trans. H. & E. Hong (Princeton: Princeton University Press), 61.

30. S. Kierkegaard (1987), 62ff.

31. S. Kierkegaard (1987), 63.

32. S. Kierkegaard (1987), 68.

33. S. Kierkegaard (1987), 68.

34. S. Kierkegaard (1987), 137.

35. S. Kierkegaard (1987), 137.

36. For examples, see R. Furtak (2010) "Kierkegaard and Platonic Eros," in J. Stewart (ed.) *Kierkegaard and the Greek World: Socrates and Plato* (London: Ashgate), 105–114; W. McDonald (2003) "Love in Kierkegaard's Symposia," *Minerva* 7, www.sorenkierkegaard.nl/artikelen/Engels/090. Love in kierkegaard.pdf, accessed on 5 May 2013. U. Carlsson (2010) "Love as a Problem of Knowledge in Kierkegaard's *Either/Or* and Plato's *Symposium*," *Inquiry*, 53, 41–57. Plato's symposium also shapes Kierkegaard's *Stages on Life's Way*, especially "In Vino Veritas."

37. S. Kierkegaard (1987), 337.

38. S. Kierkegaard (1987), 352.

39. Quoted by R. Furtak (2010), 108.

40. S. Kierkegaard (1987), 354.

41. B. Barlow (1998) "Absence and Presence: The Religious and Psychological Meaning of 'The Lily in the Field and the Bird of the Air,'" *Religious Studies and Theology*, 17, 2, 20.

42. S. Kierkegaard (1997) "The Lily in the Field and the Bird of the Air," in *Without Authority*, trans. H. and E. Hong (Princeton: Princeton University Press).

43. I develop this interpretation in detail in G. Beabout (2007), 127–146.

44. A. MacIntyre (2001), 355.

45. A. MacIntyre (2001), 355. He concludes his essay, "May the conversation continue!"

13   Transforming the Character of the Rhetorician

1. See C. Shields (2007) *Aristotle* (London: Taylor & Francis), 23.
2. Gorgias is mentioned in Plato's *Apology*, the Greater Hippias, the Meno, the Phaedrus, the Philebus, the Symposium, and the Theages.
3. Plato, *Gorgias*, 447d, trans. J. Sachs (2009).
4. The literature offering commentaries and interpretations of Plato's *Gorgias* is vast. For examples, see D. Stauffer (2006) *The Unity of Plato's Gorgias* (Cambridge: Cambridge University Press); G. Klosko (1993) "Persuasion and Moral Reform in Plato and Aristotle," *Internationale de Philosophie*, 184, 31–49; R. Weiss (2003) "Oh, Brother! The Fraternity of Rhetoric and Philosophy in Plato's *Gorgias*," *Interpretation*, 30, 195–206; R. Wardy (1996) *The Birth of Rhetoric: Gorgias, Plato and Their Successors* (London: Routledge); S. Benardete (1991) *The Rhetoric of Morality and Philosophy: Plato's Gorgias and Phaedrus* (Chicago: University of Chicago); G. Vlastos (1991) *Socrates, Ironist and Moral Philosopher* (Ithaca: Cornell University Press); I. Dilman (1979) *Morality and the Inner Life: A Study in Plato's Gorgias* (New York: Barnes & Noble); E. Dodds (1959) *Plato: Gorgias* (Oxford: Clarendon Press); Olympiodorus the Younger (1998) *Commentary on Plato's Gorgias*, trans. R. Jackson, et al. (Leiden: Brill).
5. Plato, *Gorgias*, 453a. As Gorgias puts it, the rhetorician is a producer of persuasion "able to persuade people by speeches...the one with the power to speak and persuade the multitudes," 452e.
6. Plato, *Gorgias*, 472c–472d, 487e–488a, 500c.
7. Plato, *Gorgias*, 452e, 455c.
8. Gorgias, 456a–457c. In a similar way, this view is attributed to Gorgias by Meno: see Plato, *Meno* 95c.
9. These three are discussed in Plato's *Gorgias*, 486e–487e. Aristotle likewise identifies these three elements as crucial for establishing trust. Aristotle, *Rhetoric* 1378a7.
10. Plato, *Gorgias*, 459–460.
11. Plato, *Gorgias*, 463a.
12. Plato, *Gorgias*, 527c.
13. Plato, *Gorgias*, 485b.
14. Plato, *Gorgias*, 486a–486b.
15. Plato, *Gorgias*, 465b.
16. Plato, *Gorgias*, 527c.
17. Plato, *Republic*, 607b.
18. Plato, *Phaedrus*, 258d.
19. Plato, *Phaedrus*, 269b.
20. Plato, *Sophist*, 223b.
21. Plato, *Gorgias*, 465c.
22. For example, see Plato, *Sophist*, 221c–221d.
23. For an excellent account from which I have greatly benefited, see E. Garver (1994) *Aristotle's Rhetoric: An Art of Character* (Chicago: University of Chicago Press). See also A. Rorty (2011) "Aristotle on the Virtues of Rhetoric," *The Review of Metaphysics* 54, 715–733; K. Quinn (1996) "A Rhetorical Conception of Practical Rationality," *Journal of Economic Issues*, 30, 1127–1142; C. Rapp (2009) "The Nature and Goals of Rhetoric," in G. Anagnostopoulos (ed.) *A Companion to Aristotle* (Oxford: Blackwell), 579–596.

24. Aristotle, *On Sophistical Refutations*, 1834a3.
25. Aristotle, *Rhetoric*, 1355b11. With regard to Aristotle's *Rhetoric*, in addition to the translation of W. Rhys Roberts included in the McKeon edition of *The Complete Works of Aristotle*, I have benefitted from the translation of Joe Sachs, Newburyport, MA: Focus Publishing, 2009.
26. Aristotle, *Rhetoric*, 1355b18.
27. Aristotle, *Rhetoric*, 1354a14. In the *Nicomachean Ethics*, Aristotle defines *techne* (art, craft) as a "power for making, accompanied by true reasoning" (1140a10).
28. Aristotle, *Rhetoric*, 1354a18.
29. Aristotle, *Rhetoric*, 1355a31.
30. Aristotle, *Rhetoric*, 1355a22.
31. Aristotle, *Rhetoric*, 1355b14.
32. E. Garver (1984), 484.
33. Aristotle, *Rhetoric*, 1355b11.
34. Aristotle, *Rhetoric*, 1356a14.
35. Aristotle, *Rhetoric*, 1378a9.
36. Aristotle, *Rhetoric*, 1360b3–1360b 18.
37. Aristotle, *Rhetoric*, 1364a4–1364a 10.
38. Aristotle, *Rhetoric*, 1369a27.
39. Aristotle, *Rhetoric*, 1364a25–1364a 29.

14   The Manager as Wise Steward: Activities, Practice, and Virtue

1. E. Garver (1984), 484.
2. G. Moore (2002), 19–32. Also see G. Moore (2005a), 659–685 and (2005b), 237–255; G. Moore (2008), 483–511; G. Moore and R. Beadle (2006), 369–389; G. Moore (2012b) "Virtue in Business: Alliance Boots and an Empirical Exploration of MacIntyre's Conceptual Framework," *Organization Studies*, 33, 363–387; G. Moore (2012a), 293–318.
3. G. Moore (2002), 22.
4. These are the productive practices that MacIntyre lists in response to objections raised by David Miller to his account of social practices. See A. MacIntyre (1994), 284–286.
5. A. MacIntyre (1994), 285.
6. A. MacIntyre (1981), 194.
7. A. MacIntyre (1981), 194. For further discussion of productive practices and interlocking social practices, see A. MacIntyre (1994), 284.
8. M. Hernandez (2008) "Promoting Stewardship Behavior in Organizations: A Leadership Model," *Journal of Business Ethics*, 80, 122.
9. M. Hernandez (2008), 122.
10. P. Block (1993) *Stewardship* (San Francisco: Berrett-Koehler), xx.
11. P. Block (1993), xx.
12. P. Block (1993), 18. Block provides many examples of how the manager-as-steward can empower members of the organization to become active participants in decision-making. Block provides suggestions for redesigning management practices, flattening the organizational structure, rethinking staff functions, and redesigning reward systems.

13. P. Block (1993), 41.
14. P. Block (1993), xx.
15. L. Spears (1977) *Servant Leadership: A Journey in the Nature of Legitimate Power and Greatness* (New Jersey: Wiley), 4–6.
16. Spears (1997), 85.
17. B. Bass (2008) *The Bass Handbook of Leadership: Theory, Research, and Managerial Applications*, Fourth edition (New York: The Free Press), 50.
18. P. Drucker (1985) *The Practice of Management* (New York: Harper & Row), from the preface to the 1985 edition, viii.
19. H. Fayol (1916 [1949]) *General and Industrial Management*, trans. C. Storrs (London: Sir Isaac Pitman & Sons).
20. L. Gulick (1937) "Notes on the Theory of Organization," in L. Gulick and L. Urwick (eds) *Papers on the Science of Administration* (New York: Institute of Public Administration), 3–35.
21. Drucker (1985), x.
22. Drucker (1985), 17. Drucker uses this threefold division to structure his book.
23. Drucker (1985), 343–344.
24. H. Mintzberg (1973).
25. H. Mintzberg (1973).
26. H. Mintzberg (2009), 5–6.
27. H. Mintzberg (1973), 28–48.
28. H. Mintzberg (1973), 10.
29. H. Mintzberg (1973), 55.
30. H. Mintzberg (1973), 55.
31. H. Mintzberg (1973), 57–58.

15   Management Is a Domain-Relative Practice

1. J. Dunne (2002) "Alasdair MacIntyre on Education: In Dialogue with Joseph Dunne," *Journal of Philosophy of Education*, 36, 1–19.
2. Dunne (2002), 4.
3. Dunne (2002) 5.
4. Dunne (2002), 4.
5. Dunne (2002), 5.
6. Dunne (2002), 5.
7. Dunne (2002), 9.
8. Dunne (2002), 7.
9. Dunne (2002), 7–8.
10. J. Dunne (2003), 353.
11. In the follow-up issue of the *Journal of Philosophy of Education* that explores themes raised by the Dunne/MacIntyre conversation, five of the eleven essays focus on the question of whether teaching is a practice; each, in various ways, took issue with MacIntyre's unexpected response. See the essays in the 2003 issue of the *Journal of Philosophy of Education* (37, 2) by J. Dunne (2003); P. Hogan (2003) "Teaching and Learning as a Way of Life," *Journal of Philosophy of Education*, 37, 2, 207–223; K. Katayama (2003) "Is the Virtue Approach to Moral Education Viable in a Plural Society," *Journal of Philosophy of Education*, 37, 2, 325–338; T. McLauglin (2003) "Teaching as a Practice and a Community of Practice: The Limits of Commonality and the Demands of

Diversity," *Journal of Philosophy of Education*, 37, 2, 339–352; and N. Noddings (2003). The chief strategy, of course, of those who argue that teaching is a practice is to consider the well-known definition of a practice that MacIntyre presents on p. 187 of *After Virtue*, and then to show that the activity of teaching fits this definition.

12. A. MacIntyre (1981), 33–34, 218. Also see D'Andrea (2006), 396.
13. A. MacIntyre (1981), 202.
14. C. Higgins (2010) "The Good Life of Teaching," *Journal of Philosophy of Education*, 44, 2–3, 189–208. In his book-length manuscript (2011), *The Good Life of Teaching: An Ethics of Professional Practice* (Hoboken, NJ: Wiley-Blackwell), Higgins develops the notion of "para-practices" (260–262). Higgins writes, "Many practices, and especially those that have communication built into them, attract cultures of criticism, interpretation, and commentary. These are situated neither wholly within nor wholly without the artistic and athletic practices (to choose the most obvious examples) they serve to explicate. Such para-practices tend to be interstitial: an architecture critic may be part newspaperman, part architect, and part art historian; a baseball broadcaster will have one foot in the world of baseball and one foot in the world of broadcast journalism. Indeed, a broadcast team is usually composed of two commentators, a play-by-play announcer (in the UK, the commentator) who comes from the culture of broadcasting and a color commentator or analyst (in the UK, the cocommentator) who is almost always a former player or coach. Between the two of them, they try to find words to evoke the achievements and real drama of the practical episode before them" (260). Higgins goes on to develop several examples from the world of sports broadcasting to develop his point about para-practices. He recounts the answer given by a sportscaster who was asked to describe the difference between working as a broadcaster at a baseball game compared to an ice hockey game. "He stumbled at first, and then, surprising himself it seemed, answered that the two experiences had very little in common. The dramatically different pacing of the games meant that in one case he is painting a picture of rapidly unfolding action and the other he is telling a slowly developing story" (261). So when Higgins calls broadcasting a para-practice, I think he is getting at something similar to what I mean by a domain-relative practice. Another way to clarify what I mean by a domain-relative practice would be to employ the medieval doctrine of analogy. For example, a basketball coach and a baseball coach are both engaged in the same practice, analogically understood. That both are "coaches" might seem puzzling when we limit the use of language to only univocal or equivocal uses.
15. I am limiting my discussion of "coaching" to its natural home in the domain of athletics. Over the last several decades, the notion of a coach has been broadened. There are many people now claiming expertise in coaching, including not only singing coaches and acting coaches, but also career coaches, dating coaches, personal life coaches, etc.
16. J. Dewey (1933) *How We Think* (Chicago: Henry Regnery), 35–36.
17. J. Dewey (1933) 36.
18. J. Dunne (2002), 5.
19. J. Dunne (2002), 8.
20. J. Dunne (2002), 9.

21. N. Noddings (2003), 250.
22. N. Noddings (2003), 250.
23. N. Noddings (2003), 244
24. A. MacIntyre (1981), 32.
25. T. Whetstone (2003), 344.
26. T. Whetstone (2003), 354.
27. T. Whetstone (2003), 352.
28. T. Whetstone (2003), 352.

16   The Dispositions of the Wise Steward and the Parts of Practical Wisdom

1. For examples, see S. Covey (1989); D. Goleman (2000); L. Segil (2002); G. Kaupins (2006).
2. Aristotle, *Nicomachean Ethics*, Book VI, especially Chapters 5 and 8–13; Thomas Aquinas, *Summa theologiae*, II–II, 47–56.
3. For a helpful summary and explanation of this virtue, see Josef Pieper's treatment of prudence in *The Four Cardinal Virtues* (1966).
4. Thomas Aquinas describes this virtue as "foremost among all the moral virtues." Summa Theologiae, II–II, 56, 1. Also see J. Pieper (1966); W. May (1995) "The Virtues of the Business Leader," in *On Moral Business: Classical and Contemporary Resources for Ethics in Economic Life*, ed. M. Stackhouse, et al. (Grand Rapids, MI: William B. Eerdmans Publishing), 692–700.
5. Pieper (1966), 14–17.
6. Aristotle, *Nicomachean Ethics* 1141b18–1141b 20.
7. G. Klubertanz (1952) *The Discursive Power* (Saint Louis: Modern Schoolman), 161.
8. M. Gladwell (2005) *Blink: The Power of Thinking Without Thinking* (New York: Little, Brown, and Company), 3–8.
9. These are the vices that St Thomas Aquinas lists as forms of imprudence. See his *Summa Theologiae*, II–II, 53–55.
10. Aristotle *Nicomachean Ethics* 1140a28.
11. D. Moberg (2007) "Practical Wisdom and Business Ethics," *Business Ethics Quarterly*, 17,3, 535.
12. G. Weaver (2006) "Virtue in Organizations: Moral Identity as a Foundation for Moral Agency," *Organization Studies*, 27, 358.
13. R. Solomon (1993); R. Solomon (1992) '328–329; T. Morris (1997) *If Aristotle Ran General Motors* (New York: Henry Holt).
14. R. Sternberg (1990) *Wisdom: Its Nature, Origins, and Development* (Cambridge: Cambridge University Press). See also R. Kilburg (2012) *Virtuous Leaders: Strategy, Character, and Influence in the 21st Century* (Washington, D.C.: American Psychological Association); R. Kilburg (2006) *Executive Wisdom: Coaching and the Emergence of Virtuous Leaders* (Washington, D.C.: American Psychological Association); R. Kilburg (2000) *Executive Coaching: Developing Managerial Wisdom in a World of Chaos.* (Washington, D.C.: American Psychological Association).
15. A. Sison and I. Ferrero (2012) "A Survey of Virtue in Business and Management Literature (1980–2010)," presented August 4, 2012 at the annual meeting of

the Society of Business Ethics, Boston, MA; Also see B. Schwartz and K. Sharpe (2010) *Practical Wisdom* (New York: Riverhead); C. Clarke (2010) "Practical Wisdom and Understanding the Economy," *Journal of Management Development*, 29, 678–685; A. Yuengert (2013) *Approximating Prudence: Aristotelian Practical Wisdom and Economic Models of Choice* (London: Palgrave MacMillan). Also see the special issues of the *Journal of Management Development* in 2010 and 2011 focusing on practical wisdom, especially D. Melé (2010) "Practical Wisdom in Managerial Decision Making," *Journal of Management Development*, 29,7/8, 637–645; H. Alford (2010) "The Practical Wisdom of Personalism," *Journal of Management Development*, 29,7, 697–705; W. Grassl (2010) "Aquinas on Management and Its Development," *Journal of Management Development* 29,7, 706–715; D. Tredget (2010) "Practical Wisdom and the Rule of Benedict," *Journal of Management Development*, 29,7, 716–723.

16. B. Schwartz and K. Sharpe (2010), 25.
17. B. Fowers (2005) *Virtue and Psychology: Pursuing Excellence in Ordinary Practices* (Washington D.C.:American Psychological Association), 117; E. Pellegrino and D. Thomasma(1993) *The Virtues in Medical Practice* (Oxford: Oxford University Press), 90; T. Morris (1997) 160–169.
18. D. Moberg (2007), 536.
19. D. Moberg (2007), 536.
20. D. Moberg (2007), 537–540.
21. For example, see J. Boatright (2009) *Ethics and the Conduct of Business* (London: Pearson) 1.
22. Boatright (2009), 3.
23. Aristotle *Nicomachean Ethics* 1112a18–1112a19.
24. Aristotle *Nicomachean Ethics* 1112b12.
25. Aristotle *Nicomachean Ethics* 1112b13.
26. Aristotle *Nicomachean Ethics* 1112b15–1112b17.
27. Aristotle *Nicomachean Ethics* 1112b31.
28. Aristotle *Nicomachean Ethics* 1113a14.
29. Aristotle *Nicomachean Ethics* 1140a25.
30. Aristotle *Nicomachean Ethics* 1140a30.
31. Aristotle *Nicomachean Ethics* 1140a30.
32. Aristotle *Nicomachean Ethics* 1140b21.
33. Aristotle *Nicomachean Ethics* 1140b7.
34. Aristotle *Nicomachean Ethics* 1142b28.
35. Aristotle *Nicomachean Ethics* 1142b19–1142b21.
36. Aristotle *Nicomachean Ethics* 1142b22.
37. Aristotle *Rhetoric* 1355a30–1355a32.
38. Plato *Republic* V:473d.
39. Aristotle draws these distinctions both in Book VI, Chapter 2 of the *Nicomachean Ethics* and in the first chapters of Book I of *Metaphysics*.
40. For example, see Thomas Aquinas (1993) *Commentary on Aristotle's Nicomachean Ethics* trans. C. Litzinger (Notre Dame, IN: Dumb Ox Books), 1. Thomas Aquinas makes the statement about the business of the wise person in reference to Aristotle, *Metaphysics* I:982a18.

Bibliography

H. Alford (2010) "The Practical Wisdom of Personalism," *Journal of Management Development*, 29, 7, 697–705.

W. Amann et al. (eds) (2011) *Business Schools Under Fire: Humanistic Management as the Way Forward* (London Palgrave Macmillan).

W. Amann and A. Stachowicz-Stanusch (eds) (2012) *Integrity in Organizations: Building the Foundations for Humanistic Management* (London: Palgrave Macmillan).

D. Amaral-Phillips (2001) "Traits of Successful Managers" (available at: http://www2.ca.uky.edu/afsdairy-files/extension/nutrition/Traits_of_Successful_Managers.pdf>), accessed 5 May 2013.

E. Anscombe (1958) "Modern Moral Philosophy," *Philosophy*, 33, 1–19.

Aristotle (1941) *The Basic Works of Aristotle*, ed. R. McKeon (New York: Random House).

Aristotle (2002) *Nicomachean Ethics*, trans. C. Rowe (Oxford: Oxford University Press).

H. Arendt (1992) *Eichmann in Jerusalem: A Report on the Banality of Evil* (New York: Penguin).

R. Arum and J. Roksa (2011) *Academically Adrift: Limited Learning on College Campuses* (Chicago: University of Chicago Press).

A. J. Ayer (1936) *Language, Truth, and Logic* (New York: Dover).

J. Badaracco (2006) Questions of Character: Illuminating the Heart of Leadership Through Literature (Boston, MA: Harvard Business Review Press).

J. Bakan (2004) *The Corporation* (New York: Free Press).

B. Ballard (2000) *Understanding MacIntyre* (Lanham, MD: University Press of America).

K. Balstad Brewer (1997) "Management as a Practice: A Response to Alasdair MacIntyre," *Journal of Business Ethics*, 16, 825–833.

B. Barlow (1998) "Absence and Presence: The Religious and Psychological Meaning of 'The Lily in the Field and the Bird of the Air,'" *Religious Studies and Theology*, 17, 2, 20.

B. Bass (2008) *The Bass Handbook of Leadership: Theory, Research, and Managerial Applications*, Fourth edition (New York: The Free Press).

G. Beabout (1996, 2009) *Freedom and Its Misuses: Kierkegaard on Anxiety and Despair* (Milwaukee: Marquette University Press).

G. Beabout (1999) "Business or Medicine: Challenging the Stereotypes," *National Catholic Register*, 1 August, 9.

G. Beabout et al. (2002) *Beyond Self-Interest: A Personalist Account of Human Action* (Lanham, MD: Rowman and Littlefield).

G. Beabout (2007) "The Silent Lily and Bird as Exemplars of the Virtue of Active Receptivity," in R. Perkins (ed.) *Without Authority: International Kierkegaard Commentary*, Volume 18 (Macon, GA: Mercer University Press).

G. Beabout (2012) "Management as a Domain-Relative Practice that Requires and Develops Practical Wisdom," *Business Ethics Quarterly*, 22, 405–432.

R. Beadle (2001) "MacIntyre and the Amorality of Management," http://www.mngt.waikato.ac.nz/ejrot/cmsconference/2001/Papers/Management_and_Goodness/Beadle.pdf, accessed 5 May 2013.

R. Beadle (2002) "The Misappropriation of MacIntyre," *Reason in Practice*, 2, 2, 45–54.

R. Beadle (2008a) "Rand and MacIntyre on Moral Agency," *The Journal of Ayn Rand Studies*, 9, 2, 221–243.

R. Beadle (2008b) "Why Business Cannot Be a Practice," *Analyse und Kritik*, 30, 1, 227–241.

R. Beadle and G. Moore (2006) "MacIntyre on Virtue and Organization," *Organization Studies*, 27, 323–340.

R. Beadle and G. Moore (2008) "MacIntyre, Empirics and Organisation," *Philosophy of Management*, 7, 1–2.

R. Beadle and K. Knight (2012) "Virtue and Meaningful Work," *Business Ethics Quarterly*, 22, 433–450.

F. C. Beiser (2005) *Schiller as Philosopher: A Re-Examination* (Oxford: Oxford University Press).

R. Bellah et al. (2007) *Habits of the Heart: Individualism and Commitment in American Life*, Third edition (Berkeley, CA: University of California Press).

S. Benardete (1991) *The Rhetoric of Morality and Philosophy: Plato's Gorgias and Phaedrus* (Chicago: University of Chicago).

P. Blackledge and N. Davidson (eds) (2006) *Alasdair MacIntyre's Engagement with Marxism* (Leiden: Brill).

P. Blackledge and K. Knight (eds) (2011) *Virtue and Politics: Alasdair MacIntyre's Revolutionary Aristotelianism* (Notre Dame, IN: University of Notre Dame Press).

D. Blagg and S. Young (2001) "What Makes a Good Leader?" *Harvard Business School Bulletin* (available at: <www.alumni.hbs.edu/bulletin/2001/february/leader.html> , accessed 5 May 2013).

P. Block (1993) *Stewardship* (San Francisco: Berrett-Koehler).

R. Bodéüs (1993) *The Political Dimensions of Aristotle's Ethics*, trans. J. Garrett (Albany: State University of New York Press).

W. C. Booth (1989) *The Company We Keep: An Ethics of Fiction* (Berkeley, CA: University of California Press).

N. Bowie (1999) *Business Ethics: A Kantian Perspective* (Oxford: Blackwell).

J. Boatright (2009) *Ethics and the Conduct of Business* (London: Pearson).

I. Briggs-Meyers (1995) *Gifts Differing: Understanding Personality Type* (Palo Alto, CA: Davies-Black).

H. Brody (2002) *Stories of Sickness*, Second edition (Oxford: Oxford University Press).

B. Burrough and J. Helyar (2009) *Barbarians at the Gate: The Fall of RJR Nabisco* (New York: HarperBusiness).

J. Burtchaell (1998) *The Dying of the Light* (Grand Rapids: Eerdmans), 563–633.

H. Bush (2008) *Mark Twain and the Spiritual Crisis of His Age* (Tuscaloosa, AL: University of Alabama).

M. Calkins and J. B. Wight (2008) "The Ethical Lacunae in Friedman's Concept of the Manager," *The Journal of Markets and Morality*, 11, 2, 221–238.

U. Carlsson (2010) "Love as a Problem of Knowledge in Kierkegaard's *Either/Or* and Plato's *Symposium*," *Inquiry*, 53, 41–57.

T. Chambers (1999) *The Fiction of Bioethics* (New York: Routledge).

R. Charon and M. Montello (2002) *Stories Matter: The Role of Narrative in Medical Ethics* (New York: Routledge).

G. Chaucer and W. Skeat (eds) (1912) *The Complete Works of Geoffrey Chaucer,* Volume 5 (London: Oxford University Press).

A. Clark and J. Treanor (2008) "Greenspan – I Was Wrong about the Economy. Sort of,' *The Guardian*. Available at: <http://www.guardian.co.uk/business/2008/oct/24/economics-creditcrunch-federal-reserve-greenspan>), accessed on July 11, 2012.

C. Clarke (2010) "Practical Wisdom and Understanding the Economy," *Journal of Management Development*, 29, 678–685.

N. Clarke (1993) *Person and Being* (Milwaukee, WI: Marquette University Press).

A. Colby et al. (2011) *Rethinking Undergraduate Business Education* (New Jersey: Jossey-Bass).

H. Cook (2010) "Borderlands: A Historian's Perspective on Medical Humanities in the U.S. and the U.K.," *Medical Humanities*, 36, 1, 3–4.

L. Cooper (2009) *An Aristotelian Theory of Comedy: With an Adaptation of the Poetics, and a Translation of the "Tractatus Coislinianus"* (Ithaca, NY: Cornell University Press).

J. Cornwall and M. Naughton (2008) *Bringing Your Business to Life: The Four Virtues That Will Help You Build a Better Business and a Better Life* (Ventura, CA: Regal).

J. Cornwell (2010) "MacIntyre on Money," *Prospect*, 176, 58–61.

N. Cousins (1982) *The Physician in Literature* (Philadelphia, PA: WB Saunders).

S. Covey (1989) *Seven Habits of Highly Effective People* (New York: Free Press).

C. Cowton (2008) "On Setting the Agenda for Business Ethics Research," in C. Cowton and M. Haase (eds) *Trends in Business and Economic Ethics* (New York: Springer), 11–30.

L. Cunningham (ed.) (2009) *Intractable Disputes about the Natural Law* (Notre Dame, IN: University of Notre Dame).

T. D' Andrea (2006) *Tradition, Rationality, and Virtue* (London: Ashgate).

R. Daft (2011) *Management* (Mason, OH: Southwestern).

S. Datar et al. (2010) *Rethinking the MBA* (Boston: Harvard Business Press).

J. Davenport and A. Rudd (eds) (2001) *Kierkegaard After MacIntyre* (Chicago: Open Court).

D. Dawson and C. Bartholomew (2003) "Virtues, Managers and Business People: Finding a Place for MacIntyre in a Business Context," *Journal of Business Ethics*, 48, 127–138.

R. DeGeorge (1982) *Business Ethics* (New York: Macmillan).

J. Dewey (1933) *How We Think* (Chicago: Henry Regnery).

C. Dierksmeier (2011a) "The Freedom–Responsibility Nexus in Management Philosophy and Business Ethics," *Journal of Business Ethics*, 101, 263–283.

C. Dierksmeier (2011b) *Humanistic Ethics in the Age of Globality* (London: Palgrave Macmillan).

C. Dierksmeier and D. Mele (2012) *Human Development in Business: Values and Humanistic Management in the Encyclical Caritas in Veritate* (New York: Palgrave Macmillan).

I. Dilman (1979) *Morality and the Inner Life: A Study in Plato's Gorgias* (New York: Barnes & Noble).

J. Dobson (1996) "The Feminist Firm: A Comment," *Business Ethics Quarterly*, 6, 227–232.

J. Dobson (1997) "MacIntyre's Position on Business: A Response to Wicks," *Business Ethics Quarterly*, 7, 125–132.

J. Dobson (2009) "Alasdair Macintyre's Aristotelian Business Ethics: A Critique," *Journal of Business Ethics*, 86, 43–50.

E. Dodds (1959) *Plato: Gorgias* (Oxford: Clarendon Press).

T. Donaldson and T.W. Dunfee (1999) *Ties That Bind: A Social Contracts Approach to Business Ethics* (Boston, MA: Harvard University Press).

R. S. Downie (2000) *The Healing Arts* (Oxford: Oxford University Press).

P. Drucker (1954, 1985) *The Practice of Management* (New York: Harper & Row).

P. Drucker (2002) *The Essential Drucker* (New York: Harper Business).

J. Dunne (2002) "Alasdair MacIntyre on Education: In Dialogue with Joseph Dunne," *Journal of Philosophy of Education*, 36, 1–19.

J. Dunne (2003) "Arguing for Teaching as a Practice: A Reply to Alasdair MacIntyre," *Journal of Philosophy of Education*, 37, 2, 353–369.

M. Edmundson (2012) "Do Sports Build Character or Damage It?" *The Chronicle of Higher Education*. Retrieved from http://chronicle.com/article/Do-Sports-Build-Character- or/130286/.

G. Enderle (1996) "Towards Business Ethics as an Academic Discipline," *Business Ethics Quarterly*, 6, 43–65.

M. Evans and D. Greaves (2000) "Medical Humanities," *Medical Humanities*, 26, 1, 1–2.

M. Evans and D. Greaves (2010) "Ten Years of Medical Humanities," *Medical Humanities*, 36, 1, 66–68.

H. Fayol (1916 [1949]) *General and Industrial Management*, trans. C. Storrs (London: Sir Isaac Pitman).

H. Fayol (1930) *Industrial and General Administration*, trans. J. Coubrough (Geneva: International Management Institution).

P. Foot (1978) *Virtues and Vices* (Oxford: Blackwell).

B. Fowers (2005) *Virtue and Psychology: Pursuing Excellence in Ordinary Practices* (Washington, D.C.: American Psychological Association).

M. Friedman (1970) "The Social Responsibility of Business Is to Increase Its Profits," *The New York Times Magazine*, September 13, 122–126.

R. Furtak (2010) "Kierkegaard and Platonic Eros," in J. Stewart (ed.) *Kierkegaard and the Greek World: Socrates and Plato* (London: Ashgate).

J. Garff (2005) *Søren Kierkegaard: A Biography*, trans. Bruce H. Kirmmse (Princeton: Princeton University Press).

E. Garver (1984) "Aristotle's Genealogy of Morals," *Philosophy and Phenomenological Research*, 44, 4, 471–492.

E. Garver (1994) *Aristotle's Rhetoric: An Art of Character* (Chicago: University of Chicago Press).

P. du Gay (1998) "Alasdair MacIntyre and the Christian Genealogy of Management Critique," *Cultural Values*, 2, 421–444.

P. Geach (1977) *The Virtues* (Cambridge: Cambridge University Press).

D. Goleman (1995) *Emotional Intelligence* (New York: Bantam).

M. Gladwell (2005) *Blink: The Power of Thinking without Thinking* (New York: Little, Brown, and Company).

M. Gladwell (2008) *Outliers: The Story of Success* (New York: Little Brown).

D. Goleman (2000) *Working with Emotional Intelligence* (New York: Bantam).

P. W. Gooch (1987) "Socratic Irony and Aristotle's 'Eiron': Some Puzzles," *Phoenix*, 41, 2, 95–104.

K. Goodpaster (2006) *Conscience and Corporate Culture* (Malden, MA: Wiley-Blackwell).

W. Grassl (2010) "Aquinas on Management and Its Development," *Journal of Management Development*, 29, 7, 706–715.

R. Greenleaf (1977) *Servant Leadership: A Journey into the Nature of Legitimate Power and Greatness* (New York: Paulist Press).

L. Gulick (1937) "Notes on the Theory of Organization," in L. Gulick and L. Urwick (eds) *Papers on the Science of Administration* (New York: Institute of Public Administration).

P. Hadot (1995) *Philosophy as a Way of Life* trans. M. Chase (Oxford: Blackwell).

J. Haldane, "MacIntyre's Thomist Revival: What Next?" in J. Horton and S. Mendus, eds,(1994) *After MacIntyre*.

G. Hamel (2007) *The Future of Management* (Boston, MA: Harvard Business School Press).

G. Hamel (2012) *What Matters Now: How to Win in a World of Relentless Change, Ferocious Competition, and Unstappable Innovation* (San Francisco, CA: Jossey-Bass).

A. Hannay (2001) *Kierkegaard: A Biography* (Cambridge: Cambridge University Press).

R. Hare (1992) "One Philosopher's Approach to Business and Professional Ethics," *Business and Professional Ethics Journal*, 11, 3, 3–19.

S. Hauerwas (2001) *The Hauerwas Reader* (Durham, NC: Duke University Press).

S. Hauerwas (2007) "The Virtues of Alasdair MacIntyre," *First Things*, 37, October.

C. Helman (2003) *Doctors and Patients: An Anthology* (Oxford: Radcliffe Medical Press).

M. Hernandez (2008) 'Promoting Stewardship Behavior in Organizations: A Leadership Model,' *Journal of Business Ethics*, 80, 122.

C. Higgins (2010) "The Good Life of Teaching," *Journal of Philosophy of Education*, 44, 2–3, 189–208.

C. Higgins (2011) *The Good Life of Teaching: An Ethics of Professional Practice* (Hoboken, NJ: Wiley-Blackwell).

J. Hine (2007) "The Shadow of MacIntyre's Manager in the Kingdom of Conscience Constrained," *Business Ethics*, 16, 357–371.

P. Hogan (2003) "Teaching and Learning as a Way of Life," *Journal of Philosophy of Education*, 37, 2, 207–223.

M. Horkheimer (1992, originally 1939) "The Social Function of Philosophy," in *Critical Theory. Selected Essays* (New York: Continuum).

J. Horton and S. Mendus (eds) (1994) *After MacIntyre: Critical Perspectives on the Work of Alasdair MacIntyre* (Notre Dame, IN: University of Notre Dame Press).

C. Horvath (1995) "Excellence v. Effectiveness: MacIntyre's Critique of Business," *Business Ethics Quarterly*, 5, 499–532.

K. M. Hunter (1993) *Doctor's Stories* (Princeton, NJ: Princeton University Press).

R. Hursthouse (1999) *On Virtue Ethics* (Oxford: Oxford University Press).

F. Jensen (2009) "Poul Martin Møller: Kierkegaard and the Confidant of Socrates," in J. Stewart (ed.) *Kierkegaard and His Danish Contemporaries – Philosophy, Politics and Social Theory*, Volume 7 (Farnham: Ashgate).

M. C. Jensen and W. H. Meckling (1976) "Theory of the Firm: Managerial Behavior, Agency Costs and Ownership," *Journal of Financial Economics*, 3, 4, 305–360.

K. Katayama (2003) "Is the Virtue Approach to Moral Education Viable in a Plural Society," *Journal of Philosophy of Education*, 37, 2, 325–338.

G. Kaupins (2006) "The Characteristics and Traits of Successful Managers and Supervisors," *Academy of Business and Public Administration Proceedings*, Dallas, TX, April.

R. Keat (2000) *Cultural Goods and the Limits of the Market* (New York: Palgrave Macmillan).

R. G. Kennedy (2006) *The Good that Business Does* (Grand Rapids: Acton Institute Christian Thought Series).

S. Kierkegaard (1987) *Either/Or*, Volume 2, trans. H. & E. Hong (Princeton: Princeton University Press).

S. Kierkegaard (1992) *The Concept of Irony* trans. H. & E. Hong (Princeton: Princeton University Press).

S. Kierkegaard (1997) "The Lily in the Field and the Bird of the Air," in *Without Authority*, trans. H. and E. Hong (Princeton: Princeton University Press).

S. Kierkegaard (2001) *The Essential Kierkegaard* (Princeton: Princeton University Press).

R. Kilburg (2000) *Executive Coaching: Developing Managerial Wisdom in a World of Chaos* (Washington, D.C.: American Psychological Association).

R. Kilburg (2006) *Executive Wisdom: Coaching And the Emergence of Virtuous Leaders* (Washington, D.C.: American Psychological Association).

R. Kilburg (2012) *Virtuous Leaders: Strategy, Character, and Influence in the 21st Century* (Washington, D.C.: American Psychological Association).

E. von Kimakowitz et al. (eds) (2011) *Humanistic Management in Practice* (New York: Palgrave Macmillan).

G. Klosko (1993) "Persuasion and Moral Reform in Plato and Aristotle," *Internationale de Philosophie*, 184, 31–49.

G. Klubertanz (1952) *The Discursive Power* (Saint Louis: Modern Schoolman).

K. Knight (1998) (ed.) *The MacIntyre Reader* (Notre Dame, IN: University of Notre Dame Press).

K. Knight (2007) *Aristotelian Philosophy: Ethics and Politics from Aristotle to MacIntyre* (Cambridge: Polity).

D. Koehn (1995) "A Role of Virtue Ethics in the Analysis of Business Practice," *Business Ethics Quarterly*, 5, 533–539.

E. B. Lambeth (1990) "Waiting for a New St. Benedict: Alasdair MacIntyre and the Theory and Practice of Journalism," *Journal of Mass Media Ethics*, 5, 2, 75–87.

J. Lantos (1999) *Do We Still Need Doctors? A Physician's Personal Account of Practicing Medicine Today* (New York: Routledge).

S. Lewis (1922) *Babbitt* (New York: Grosset & Dunlap).

J. Lippitt (2007) "Getting the Story Straight: Kierkegaard, MacIntyre, and Some Problems with Narrative," *Inquiry*, 50, 1, 34–69.

C. Lutz (2004) *Tradition in the Ethics of Alasdair MacIntyre: Relativism, Thomism, and Philosophy* (Lanham, MD: Lexington Books).

C. Lutz (2012) *Reading Alasdair MacIntyre's After Virtue* (London: Continuum).

A. MacIntyre (1958) "On not Misrepresenting Philosophy," *Universities and Left Review*, 4, 72.

A. MacIntyre (1958–1959) "Notes from the Moral Wilderness," *The New Reasoner*, 7 and 8.

A. MacIntyre (1966) *A Short History of Ethics* (New York: Macmillan).

A. MacIntyre (1970) *Herbert Marcuse* (New York: Viking Press).

A. MacIntyre (1977a) "Utilitarianism and Cost–Benefit Analysis: An Essay on the Relevance of Moral Philosophy to Bureaucratic Theory," in K. Sayre (ed.) *Values in the Electric Power Industry* (Notre Dame: University of Notre Dame Press), 217–237.

A. MacIntyre (1977b) "Epistemological Crises, Dramatic Narrative, and the Philosophy of Science," *The Monist*, 60, 4, 453–472.

A. MacIntyre (1979a) "Corporate Modernity and Moral Judgment: Are They Mutually Exclusive?" in K. E. Goodpaster and K. M. Sayre (eds) *Ethics and Problems of the 21st Century* (Notre Dame: University of Notre Dame Press), 122–135.

A. MacIntyre (1979b) "Social Science Methodology as the Ideology of Bureacratic Authority," in M. J. Falco (ed.) *Through the Looking Glass: Epistemology and the Conduct of Enquiry. An Anthology* (Washington, D.C.: University Press of America).

A. MacIntyre (1979c) "Why Is the Search for the Foundations of Ethics so Frustrating?," *Hastings Center Report*, 9, 4, 22.

A. MacIntyre (1981, 1984, 2007) *After Virtue* (Notre Dame, IN: University of Notre Dame Press).

A. MacIntyre (1982) "Why are the Problems of Business Ethics Insoluble," in B. Baumrin and B. Friedman (eds) *Moral Responsibility and the Professions* (New York: Haven Publishing), 99–107.

A. MacIntyre (1984a) "Does Applied Ethics Rest on a Mistake?," *The Monist*, 67, 598–613.

A. MacIntyre (1984b) *Marxism and Christianity* (Notre Dame, IN: University of Notre Dame).

A. MacIntyre (1990a) *Three Rival Versions of Moral Inquiry: Encyclopedia, Geneaology, Tradition* (Notre Dame, IN: University of Notre Dame Press).

A. MacIntyre (1990b) *First Principles, Final Ends, and Contemporary Philosophical Issues* (Milwaukee, WI: Marquette University Press).

A. MacIntyre (1992) "Plain Persons and Moral Philosophy: Rules, Virtues and Goods," *American Catholic Philosophical Quarterly*, 66, 1, 3–7.

A. MacIntyre (1994) "A Partial Response to My Critics," in J. Horton and S. Mendus (eds) *After MacIntyre* (Notre Dame: University of Notre Dame Press).

A. MacIntyre (1997) *A Short History of Ethics* (London: Routledge).

A. MacIntyre (1999a) *Dependent Rational Animals: Why Human Beings Need the Virtues* (Chicago: Open Court).

A. MacIntyre (1999b) "Social Structures and Their Threat to Moral Agency," *Philosophy*, 74, 311–329.

A. MacIntyre (2000) "Theories of Natural Law in the Culture of Advanced Modernity," in E. B. McLean (ed.) *Common Truths: New Perspectives on Natural Law* (Wilmington, DE: Intercollegiate Studies Institute).

A. MacIntyre (2001) "Once More on Kierkegaard," in J. Davenport and A. Rudd (eds) *Kierkegaard After MacIntyre* (Chicago: Open Court).

A. MacIntyre (2006a) *Selected Essays*, 2 Volumes (Cambridge: Cambridge University Press).

A. MacIntyre (2006b) *Edith Stein: A Philosophical Prologue* (London: Rowman and Littlefield).

A. MacIntyre (2008) "How Aristotelianism Can Become Revolutionary: Ethics, Resistance, and Utopia," *Philosophy of Management*, 7, 1, 3.

A. MacIntyre (2011) *God, Philosophy, Universities: A Selective History of the Catholic Philosophical Tradition* (London: Rowman and Littlefield).

A. MacIntyre and J. Dunne (2002) "Alasdair MacIntyre on Education: In Dialogue with Joseph Dunne," *Journal of Philosophy of Education*, 36, 1, 1–19.

L. Mackey (1971) *Kierkegaard: A Kind of Poet* (Philadelphia, PA: Univeristy of Pennsylvania Press).

I. Mangham (1995) "MacIntyre and the Manager," *Organization*, 2, 181–204.

G. Marino (2001) "Avoiding Moral Choices: Call in the Ethics Experts," *Commonweal*, March 23, 11–15.

W. May (1995) "The Virtues of the Business Leader," in M. Stackhouse et al. (eds) *On Moral Business: Classical and Contemporary Resources for Ethics in Economic Life* (Grand Rapids, MI: William B. Eerdmans Publishing), 692–700.

W. McDonald (2003) "Love in Kierkegaard's Symposia," *Minerva* 7, www.sorenkierkegaard.nl/artikelen/Engels/090. Love in kierkegaard.pdf, accessed on 5 May 2013.

D. McCann and M. Brownsberger (1990) "Management as a Social Practice: Rethinking Business Ethics After MacIntyre," in M. Stackhouse et al. (eds) *On Moral Business* (Grand Rapids, MI: Eerdmans), 508–514.

D. McGregor (1960) *The Human Side of Enterprise* (New York: McGraw Hill).

D. McGregor (1966) "The Human Side of Enterprise," in W. Bennis and E. Schein (eds) *Leadership and Motivation, Essays of Douglas McGregor* (Cambridge, MA: MIT Press).

T. McLauglin (2003) "Teaching as a Practice and a Community of Practice: The Limits of Commonality and the Demands of Diversity," *Journal of Philosophy of Education*, 37, 2, 339–352.

B. McLean and P. Elkind (2004) *The Smartest Guys in the Room: The Amazing Rise and Scandalous Fall of Enron* (New York: Penguin).

M. McLuhan and B. Powers (1992) *The Global Village* (Oxford: Oxford University Press).

P. McMylor (1994) *Alasdair MacIntyre: Critic of Modernity* (New York: Routledge).

D. Melé (2010) "Practical Wisdom in Managerial Decision Making," *Journal of Management Development*, 29, 7/8, 637–645.

J. S. Mill (1859) *On Liberty* (London: Parker and Son).

D. Miller (1994) "Virtues, Practices, and Justice," in J. Horton and S. Mendus (eds) *After MacIntyre* (Notre Dame, IN: University of Notre Dame Press).

H. Mintzberg (1973) *The Nature of Managerial Work* (New York: Harper & Row).

H. Mintzberg (2005) *Managers, not MBAs* (San Francisco, CA: Berrett Koehler).

H. Mintzberg (2009) *Managing* (San Francisco, CA: Berrett-Koehler Publishers).

L. Mises (1944) *Bureaucracy* (New Haven, CT: Yale University Press).

D. Moberg (2007) "Practical Wisdom and Business Ethics," *Business Ethics Quarterly*, 17, 3, 535–561.

E. Mooney (2007) *On Søren Kierkegaard: Dialogue, Polemics, Lost Intimacy, and Time* (London: Ashgate).

G. Moore (2002) "On the Implications of the Practice–Institution Distinction: MacIntyre and the Application of Modern Virtue Ethics to Business," *Business Ethics Quarterly*, 12, 19–32.

G. Moore (2005a) "Corporate Character: Modern Virtue Ethics and the Virtuous Corporation," *Business Ethics Quarterly*, 15, 4, 659–685.

G. Moore (2005b) "Humanizing Business: A Modern Virtue Ethics Approach," *Business Ethics Quarterly*, 15, 2, 237–255.

G. Moore (2005c) "Corporate Character: Modern Virtue Ethics and the Virtuous Corporation," *Business Ethics Quarterly*, 15, 4, 659–685.

G. Moore (2008) "Re-Imagining the Morality of Management: A Modern Virtue Ethics Approach," *Business Ethics Quarterly*, 18, 483–511.

G. Moore (2012a) "The Virtue of Governance, the Governance of Virtue," *Business Ethics Quarterly*, 22, 293–318.

G. Moore (2012b) "Virtue in Business: Alliance Boots and an Empirical Exploration of MacIntyre's Conceptual Framework," *Organization Studies*, 33, 363–387.

G. Moore and R. Beadle (2006) "In Search of Organizational Virtue in Business: Agents, Goods, Practices, Institutions and Environments," *Organization Studies*, 27, 369–389.

T. Morris (1997) *If Aristotle Ran General Motors* (New York: Henry Holt).

L. Nash (1995) "Whose Character? A Response to Mangham's 'MacIntyre and the Manager,'" *Organization*, 2, 226–232.

J. Nicholas (2012) *Reason, Tradition, and the Good: MacIntyre's Tradition Constituted Reason and Frankfurt School Critical Theory* (Notre Dame, IN: University of Notre Dame Press).

N. Noddings (2003) "Is Teaching a Practice?," *Journal of Philosophy of Education*, 37, 2, 241–251.

Olympiodorus the Younger (1998) *Commentary on Plato's Gorgias,* trans. R. Jackson et al. (eds) (Leiden: Brill).

W. Ong (1975) "The Writer's Audience Is Always a Fiction," *PMLA*, 90, 1, 9–21.

W. Ong (2002) *Orality and Literacy* (New York: Routledge).

T. Overbury (1614) *New and Choise Characters, of Seuerall Authors* (London: Thomas Creede).

C. Pavur (2005) *The Ratio Studiorum: The Official Plan for Jesuit Education* (The Institute of Jesuit Sources), available online at: http://www.slu.edu/colleges/AS/languages/classical/latin/tchmat/pedagogy/rs/rs1.html, accessed on 5 May 2013.

E. Pellegrino and D. Thomasma (1993) *The Virtues in Medical Practice* (Oxford: Oxford University Press).

T. Peters (2003) *Re-Imagine: Business Excellence in a Disruptive Age* (London: Dorling Kindersle).

J. Pieper (1966) *The Four Cardinal Virtues* (Notre Dame, IN: University of Notre Dame Press).

Plato (1961) *Collected Dialogues,* ed. E. Hamilton and H. Cairns (Princeton: Princeton University Press).

S. Posen (2005) *The Doctor in Literature: Satisfaction of Disappointment?* (Oxford: Oxford University Press).

G. Press (2007) *Plato: A Guide for the Perplexed* (London: Continuum).

T. Prindle (trans. and ed.) (1991) *Made in Japan: And Other Japanese Business Novels* (New York: Sharpe).

S. M. Puffer (2004) *International Management: Insights from Fiction and Practice* (New York: Sharpe).

K. Quinn (1996) "A Rhetorical Conception of Practical Rationality," *Journal of Economic Issues*, 30, 1127–1142.

C. Rapp (2009) "The Nature and Goals of Rhetoric," in G. Anagnostopoulos (ed.) *A Companion to Aristotle* (Oxford: Blackwell), 579–596.

R. Reynolds and J. Stone (2010) *On Doctoring*, Third edition (New York: Simon & Schuster).

S. Robbins et al. (2005) *Management*, Eighth edition (Englewood Cliffs, NJ: Prentice Hall).

S. Robbins and M. Coulter (2011) *Management* (Saddle River, NJ: Prentice Hall).

L. Rohrer (2009) "Can Business Managers Be Virtuous?," MacIntyre Conference Proceedings, Lincoln University, October.

A. Rorty (2011) "Aristotle on the Virtues of Rhetoric," *The Review of Metaphysics*, 54, 715–733.

R. Rorty (1979) *Philosophy and the Mirror of Nature* (Princeton, NJ: Princeton University Press).

R. Rorty (1998) *Achieving Our Country* (Boston: Harvard University Press).

M. Rothbart (2007) "Temperament, Development, and Personality," *Current Directions in Psychological Science*, 16, 4, 207–212.

A. Rudd (2012) "Alasdair MacIntyre: A Continuing Conversation," in J. Stewart (ed.) *Kierkegaard's Influence on Philosophy: Anglophone Philosophy* (London: Ashgate), 117–134.

J. Sachs (2009) *Plato's Gorgias and Aristotle's Rhetoric: Translation, Glossary and Introductory Essay* (Newburyport, MA: Focus Publishing).

J. Salinsky (2004) *Medicine and Literature: The Doctor's Companion to the Classics* (Oxford: Radcliffe Medical Press).

J. Sallis (1996) *Being and Logos: Reading the Platonic Dialogues*. Third edition (Bloomington, IN: Indiana University Press).

S. Sanghera (2003) "You Should Be Bonkers in a Bonkers' Time," *Financial Times*, September 23.

P. Santilli (1984) "Moral Fictions and Scientific Management," *Journal of Business Ethics*, 3, 279–286.

F. Schiller (2004) *On the Aesthetic Education of Man*, trans. R. Snell (New York: Dover Publications).

D. Schindler (1993) "Norris Clarke on Person, Being, and St. Thomas," *Communio*, 20, 580–598.

D. Schindler (1996) *Heart of the World, Center of the Church: Communio Ecclesiology, Liberalism, and Liberation* (Grand Rapids: Eerdman's).

F. Schlegel (1971) *Friedrich Schlegel's Lucinde and the Fragments*, trans. Peter Firchow (Minneapolis: University of Minnesota Press).

V. Schmidt (2001) *45 Master Characters: Mythic Models for Creating Original Characters* (Cincinnati, OH: Writer's Digest Books).

D. Schoen (2011) "Polling the Occupy Wall Street Crowd," *Wall Street Journal*, October 18.

R. Scholes and R. Kellogg (1966) *The Nature of Narrative* (Oxford: Oxford University Press).

M. Schwartz (2010) "Moral Vision: Iris Murdoch and Alasdair MacIntyre," *Journal of Business Ethics*, 90, 315–327.

B. Schwartz and K. Sharpe (2010) *Practical Wisdom* (New York: Riverhead).

L. Segil (2002) *Ten Essential Traits for Managers* (Somerset, NJ: Wiley).

F. Sejersted (1996) "Managers and Consultants as Manipulators: Reflections on the Suspension of Ethics," *Business Ethics Quarterly*, 6, 1, 67–86.

D. Sellman (2000) "Alasdair MacIntyre and the Professional Practice of Nursing," *Nursing Philosophy*, 1, 26–33.

P. Senge (1990) *The Fifth Discipline: The Art and Practice of the Learning Organization* (New York: Doubleday).

W. Shaw (2011) *Business Ethics*. Eighth Edition (Boston, MA: Cengage).

C. Shields (2007) *Aristotle* (London: Taylor & Francis).

H. Simon (1947) *Administrative Behavior: A Study of Decision-Making Processes in Administrative Organization* (New York: Macmillan).

H. Simon (1955) "A Behavioral Model of Rational Choice," *Quarterly Journal of Economics*, 69, 99–118.

A. Sison (2003) *The Moral Capital of Leaders: Why Virtue Matters* (Cheltenham, UK: Edward Elgar).

A. Sison, E. Hartman, and J. Fontrodona (2012) "Reviving Tradition: Virtue and the Common Good in Business and Management," *Business Ethics Quarterly*, 22, 207–10.

A. Sison and I. Ferrero (2012) "A Survey of Virtue in Business and Management Literature (1980–2010)," presented August 4, 2012 at the annual meeting of the Society of Business Ethics, Boston, MA.

M. Slote (1992) *From Morality to Virtue* (Oxford: Oxford University Press).

R. Solomon (1992) *Ethics and Excellence: Cooperation and Integrity in Business* (Oxford: Oxford University Press).

R. Solomon (1993) "Corporate Roles, Personal Virtues: An Aristotelean Approach to Business Ethics," *Business Ethics Quarterly*, 2, 337.

L. Spears (1977) *Servant Leadership: A Journey in the Nature of Legitimate Power and Greatness* (New Jersey: Wiley).

L. Spears (1997) *Insights on Leadership: Service, Stewardship, Spirit, and Servant-Leadership* (New Jersey: Wiley).

H. Spitzeck et al. (eds) (2009) *Humanism in Business* (Cambridge: Cambridge University Press).

H. Spitzeck et al. (eds) (2011) *Banking with Integrity* (London: Palgrave Macmillan).

M. Stackhouse et al. (1995) *On Moral Business: Classical and Contemporary Resources for Ethics in Economic Life* (Grand Rapids, MI: Eerdmans).

D. Stauffer (2006) *The Unity of Plato's Gorgias* (Cambridge: Cambridge University Press).

R. Sternberg (1990) *Wisdom: Its Nature, Origins, and Development* (Cambridge: Cambridge University Press).

J. Stewart (ed.) (2009) *Kierkegaard and His Danish Contemporaries – Philosophy, Politics and Social Theory*, Volume 7 (Farnham: Ashgate).

J. Stewart (ed.) (2010) *Kierkegaard and the Greek World: Socrates and Plato* (London: Ashgate).

L. Stout (2012) *The Shareholder Value Myth* (San Francisco: Berrett-Koehler).

B. Taylor (2003) *Management Science*, Eighth edition (Englewood Cliffs, NJ: Prentice Hall).

C. Taylor (1989) *Sources of the Self: The Making of the Modern Identity* (Harvard, MA: Harvard University Press).

C. Taylor (2007) *A Secular Age* (Harvard, MA: Harvard University Press).

F. Taylor (1903) *Shop Management* (New York: Harper and Row).

F. Taylor (1911) *The Principles of Scientific Management* (New York: Harper & Row).

Theophrastus (2003) *Characters*, ed. and trans. J. Rusten and I. C. Cunningham, Third edition (London: Loeb Classical Library).

Thomas Aquinas (1993) *Commentary on Aristotle's Nicomachean Ethics* trans. C. Litzinger (Notre Dame, IN: Dumb Ox Books).

Thomas Aquinas (1948) *Summa Theologica*, trans. Fathers of the English Dominican Province (New York: Benziger Brothers).

L. Tolstoy (2003) *Anna Karenina*, trans. Constance Garnett (New York: Barnes and Noble).

D. Tredget (2010) "Practical Wisdom and the Rule of Benedict," *Journal of Management Development*, 29, 7, 716–723.

M. Velasquez (1982) *Business Ethics: Concepts and Cases* (Englewood Cliffs, NJ: Prentice Hall).

G. Vlastos (1991) *Socrates, Ironist and Moral Philosopher* (Ithaca: Cornell University Press).

S. Walsh (1994) *Living Poetically: Kierkegaard's Existential Aesthetics* (University Park, PA: Pennsylvania State University Press).

R. Wardy (1996) *The Birth of Rhetoric: Gorgias, Plato and Their Successors* (London: Routledge).

G. Weaver (2006) "Virtue in Organizations: Moral Identity as a Foundation for Moral Agency," *Organization Studies*, 27, 3, 341–368.

M. Weber (1947) *The Theory of Social and Economic Organization*, trans. A. M. Henderson and T. Parsons (New York: The Free Press).

M. Weber (1997) *The Methodology of the Social Sciences*, trans. and ed. A. Shils and H. A. Finch (New York: Free Press).

R. Weiss (2003) "Oh, Brother! The Fraternity of Rhetoric and Philosophy in Plato's *Gorgias*," *Interpretation* 30, 195–206.

P. Werhane (1999) *Moral Imagination and Management Decision-Making* (Oxford: Oxford University Press).

P. Werhane and R. Freeman (1999) "Business Ethics: The State of the Art," *International Journal of Management Review*, 1, 1–16.

T. Whetstone (2003) "The Language of Managerial Excellence: Virtues as Understood and Applied," *Journal of Business Ethics*, 44, 4, 343–357.

A. Whitehead (1979) *Process and Reality* (New York: Free Press).

A.C. Wicks (1996) "Reflections on the Practical Relevance of Feminist Thought to Business," *Business Ethics Quarterly*, 6, 523–532.

A.C. Wicks (1997) "On MacIntyre, Modernity and the Virtues: A Response to Dobson," *Business Ethics Quarterly*, 7, 133–135.

O. Williams (ed.) (1998) *The Moral Imagination* (Notre Dame, IN: University of Notre Dame Press).

F. P. Wilson (1969) *The English Drama, 1485–1585* (Oxford: Oxford University Press).

T. Wright and J. Goodstein (2007) "Character is not 'Dead' in Management Literature: A Review of Individual Character and Organizational-Level Virtue," *Journal of Management December*, 33, 6, 928–958.

A. Yuengert (2012) *Approximating Prudence: Aristotelian Practical Wisdom and Economic Models of Choice* (London: Palgrave MacMillan).

E. Ziolkowski (2011) *The Literary Kierkegaard* (Evanston, IL: Northwestern University Press).

Index